BEYOND CARING LABOUR
TO PROVISIONING WORK

Although women have long been members of the labour force, the proportion of domestic, caring, and community work they provide compared to men or the state has yet to decrease substantially. *Beyond Caring Labour to Provisioning Work* offers a powerful new framework for understanding women's work in a holistic sense, acknowledging both their responsibilities in supporting others as well as their employment duties.

Beyond Caring Labour to Provisioning Work is based on a four-year, multi-site study of women who are members of contemporary community organizations. The authors reveal the complex ways in which these women define and value their own work, investigating what supports and constrains their individual and collective efforts. Calling on the state to assist more with citizens' provisioning responsibilities, *Beyond Caring Labour to Provisioning Work* provides an excellent basis for new discussions on equitable and sustainable public policies.

SHEILA M. NEYSMITH is a professor in the Factor-Inwentash School of Social Work at the University of Toronto.

MARGE REITSMA-STREET is a professor emerita in the Studies in Policy and Practice Program and the School of Social Work at the University of Victoria.

STEPHANIE BAKER COLLINS is an associate professor in the School of Social Work at McMaster University.

ELAINE PORTER is an associate professor in the Department of Sociology at Laurentian University.

Beyond Caring Labour to Provisioning Work

SHEILA M. NEYSMITH,
MARGE REITSMA-STREET,
STEPHANIE BAKER COLLINS,
AND ELAINE PORTER

with JUDY CERNY and SANDRA TAM

UNIVERSITY OF TORONTO PRESS
Toronto   Buffalo   London

© University of Toronto Press 2012
Toronto   Buffalo   London
www.utppublishing.com
Printed in Canada

ISBN 978-1-4426-4325-3 (cloth)
ISBN 978-1-4426-1175-7 (paper)

∞

Printed on acid-free, 100% post-consumer recycled paper with vegetable-based inks.

Library and Archives Canada Cataloguing in Publication

Beyond caring labour to provisioning work/Sheila M. Neysmith . . . [et al.].

Includes bibliographical references and index.
ISBN 978-1-4426-4325-3 (bound). – ISBN 978-1-4426-1175-7 (pbk.)

1. Poor women – Canada.   2. Poor women – Employment – Canada.
3. Poor women – Canada – Social conditions.   4. Informal sector
(Economics) – Canada.   I. Neysmith, Sheila

HD6099.B49 2012   331.4086′240971   C2011-908091-5

University of Toronto Press acknowledges the financial assistance to its
publishing program of the Canada Council for the Arts and the Ontario
Arts Council.

 Canada Council   Conseil des Arts
for the Arts   du Canada

 ONTARIO ARTS COUNCIL
CONSEIL DES ARTS DE L'ONTARIO

University of Toronto Press acknowledges the financial support of the
Government of Canada through the Canada Book Fund for its publishing
activities.

We dedicate this book to all those in our lives whose provisioning has been, and continues to be, a source of inspiration and love.

Contents

Part Three

Appendix: Principles and Practices in the 'Women Provisioning in Community' Research Project   163

MARGE REITSMA-STREET

Preface

Women's work matters. This book is fuelled by a desire to imagine in new ways the dimensions and consequences of women's work within households, organizations, and communities. By the end of the twentieth century, collective spaces that support women in their daily and transformative labours faced significant threats to their survival and mission. A decade later, more groups and organizations are disappearing, especially those situated in communities that are marginalized by income, race, and age as governments, businesses, and communities respond to financial and environmental crises.

As one way to document and bear witness to the struggles of women living in these difficult times, we initiated the Women Provisioning in Community Research Project. In this multi-site project we explored women's provisioning relationships and responsibilities as they respond to being on the edges of the new global economies Throughout the book chapters we probe how women and their organizations engage with 'the values we want to hold that are dear to us,' in the words of one research participant, while 'surviving and changing at the same time,' in the words of another.

This book would not exist without the sustained help of many people. We deeply appreciate the generosity of those who participated in the research interviews, focus groups, countless conversations, and feedback sessions between 2003 and 2007. The approval and practical support of the six organizations who agreed to become research sites were invaluable. Of particular assistance were the steadfast and enjoyable contributions of the community advisory groups who worked alongside the university researchers and students. They piloted the research activities, strategized how data would be collected, and debated preliminary results. Neither individual nor organizational participants are named in the book, in accordance with our community research ethics and conventions of the Ethics Review Boards in Canadian universities. Confidentiality was also required to respect the restrictions women's community organizations may encounter when they criticize their funders or advocate for changes. We are pleased the organizations and communities in the project were able to use research project findings to legitimize to themselves the value of their daily work, and the importance of holding on as best they can to what they name as valuable organizational work. Some of the advisory groups became significant relational arenas to spark discussions about what could be different, and to mourn what was being lost. Several times the information and relationships generated during the course of the research helped to leverage new policies and funding proposals.

We wish to acknowledge the following people for their contributions, much of it voluntary and beyond the call of duty. Pat Rogerson, Silvia Vilches, and Arlene Wells gave freely of themselves, providing prompt, positive feedback, creative suggestions, and wonderful food at every stage of the research. Thank you Crystal Gartside for choosing this project to work on during your graduate studies, and for your efficient and accurate coding, and quiet, profound questions. We thank Aleks McHugh for thorough literature reviews and setting up the web board, and Corrine Lowen for adding substantial data on changes in organizational policies and for writing reports that helped an organization in negotiations with a funder. Thanks to Oxana Mian for a photographic record of the project questions acted out in skits, and for comprehensive, conceptual minutes of cross-site meetings. Above all, we appreciate how strongly these women, and many others, including Jane Aronson, Xiobei Chen, Mehmoona Moosa Mitha, Ana Maria Peredo, Viki Prescott, and Karen Swift, valued the task of examining women's individual and collective provisioning and thereby helped to make this book a reality.

A particular thanks to three people. Catherine van Mossel, doctoral student in Studies in Policy and Practice and the School of Nursing at the University of Victoria, began as a site research associate and became our project coordinator extraordinaire. She orchestrated the project team relationships, research processes, and data analysis across thousands of physical miles and Internet spaces – with friendliness, competence, and analytical astuteness. Furthermore, we wish to express our appreciation for Catherine's conceptual contributions to the chapter on collective provisioning. We owe special thanks to Tracy Smith-Carrier, doctoral student at the Factor-Inwentash Faculty of Social Work, University of Toronto, who also began as a research associate of the project and then served as our outstanding editorial assistant on all the stages of the book. Donna Barker, office manager in the School of Social Work at the University of Victoria, served as research secretary and financial administrator throughout the project. We depended on her efficiency, laughter, and administrative acumen.

We appreciate funding from the Social Sciences and Humanities Research Council – which supported our work through both a development grant and then a multi-year project grant. Those monies made it possible to pay modest honorariums to research participants, to organize community and cross-site team meetings and feedback workshops, and to hire and mentor thirteen graduate students as research associates. Three of those students used the data to complete graduate theses, while several others presented project findings at local community events as well as academic and international conferences. We are thankful to Laurentian, McMaster, Toronto, Victoria, and York Universities for their institutional support of the authors. Special mention needs to be made of the contributions of Laura Proctor and Katy Chan, computer support personnel at the University of Victoria, for creating and maintaining a password-protected web board for the project data. For researchers living in different cities, the web board became our filing cabinet 'in the sky,' making papers and data stripped of confidential information efficiently accessible to the researchers wherever they lived and worked. Finally, this book would not have been published if Virgil Duff, before he retired as Executive Editor of University of Toronto Press, had not encouraged us to pursue a prospectus we showed him. We thank him, Doug Richmond, Associate Acquisitions Editor, and Wayne Herrington, Associate Managing Editor, who together shepherded the manuscript through the many stages of publication.

There is the invisible emotional and material work of many who helped to make this book possible. We thank the anonymous reviewers who examined the book manuscript and papers submitted to journals. They strongly encouraged us to continue and develop the analysis. We thank them for provocative analytical threads and clear suggestions on how to proceed, particularly in the multiple ways women build collectivity, contest provisioning obligations, and expand notions of worthy citizens. We thank our kith, kin, and close friends who encouraged us throughout the project, the writing of articles, and this book. Beyond words are debts of gratitude to our partners Jason Boyd, Steve Collins, Michael Milner, K.V. Nagarajan, Harry Street, and Bill Tassie for their ongoing support and practical help. Profound gratitude is due to Anne Wilson for her exquisite attention to the craft of writing, steeped in friendship.

In the early years of the research project on women's provisioning, we developed principles and policies about how we would work together. This Memorandum of Understanding, included as the Appendix in this book, was written after discussions with community groups and research associates. It aims to capture, in writing, our approach to the feminist research commitment, to enjoying personal relationships and tasks and contesting privileges that are taken for granted when making decisions about data collection, analysis, writing, and dissemination. One of our research principles was 'to practise healthy ways of provisioning amongst ourselves and in the sites.' We thank each other for all the ways we tried to practise this principle. Sometimes we did so with tact and joy; other times with stilted awkwardness. Throughout our time together, this principle served as an inspiration for a way of working and being together – when babies were born and children married, while coping with serious illnesses and deaths of parents, and as new obligations were taken on along the way.

Provisioning follows pathways of relationships across arenas of life. This is not just the key point of the book: it is what we wanted to value and create in our work with each other.

Marge Reitsma-Street
with
Stephanie Baker Collins
Judy Cerny
Sheila Neysmith
Elaine Porter
Sandra Tam

August 2010

BEYOND CARING LABOUR
TO PROVISIONING WORK

1 Introduction: Conceptualizing the Work of Women in the Twenty-First Century

Since the ground-breaking work of Marilyn Waring (1988) there has been an explosion of research and theory about the work that women do, where and how the work is done, its characteristics, and perhaps most contentiously, how it is valued. There is now little doubt that charting and accounting for all the work that women do is important. The debate is about approaches that best capture its depth and complexity and then the relative merits of different strategies for imputing its value (Craig, 2007; Hoskyns & Rai, 2007; Neysmith & Reitsma-Street, 2000; Statistics Canada, 2005a). Although the different approaches that make up this literature have implications for research and theory, of particular concern to the authors of this book is how their associated policies affect the quality of life experienced by different groups of women.

We start from the premise that it is time to reframe the 'problem' facing women as they strive to acquire resources for meeting the responsibilities they carry for their well-being and that of others. Attempts to address their economic needs all too often turn women into female equivalents of male breadwinners. This model fails to incorporate the unpaid work that women do, undervalues caring labour, whether paid or not, and ignores all other types of work that women do as they engage in what political economists refer to as social reproduction – 'the activities and attitudes, behaviours and emotions, responsibilities and relations directly involved in the maintenance of life on a daily basis, and intergenerationally' (Laslett & Brenner, 1989, p. 382, as cited in Bezanson & Luxton, 2006, p. 35). The contradictions in women's lives remain hidden when theory, research, and policy reinforce the separation of the worlds of employment, community, and domestic labour from one another. These divisions and boundaries are not drawn by women and cannot account for the complexities of women's lives. In this book we use the concept of provisioning, as developed by feminist economists, to explore the multiple dimensions of women's work experiences. We investigate what happens – what different types of questions are posed – when women are positioned as citizens with responsibilities, actively engaged in trying to marshal the resources they need to meet the obligations they carry as individuals and members of community groups.

Building on the work of feminist economists (Beneria, 1995; Day, 1995; Donath, 2000; Gardiner, 1997; MacDonald, 1995; Moser, 1989; J.A. Nelson, 1996, 1998, 1999; Power, 2004), but dimming the spotlight on the market, in this book we directly address the issue of provisioning – the work needed to realize the necessities and conveniences of life. Although paid labour in a capitalist society supposedly enables individuals to do this work, women's experiences and research referenced throughout the book suggest otherwise. Through provisioning we expand the meaning of work to include all activities that secure resources and provide the necessities of life to those for whom one has relationships of responsibility. This definition speaks to a range of activities that are never finished, must be performed regularly, and require energy and attention. These activities cannot be isolated or separated from the context of social relationships because provisioning consists of those daily activities performed to ensure the survival and well-being of oneself and others. Both the activities and the relationships may be voluntary or prescribed. The point is that the activities are necessary; without them, people would not survive. Articulating their policy implications has a particular urgency, given the realities facing people who live with increasing poverty, instability, regulations, and penalties that accompany decreases in public supports. In Canada, these decreases were particularly stark in Ontario and British Columbia, following their regime shifts in 1995 and 2001, respectively. These shifts had occurred before the data that inform the analyses in the following chapters were collected.

The term *provisioning*, as used by feminist economists, directs attention to the purpose of economic activity. Passive images of workers and consumers are replaced with those of people facing challenges about how to meet their needs and obligations (Langley & Mellor, 2002). Use of the concept also facilitates challenges to assumptions that the primary work of governments, financial institutions, and social organizations is development based on increasing productivity. Such a position calls into question assertions that keeping the market economy growing is a prerequisite for social progress, that issues like health care and environmental protection can be addressed only after industry is developed. As the economic recession of 2008–9 so dramatically revealed, under such assumptions bailing out banks is defined as necessary economic activity; bailing out families is not. Importantly, focusing on the multiple dimensions of provisioning also disturbs the gendered assumptions underlying familial and employee relationships.

Our investigation into provisioning struck a chord with many of the participants, because it made them aware of the breadth and depth of their work in ways that justified our selection of this concept as the basis for our study. Other concepts such as *social capital* (see Lowndes, 2000; Rankin, 2002), *empowerment* (Adams, 2003), and *social exclusion* (Bryne, 1999; Levitas, 1996; Littlewood & Herkommer, 1999; Room, 1999) had been considered. Although these concepts address some of the same concerns, it was ultimately decided that they could not capture the complicated lives of our participants nor explicate how they, as individuals and as members of community groups, attempted to change and resist the oppressive conditions that limited their options. All three concepts tend to assume an outsider perspective, one of looking into and downward onto the lives of women, fitting them into identities as entrepreneurs, consumers, victims, clients, or 'others,' who must be helped up, or expected to pull themselves up, to be included. Thus they can recreate positions of marginality and reinforce states of privilege, missing or devaluing the dynamic, changing nature of the work women do to provision on behalf of those with whom they have relationships of responsibility today and will have in the future. As such, these concepts did not open up avenues for exploring who benefits from increasing poverty and why the capacities of households and communities to provide are being undermined so systematically. Closer to our analytical perspective was the concept of social reproduction (Bakker, 2007; Bezanson & Luxton, 2006). This concept pinpoints the interactions between the public and private spheres. However, we needed something more concrete, a concept that allowed us to examine its empirical dimensions, adding more depth to understanding women's agency in their roles in social reproduction. As does *social reproduction*, the term *provisioning* emphasizes social relations, but it has the advantage of focusing on the strategic nature of women's managing day to day.

Provisioning, operationalized as women's strategies to secure resources to provide the necessities of life to those for whom they have responsibility, is a conceptual segue into developing a more robust understanding of the working experiences of women and the social conditions needed to support the obligations that women carry – those assumed and those thrust upon them by the state and the market. The neoliberal discourse of restructuring claim that short-term pain is required for long-term gain in the 'new reality' of globalization is an old reality for many women (Cohen & Brodie, 2007). This book documents the short-term reality. More importantly, it shows how women, as individuals, but also as members of collectivities, struggle to develop strategies for survival – strategies that must take into account the responsibilities they carry, not only for themselves but for others. In the conversations about provisioning, as suggested by Vobruba (2000), we focused on specific situations where women had to negotiate the resources they needed for living.

Situating the Actors

The book draws on data from a longitudinal, multi-year research project that explores the question 'What supports and what limits the provisioning work of women who are members of poor households and marginalized communities?' The examination of how women and groups interpret their provisioning responsibilities and options took place in six communities in two Canadian provinces. The sites were selected for their innovative work with marginalized groups, as examples of contemporary collectivities responding creatively to the material and gender concerns of communities marginalized by poverty, ageism, and racism (Bannerji, 2000; Dua & Robertson, 1999; Fraser, 1997). Three of the sites were in large urban centres, while the others were in medium-sized cities. All were in provinces that had introduced sweeping cuts to social assistance and other services to women and communities (Creese & Strong-Boag, 2005; Klein & Long, 2003; Neysmith, Bezanson, & O'Connell, 2005). The groups were: (1) a food cooperative programme within a multi-resource neighbourhood services centre; (2) a provincial network of older women with local chapters; (3) a small incorporated women's society offering employability training to women who have left abusive relationships; (4) a large incorporated community resource centre for families living in two poor, multicultural neighbourhoods; (5) a programme focusing on young immigrant women that was part of a large, multi-service organization; and (6) a tenant group in a large urban social housing complex. Site differences are elaborated upon in chapters 5–8 which focus on specific communities.[1]

A total of 100 women agreed to be interviewed about their own provisioning responsibilities, and those of the site with which they were associated. The majority of the study participants were women with low or insecure income. They ranged in age from early twenties to over eighty years; most were Caucasians, but some were First Nations, African, Asian, or Latin American, and all spoke either English or French. The backgrounds, summarized in table 1.1, reflect some of the diversity expected in Canadian urban populations (Statistics Canada, 2008a). Over the four-year span of the study, 138 key informants participated in nineteen focus groups and/or interviews to better understand the context of site activities and the constraints they faced. We invited a range of people, including current members and alumni, long-term participants and those newer to the organization, paid staff, board members, and volunteers. Several key informants were involved in the sites in multiple ways, such as being both providers and receivers of an organization's activities. To complement our understanding of the context of sites and changes over time, researchers also engaged in field visits and content analysis of policy documents, such as organizational mission statements and annual reports.

All participants were asked similar questions, with the spotlight moving from their individual responsibilities and their associated work to questioning for whom they were responsible as members of a group. The invitation and consent process for research participants, as approved by the sites and ethics boards at respective universities, included a verbal and written explanation of the concept of *provisioning*, as well as why we were using it in this study rather than *work* or *care*.[2] The questions that guided the individual interviews were:

- What activities do you do to provide for the persons you are responsible for?
- How do you carry out this work?
- What helps you and what makes it difficult?
- What role does organization xxx play in assisting you to provide for those for whom you are responsible?
- What changes do you foresee in these provisioning responsibilities in the next 3–5 years?
- What do you see affecting this work in the future?

Analytically, within each site, we explored relationships of responsibility within the organizations; types and purposes of provisioning activities; external and internal changes in policies, values, and activities; approaches to negotiating and deciding boundaries of responsibilities; costs and consequences of provisioning choices; and supports and lim-

Table 1.1. Description of sites and background of women interviewed

Sites by pseudonym	Number and background of women interviewed
Pont Place is a small NGO that hosts employability and counselling programmes for women who have left abusive relationships.	$N = 13$. Ages 25–55. 3 Aboriginal or Metis; all low income; 9 with children living at home; 2 living in transitions home
Hands On is a large NGO community resource organization with free play, cultural, and educational activities for children and families in two poor, multicultural neighbourhoods.	$N = 25$. Ages, most were 25–45 but 2 over 55; 3 Aboriginal and 5 francophone; all low income; only 1 with no children at home; 13 single parents
Cascade Co-op is a medium-size food cooperative, with its own executive responsible for advocacy, food security, fundraising, and mutual aid activities; housed in a large multi-service centre for urban poor families.	$N = 21$. Ages, most were 40–55, but 3 were younger and 3 older; 3 recent immigrants; all low income; diverse household types; most responsible for children, including adult children at home or living close by; 4 without children
Heracane is a large group of older women in two cities committed to public debate and advocacy on justice, stereotypes, and the representation of older women on policy committees.	$N = 18$. Ages 55–80; 3 Aboriginal and racial minority status; none poor, but some with modest incomes; 6 living with partners; most regularly caring for grandchildren, siblings, older relatives
Gen-Y is an independent programme geared to the employment, housing, and parental concerns of young women, administered by a very large NGO committed to women's issues and needs.	$N = 15$. Ages 16–24; all but 1 woman of racial minority status; all low or no income; 7 lone mothers; 3 live on own, 5 living in a shelter, others with mother or roommate
Jane's House is a very small, fledgling tenants' self-help and advocacy group in a large urban social housing complex.	$N = 8$. Ages 25–55; 5 racial minority status; all low income; diverse household types, including multi-generational; all with 2 or more children

its to provisioning work. Mapping the diversity of individual and collective provisioning work emerged from an analysis of the taped and transcribed interviews and focus groups, as well as from reflections on informal conversations and field visits.

Preliminary findings from all sites were reviewed with the advisory panels, while community presentations, site reports, and skits provided members with results and questions for debate. All but two chapters are jointly written by the book's co-authors. Chapters 5 and 6, by Sandra Tam and Judy Cerny respectively, reflect additional research that they undertook as part of their PhD dissertations. Although they worked closely with the book authors, they assumed primary responsibility for these chapters, but the analysis reflects these additional research data.

How the Story Unfolds

Chapter 2 sets the context, theoretical questions, and practical concerns that fuelled the study and subsequent analyses. It uses excerpts from the 1912 strike song of working women, 'Bread and Roses,' to organize the content so that it is very clear how current issues come with deep historical roots. The rest of this chapter lays out the major dimensions of the chapters in the book as they are each organized into one of three sections. Part One synthesizes findings from all sites so that common themes and their theoretical implications are clarified. Thus, chapter 3 presents an overview of the individual provisioning work done by participants across all sites, while chapter 4 focuses on the ways women work together and how they define their organizational, community, and citizenship labours.

Chapter 3 was written after findings for each site had been analysed for its respective issues and insights. It charts the contours of individual participants' work, and its associated responsibilities, into two major categories – provisioning activities and provisioning strategies. The chapter conceptualizes practical and transformative ways women strategize their work, including negotiating the boundaries of their provisioning responsibilities that, we argue, flow through pathways of relationships. Our findings confirm the complex nature of the activities that make up women's work (Luxton & Corman, 2001; Staeheli & Clarke, 2003; Vosko, 2006). We end chapter 2 by viewing relationships as pathways to the incessant decisions required to meet and change those individual provisioning responsibilities.

In chapter 4 we examine collective provisioning – women working together to meet responsibilities and maintain relationships outside the household and market. These arenas include mutual aid groups and not-for-profit, non-governmental organizations (NGOs) estimated as totalling 161,000 in Canada (Imagine Canada, 2006; Meinhard & Foster, 2003). We assume that these collectivities, including religious institutions, cultural institutions, and emerging global and electronic networks, are important venues for the creation of relationships and ideas about women's provisioning. Collective provisioning in our study is located within the context of community sites and the neoliberal policies that were affecting them. Three types of collective provisioning strategies were identified, each attentive to particular obligations, yet all interdependent and necessary: (1) the creation of valued goods and services that focus on the practical needs of women, (2) the construction of alternatives that had the potential to change systemic inequities, and (3) negotiations required to map common visions while contesting differences and negotiating boundaries. We conclude that women-centred collectivities must survive because they serve as vital spaces where the struggles for 'bread and roses,' for resources and citizenship, can be negotiated in transformative ways.

Part Two highlights how, despite underlying similarities, provisioning work takes myriad forms, depending on the life circumstances of the women involved. It explores the ways that individual women living in six disparate communities define, experience, and contest their labour in households, the market, and community. Each chapter reveals site-based specifics of how the work that comes with provisioning is connected to relationships. These relationships may be familial, employment-, and/or community-based but they all come together in the lives of participants. Their effects on each other and how these were intersected by changing access to public provisions under neoliberal policy regimes highlight how policy has impact locally.

This section starts with chapter 5, which examines young women's experiences of preparing for jobs and careers while balancing school, work, and family responsibilities. Sandra Tam uses institutional ethnography (IE) to reveal how the social organization of young women's experiences departs from current knowledge about youth and work, and from related academic and policy discourses in which labour market programmes and practices are embedded. These make young women's own knowledge invisible and authorize youth employment 'experts' to define the problems and solutions to eliminate young women's 'dependence' on the state. Using the concept of provisioning to make observable the complexity of their working lives, Sandra Tam concludes that the conditions under which young women provision are shaped by social relations in the youth labour market, and programme and practice discourses that construct these young women as 'youth at risk.'

Judy Cerny explores the provisioning responsibilities of immigrant mothers and their perceptions of how Canadian childcare policy both assists and constrains their strategies for providing care for their children. The analysis reveals how low-income mothers provision under numerous constraints: a continuous shortage of money and resources; the limited availability of social and community services; lack of transportation; a high level of violence/criminal activity in their neighbourhoods; low-quality housing; and a shortage of affordable recreational opportunities. Many mothers were burdened with poor health and inadequate diets, limited English language skills, the struggles of adapting to a new country, and/or the necessity to care for children with special needs. The chapter underscores how poorly Canadian childcare policies/programmes meet the needs of these women.

Chapter 7 documents the work and responsibilities of older women, who carry large and complex provisioning responsibilities. As was the case in the other sites, where the mean age of participants was younger, this work can be summarized as provisioning activities and provisioning strategies. In addition, analysis suggests three major issues facing older women: (1) the unexpected magnitude of the provisioning work that they continue to do in their sixties, seventies, and eighties, (2) how to square the realities of an aging body with the provisioning expectations held by others, and (3) setting priorities and enforcing boundaries when time is scarce. Implications for theory and the citizenship claims of older women are considered.

The last chapter in this section, chapter 8, presents data from three research sites that were in a low-income neighbourhood in which women provisioned for households and communities. In this chapter individual provisioning efforts are examined alongside the role that community groups play in sustaining women as they struggle to provision for those with whom they have relationships that entail responsibilities. The data are from interviews with members and/or service users from two groups in Ontario and one in British Columbia. A complex web of activity – including paid employment, voluntary work, care work, exchanges of goods and services, community work, and self-provisioning – are uncovered. In the face of significant cutbacks in state provision of goods and services, women were engaging in multiple activities to compensate through private provisioning for resources that were no longer publicly available. The policy context within which these strategies were pursued is explored, and in particular, how risky policies produce risky coping strategies.

Part Three uses the data and theory about individual and collective provisioning from all sites to begin envisioning forms of social provisioning that support rather than appropriate the work of women. We posit in chapter 9 that community groups provide the necessary space to start rethinking how individuals engage with each other to sustain collective well-being. However, these spaces are sites of contradiction. As funding changes restructure the collective work done by women in community organizations, there is a concern that this work is increasingly being usurped to substitute for withdrawals of public services. Our data support these concerns.

Our findings also reveal ways in which women resist the appropriation of their community work. We argue that these spaces must be maintained because they continue to challenge an individualized notion of citizenship by offering other ways that citizenship gets enacted. Three connections between citizenship activities and community provisioning are discussed: (1) how women challenge notions of the worthy citizen in the ways in which they collectively work in community; (2) how they bring privatized need back into the public arena; and (3) how they move from solidarity to advocacy. We conclude that the work of collective provisioning in community settings can serve women's strategic interests.

In the final chapter, the conceptual and empirical data of the preceding chapters become the basis for proposing directions that have the potential to set research and policy agendas that can sustain people. The chapter picks up the challenge facing women as individuals and members of groups: how to organize, survive, and change in ways that respect a belief in collective provisioning responsibilities at personal, local, and global levels. Provisioning responsibilities are related to obligations of individuals and groups in the course of their relationships. The myths of independent individuals and abstract resources swirling around the globe untethered by time and space are revealed for what they are – myths. However, these myths power neoliberal policies that are deeply unjust to marginalized groups locally and globally who engage in the social reproduction required if there is to be a future! We conclude that this study of First World women, marginalized in Canadian society, reveals not only how the appropriation of their provisioning is one dimension of the Canadian version of neoliberalism, but that a recognition of how individual, collective, and state provisioning are tied together offers a way of thinking about what sustainable public policies need to incorporate. As a way forward, in chapter 10, we envision the dimensions of some of these needed policies.

2 Securing the Future by Positioning the Past in the Present

The literature is replete with efforts to capture the depth and breadth of women's work. One method has been to think in terms of an informal economy that allows for an expansion of the strategies available with which households seek to make ends meet (Elson, 1992; Feldman, 1992; J.A. Nelson, 1999). However, the gendered nature of this work, like that found in the formal economy, means that women do work that is different from men's. In both economies, women's caring responsibilities affect their ability to acquire resources. Consequently, women's survival strategies to meet daily needs result all too often in few opportunities to pursue longer-term goals, while, at the same time, gendered inequities are reproduced and reinforced. Research and theory need to be directed at transforming these conditions, not diverted to helping women develop better coping strategies, as necessary as these might be for short-term survival. Similarly, focusing on employment, anti-poverty, and educational programmes without looking at the broader social environment can too readily feed political agendas of privatization and state withdrawal (Caragata, 2009; Gurstein & Vilches, 2009; Morgen & Maskovsky, 2003). In fact, every chapter reveals just how readily this happens. It is the societal-level negotiations over available social and technical resources, not individual behaviour or choice, that shape options for low-income women within and across households in countries such as Canada.

The search for a fresh understanding of what constitutes work and security in the lives of individual women is required to inform public policy. Central to this is recognition that state, family, market, and community may be separate policy spheres, but their effects intersect in people's lives (Neysmith, Bezanson, & O'Connell, 2005).

Furthermore, what happens in each sphere travels along pathways of relationships that bring together concerns that ultimately shape how policies are experienced. One purpose of this book is to document these effects empirically by mapping in some detail the multiple dimensions of provisioning work done by women, including that done in the poorly understood collective arenas that are disappearing. If the contours of women's collective work are not visible, if the value of the different types of organizational work they do are not accurately assessed, under neoliberal policy assumptions they will be destroyed during restructuring, with no markers left to inform future generations of their existence.

In the first part of this chapter some of the difficulties of the dominant female breadwinner approach to meeting need are summarized. Attempts to incorporate into policy unpaid work and caring labour, both paid and unpaid, are reviewed and found to be not only theoretically awkward but unsuccessful in changing the low and insecure incomes of many women. Frequently employment and dependent care policies have actually pitted differentially located groups of women against each other. Next we explore what happens analytically when women's responsibilities are used as the starting point for understanding the what, why, and how of the options and strategies they employ to secure resources. Finally, we reflect on the capacity of the concept of provisioning to highlight aspects of women's lives that remain hidden when research is based on concepts such as coping, empowerment, and social capital. For the authors, the concept of provisioning facilitated the collection of empirical data that allowed us to document the ways women and communities meet their immediate survival needs while strategizing for the future. For those women who participated in the research, the concept seemed to have what Patti Lather (1993) calls 'catalytic validity.' It gave them space outside of the traditional domestic and employment spheres to discuss the relationships that shaped their decisions about where they put their time and energy. For the reader, we hope the concept will evoke alternative ways of thinking about how social policies shape social reproduction and, thus, affect the quality of women's lives.[1]

'We go Marching, Marching,' but . . .

Theories of work and employment practices are rooted in assumptions about how markets operate in capitalist economies. Although

debates about the validity of these assumptions are outside the parameters of this book, the point to be made here is that the centrality of the market in economic thinking throws into the shadows all
other dimensions of citizens' lives – dimensions that affect their one-
dimensional appearance as valuable employees and the decisions
they make about engaging or not in paid work. The transformation
of economics into the study of markets, and the associated processes
of supply and demand, producers and consumers, jobs and the skills
needed to acquire them, highlights the complexity of economic processes while casting citizens as unidimensional bit players in a drama
about markets. For instance, explanations of unemployment that see
the problem as arising from a person's lack of skills can be challenged
on the basis that a changing job market is ignored while workers are
blamed for not possessing adequate skills. Furthermore, globalization studies that do take account of broader economic and political
processes, or the role of technology, seldom take gender into account
(see Adam, 2002; Vosko, 2006) and market work is still privileged.
Likewise, social capital studies, even as they focus on women, tend
to emphasize their capacity to develop social capital as an alternative
route for acquiring economic capital (for assessments of this literature
from a more critical perspective, see Rankin, 2002; Stolle & Lewis,
2002). No matter the strengths of these arguments on other grounds,
such perspectives reinforce a conceptual approach in which individual citizens' relationships to the market economy become their defining feature.

Nation-state regimes such as those found in Canada, the United
States, and the United Kingdom delineate, through public policy, the
responsibilities and rights of those living within their borders. These
policies are based on important assumptions about the nature of public
and private life. The boundaries that define what is included and what
is excluded in these two spheres result in quite differing lived experiences for different groups. These boundary lines, which delineate where
something ends, are not as concrete as geographical borders. However,
they do shape the identities, and the imaginations of individuals and
collectivities (see Yuval-Davis & Stoetzler, 2002).

Neoliberalism is a term used since the early seventies to justify reductions
in government services by the enactment of national and international
policies that reflect a philosophy of liberal individualism. Programmes
that flow from such policies rest on the theory that the best approach
to securing and protecting human well-being is through individual

economic and social freedoms, and consequently, state interventions in market activities should be kept to a minimum (Bakker, 1996; Harvey, 2007; Larner, 2000). In this study, the research sites were geographically situated in two Canadian provinces, Ontario and British Columbia. By the year 2000, in both provinces, employment equity legislation was revoked, labour legislation was weakened, social assistance rates were deeply cut while eligibility criteria became very restrictive, and education, health, and social services underwent massive restructuring (Creese & Strong-Boag, 2005; Neysmith, Bezanson, & O'Connell, 2005).

Some effects of neoliberal programmes are quite visible and are documented (Bashevkin, 2002; Cohen & Brodie, 2007; Cohen & Pulkingham, 2009), especially the expectations placed on persons and communities to prioritize employment in the labour market, even if jobs are insecure and poorly paid. Less visible, and a challenge to document empirically, are the effects on women of the off-loading of responsibilities from public into private spaces. Costs to families and communities are hidden in rhetoric about strengthening the family unit and developing caring communities; those who cope with the consequences are primarily women in their front-line positions as family caregivers, neighbours, service providers, and community actors. Being in these social locations means that many women experience the associated costs personally or are in direct contact with those affected by the loss of social provisions that characterize neoliberal policies (Neysmith, Bezanson, & O'Connell, 2005). It is these policies that produce the circumstances in which women try to meet their provisioning responsibilities – responsibilities that are tied to relationships. Such relationships shape the content and the process, the what and the how, as well as the activities and the strategies that are available to women as they care for children and other kin, provide income and goods, exchange services, and develop community capacity.

Feminist scholars, bureaucrats, and activists have offered different ways of theorizing women's work so that all aspects of it are valued. As discussed in chapter 1, the dimensions that remain most invisible are those related to social reproduction. Unfortunately, as Hoskyns and Rai (2007) have concluded, the large body of research and theory on social reproduction has not fundamentally shifted policymaking, nor has it resulted in the kind of reconceptualization of the economic system that occurred after the economic importance of the service sector to the GNP became apparent. Our research does not resolve this conundrum, but it does document work and relationships crossing spheres, showing how aspects of work appear and disappear as they enter and exit the borders that delineate family, market, and state. Thus the data reveal the extent and costs of current problematic ways of valuing work to women and society.

Another approach to valuing the totality of women's work has been offered by feminist economists. They begin with the ways in which humans interact with each other and with the environment in order to sustain life (Beneria, 1995; Donath, 2000; Ferber & Nelson, 2003; Nelson, 1993, 2006; Power, 2004). Taylor (2004), for instance, suggests that the whole range of activities directed at provisioning should be considered work. She directs our attention to its relational nature: work is embedded in and defined by the social relations within which it is located. A neglected aspect, however, is the actual empirical investigation into how these activities, no matter their domain, are shaped by the character of relationships with others, whether kin or non-kin, individuals or communities.

By focusing on provisioning in this project, all the work women do to provide for themselves and others – whether paid or unpaid in the market, home, or community – is counted. Valuing different types of work across spheres, in the context of intersecting income, race, and age inequities, also means understanding how current accounts support privilege, even as they oppress some women more than others (Barker, 2005).

The Female Breadwinner: 'It is bread we fight for,' but . . .

In the 1990s, the gendered assumptions underlying theories of the welfare state were exposed. Several carefully argued feminist approaches for how to include women were developed (see Fraser, 1997; Lewis, 2001; Lister, 2001; O'Connor, Orloff, & Shaver, 1999). However, social policies in Canada, as in the United Kingdom, Australia, and the United States, took one single thread from the tapestry that these authors wove – that of recognizing women as earners and consumers – while ignoring other structural dimensions of inequality. This transformation of women into female breadwinners was effectively consistent with neoliberal premises of how citizens are supposed to create and distribute resources. The market and paid jobs take centre stage, with the state, the community, and family cast in supporting roles. In his later analysis of social welfare regimes, for example, Esping-Andersen (1999) could go no further than merely to recognize that families were important to consideration of social provisions, the organization of benefits, and the regulation of services.

However, when feminist scholars empirically examined the effects of inserting women and family into the state-market nexus (O'Connor, Orloff, & Shaver, 1999), they demonstrated how a different set of questions emerged – questions that the female breadwinner approach needed to address if it was to reflect the realities of women's lives. For instance, the model needed to specify the social conditions that would allow women to establish independent households. Unfortunately, adding an excluded group into existent models seldom de-centres structures of privilege which benefit the 'haves' and discriminates against the 'have nots.' The breadwinner was/ is gendered in that the concept assumes the presence of someone available to provide the domestic and caring labour that supports the breadwinner; market work cannot be done without household work. At the same time, a woman's caring responsibilities curtail her breadwinner capacities, making her appear as an inferior breadwinner (Neysmith, 2000).

Provisioning for themselves and for those dependent upon them remains difficult for many women, because it includes caring for others with the attendant financial and in-kind resources needed to do so. Making ends meet today frequently means taking a series of low-paying, contract jobs, which do not help build a secure tomorrow (Vosko, 2009). As Lewis (2001) notes, rhetoric about the benefits of life-long learning and higher education do not translate into women having access to better-paying jobs. The tunnel-vision version of training that moves women from welfare, to workfare, to low-paying contract jobs does not incorporate an understanding of the caring responsibilities women shoulder.[2] By negating the non-market contributions that women make to the welfare of the nation, such policies close off visions of citizenship that go beyond market and consumer claims.

Welfare state theorists have rightly pointed out that employment expansion in the service sector will lead to increasing inequality, because these jobs are poorly paid (Mahon, 2002). There is less interrogation of why they are poorly paid while other types of work are not. When explanations are offered, the usual conclusion is that such jobs are a marketization of traditional domestic tasks. For us, such conceptualizations are fundamentally flawed in two respects. First, the category of domestic labour all too frequently incorporates caring labour and thus dismisses the knowledge and skills of such work, seeing it as basic human maintenance work (for an economic interpretation, see Gardiner, 1997), traditionally done by women and servants, which 'naturally' draws a low wage when marketed. Second, entering women, family, or household into a market-model equation does not break up the two-spheres problematic of private and public worlds. In fact it could be argued that because it appears to promote inclusivity, the market model hides costs and benefits that accrue differentially to actors in each sphere – a conceptual practice that actually reproduces the problem. We therefore take issue with a policy discourse that privileges the 'working mother' even while recognizing it remains a strategic choice for particular debates. The purely conceptual paid–unpaid work split remains, as does the inadequate attention given to and accounting for how caring responsibilities affect both family and market work. The two-sphere dualism that has proven so problematic to women does not disappear in the female breadwinner approach to providing for wellbeing. The conclusion that a modified breadwinner approach to work is a poor fit when mapped onto women's lives still presents the challenge of what must be included for a better fit. We take this up more systematically in chapter 10.

Challenging prevailing norms and discourses that are fundamental to social change is conceptually and empirically demanding. Even in the case of feminist-informed welfare-regime theory, the major theoretical constructs are the separate spheres of state, market, labour, and family. Formal and informal social provisions are seen as originating in one of these. When studies reveal other arenas of provisioning, such as voluntary groups or informal support networks of friends and neighbours, these are interpreted from a male perspective as political or leisure-time activity, and are thus discretionary. These arenas are fitted into the dominant paradigm by positioning them theoretically as stand-ins for spheres of the state, market, labour, or family, depending on the situation in specific cases. However, thinking of these arenas as proxies does not challenge dominant understandings of how a separate spheres paradigm within a neoliberal era places demands on women to be breadwinners while they are also expected to take up increasing amounts of caring labour, as state services are cut and/or moved into the market. A conceptual wedge is needed to open up a space to discuss models of women's work that recognizes a range of provisioning domains *and* focuses on the pathways between them. Only then can new representations of the responsibilities and rights of women emerge (Adams & Padamsee, 2001).

More Than the Female Breadwinner: 'We fight for roses, too,' but . . .

To summarize, the rise of the female breadwinner model and resultant policies directed at getting women into the paid economy can increase costs to women and have very dubious payoffs in the jobs women get (Himmelweit, 2002). Therefore, feminist scholars from various disciplines now argue (1) that what is included in welfare needs to move beyond current models of welfare regimes (Brush, 2002) that gloss over the arena of social reproduction; (2) that well-being goes beyond sustainable material consumption and standards of health, environment, and housing to include opportunities for leisure, useful work, personal development, individual independence, and access to the resources needed for giving and receiving care over the lifetime (Perrons, 2000); and (3) that the state and civil society are potential spaces for enacting transformative strategies, and they have important roles to play in provisioning these aspects of well-being (Langley & Mellor, 2002; Stolle & Lewis, 2002). In sum, social policy that reflects a social reproduction perspective would need to encompass all the work people do that contributes to their own and others' welfare.

Descriptions of women's work outside the paid labour force are frequently captured under the term *caring labour*. There are a number of streams in this now substantial body of literature. One documents the breadth and depth of informal care provided by kin to aging family members. It reveals how, across OECD (Organisation of Economic Co-operation and Development) countries, mixed economies of care-service approaches, which combine public and market providers, continue to underestimate the costs of care borne by families (Daly, 2002; Glendinning & Means, 2004; Scourfield, 2006). Policy responses such as carers' allowances, paid volunteering, and direct payments to care users to buy help have been tried across jurisdictions, with mixed results (Kreigher, 1999; Timonen, Convery, & Cahill, 2006; Ungerson, 2004). They all underestimate the quantity and quality of caring labour needed and thus smack of tokenism.

Another stream of analysis has focused on gender differences in the types and amount of informal caring work done by women and men (Olson, 2003; Statistics Canada, 2005c). It shows that older women and men both do caring labour, but its focus and meaning vary by gender. As the result of differences in life expectancies, and the fact that women tend to marry older men, at any moment more women are providing care for longer periods of time – seldom under circumstances of their own choosing. Furthermore, taking on this work earlier in the life cycle affects women's options in the labour force, their resultant meagre pension entitlements, and the toll it takes on their own health.

Parallel to this social science and health policy literature, theory has been developed about an ethics of care (Clement, 1996; Gilligan, 1982; Hankivsky, 2004; Koehn, 1998; Nelson & England, 2002; Tronto, 1993) that challenges individualized concepts of justice and rights. Of interest here is its focus on how relationships underlie and shape women's responsibilities, and their associated notions of justice of what constitutes an ethical choice. Taken together, this body of scholarship problematizes the fact that social conditions such as need, labour such as unpaid work, and statuses such as being recipients and providers of care are not attached to social entitlements. Ensuing debates have attempted to reconcile the apparently oppositional approaches of care and justice ethics so that policies that promote the well-being of women can be developed. Women occupy differing social locations within and across national boundaries, with varying access to care. In recent years, authors like Sevenhuijsen (2004) have developed tools for analysing policies from the perspective of an ethics of care.

Feminists are divided on the effectiveness and gender implications of two policy mechanisms for valuing caring work. Focusing on policies that will divide familial caring responsibilities more equitably between men and women would ignore concerns about how this could privatize caring as a family matter. On the other hand, pursuing the development of caring services, such as national childcare and eldercare policies, that would open up options for women would not directly address gender disparities. Each analysis captures only parts of the dilemma; the challenge is how to develop policy strategies that are multi-dimensional. All sides acknowledge that women of all ages continue to do, and bear the consequences of doing, most paid and unpaid caring labour and combining it with other types of paid work (Herd & Harrington Meyer, 2002; Lister, 2003, 2007; Williams, 2001). Similarly, while care has been established as work, if it is to be valued and linked to entitlements, then providing it needs to be theorized as more than individual obligation. A policy aspect in this thread of the debate is whether kin care is a form of civic engagement, with entitlements parallel to those associated with paid employment and volunteer work, and if so, what are the types of claims that can be made by those taking up such responsibilities?

We highlight the form and distribution of non-market work because it keeps disappearing in discussions about what form post-welfare states might take. This disappearance happens in analyses that are otherwise well grounded in an appreciation of the social effects of globalization and information technologies on nation states and the future of social democracy, and on the role of NGOs and consumer groups as checks to international flows of capital (Carroll & Ratner, 2001; Castells, 1996; Giddens, 1998, 2001). Outside of the feminist literature (Beneria, Floro, Grown, & MacDonald, 2000; Brah, 2002), however, for the most part, the discussion is ungendered. The informal and unpaid work of women is curiously absent – even when women are the workers, such as in many micro-credit schemes (Rankin, 2002). Not surprisingly, time-use studies continue to show that women have less leisure time than men (Statistics Canada, 2005b). These social conditions get reproduced when the dimensions of work done by women escape scrutiny in analyses of how to modify/resist the effects of international flows of capital. Resulting social policies that leave market work central to future citizenship claims would continue to exacerbate the conditions under which women struggle to make ends meet.

If we are to include the vast amount of non-market work that sustains households conceptually, it means moving beyond a model that combines the public and private, the formal and informal economies, the paid and unpaid worlds. We need to understand how the spheres are kept separated, walled off from each other, how one sphere continues to be valued more than others. This study collected the type of open-ended data that would inform alternative understandings of women's work. Thus we documented the array of participants' responsibilities and what social, emotional, physical, and material resources they and their communities put in place to try to meet them. We positioned women as citizens who provision for themselves and others with whom they have relationships of responsibility (also see Kershaw, 2010). Provisioning seemed to have the conceptual potential for moving us beyond policies that rely on images of bridging the divide between employment and caring work. The image of a bridge does not question the foundations that anchor either end of the structure. It is these foundations that need to be disrupted in order to understand why what Barrig (1994) calls the space 'between bread and roses' continues to exist. Of importance is how women negotiate the competing demands made on them – demands that insist they perform as breadwinners or be sidelined as welfare losers, that embeds the rose of citizenship within a wreath of thorns. A lens is needed that is wider, that can take in more fields, that integrates women's work differently so that the focus crosses traditional silos. This approach is frequently referred to as assuming an analytical position of intersectionality (McCall 2005; Simien 2007).

Building Alternatives: 'We will rise to create something stronger,' but . . .

Using provisioning as a conceptual tool that could focus on intersectionality as intra-categorical complexity (McCall, 2005), the question then becomes where/how to do it. Where are the spaces for rethinking how women's provisioning responsibilities are socially constructed? To facilitate the development of a multi-sphere discourse, in mapping out provisioning work we focused on relationship pathways and explored the dimensions of boundaries and time in women's lives.

In the research interviews, participants were asked to discuss the strategies they used to meet immediate (survival) and longer-term (planning) needs. Although the specifics differed, participants saw themselves as neither victims nor heroines, but as one of the actors in their own lives who were facing more involuntary than voluntary choices in a complicated, moving web of claims, responsibilities, and few options. Although participants spoke of their efforts to create new identities, build relationships, and find more resources, responses were weighted down with commentary on the struggle to survive the negative changes of the past few years and the 'crippling cuts' in funding and services. Examples include the increase in laborious, repetitive work to find sufficient food and adequate shelter, and the time-consuming negotiations of bartering exchanges to take care of daily and unexpected necessities. Participants also engaged in numbingly careful calculations to manage the increased scrutiny of their lives by officials through regulations, forms that had to be filled repeatedly, threats of penalties, and denial of benefits.

We documented the boundaries that women draw around those for whom they were responsible. Provisioning demands made on women are marked by relationship boundaries, since relationships cannot be divided from responsibility and are key to deciding what actions will be taken. Using this approach shows that the boundaries women draw do not map neatly onto even expanded definitions of household, for they extend into other arenas, and their shape changes over time.

Relationships cannot be divided from responsibility; they are key to deciding what actions will be taken. Looking across traditional boundaries integrates women's work differently and, in the process, costs buried by the traditional silos get revealed – costs cross boundaries because relationships cross boundaries. For instance, friendships take on multiple purposes. They may be a source of social support and foster economic survival; they may make life less scary but they also mean additional burdens. Relationships are also the basis for identity, participation, and citizenship, all of which are part of understanding people's sense of belonging.

Local groups can help women build identity and capacity that the joint operation of family and market spheres in a society dominated by a neoliberal policy regime can too easily undermine. Because under such a regime women absorb the costs individually, they also become the targets for blame as problems arise. If these interpretations of cause and effects are not resisted, there is no way to claim that women bear a disproportionate degree of the cost. One result is that women are often forced to negotiate boundaries internally rather than externally, privately rather than publicly, singly rather than as part of a group. Thus, women's identity, participation, sense of belonging, and capacity to provision can be influenced not only by their individual positionings but also by the positioning of the collectivities in which they are members, whether these are local communities or international networks (Yuval-Davis, 1999). By the end of the study we concluded that negotiating boundaries could be done in positive, transformative ways if collective arenas were available.

Future Possibilities: 'A Sharing of life's Glories,' but . . .

The excerpts from the 1912 song of striking women, 'Bread and Roses,' to title the sections of this chapter were chosen to emphasize the historical roots of women's labour inequities and to signal the tenacity of important ideas. The struggle has not been just for sustainable livelihoods and equitable employment policies but also is intended to ensure the existence of social conditions that give people power to make those decisions affecting the quality of their lives, for exercising agency when assuming responsibilities. We ended the familiar phrases of the old song with 'but . . .' to underline the fact that 'life's glories' need to be defined by new ideas and policy narratives that go beyond the gendered, military struggle for bread and roses. The song captures the limits as well as the strategic necessity of market work for realizing life's glories. We have argued that the model of work embodied in the concept of the female breadwinner is just too thin, too limiting. It obscures too many dimensions of women's lives. As such, it cannot even ensure the bread needed by women, let alone the possibility of roses (Phipps & Burton, 1995). Over the years we, along with many feminist scholars, have used the concepts of caring labour, paid and unpaid work, and the informal economy to push the boundaries or thicken up ideas of work (see Neysmith, 2000). However, such concepts ultimately could not cut their tethers to social economic theory which reproduces those conditions that will result in future cohorts of women living lives that will 'be sweated from birth until life closes,' as the song says.

Participants' interpretations of their options and their resulting actions are the core of the empirical research. We asked about a wide range of strategies for coming to terms with their reality, including those that would collide with official definitions of legality and legitimacy as their measures of last resort. Participants articulated loss and anger when developing accounts of who benefits and who pays when public provisions are withdrawn, making life so much more difficult when they, and those around them, are forced to take up the slack. Fortunately, some had a desire to imagine other ways, ideas, policies, and practices. Policymakers, researchers, and the women in this study speak of the need for 'new words' to understand the realities and possibilities of action. However, they need to be created within dialogue, discussion, and activities engaged in with others – that is, in community. As one women stated, 'I need to be part of a community, not just to survive today, but to live, and survive in the future.' Alternative policies that support women cannot be developed without understanding the communities in and through which women exercise agency as they strive to meet their provisioning responsibilities.

Governments, voluntary organizations, co-ops, and social networks can all provide resources, but these patterns are strongly influenced by male-dominated traditions and prevailing values or norms (England & Folbre, 2003; Nelson, 1998). Feminist scholars have repeatedly called for specifying the relationships between the productive and reproductive economies, but the role of relationships between people and between social institutions continues to be underplayed in traditional economic and social policy (Emirbayer, 1997; Peterson, 2002). Even when using the broader concept of provisioning, we can predict that the social location of different groups of women will determine what options are available to them. Furthermore, provisioning by women will continue to be more difficult than for many men because the work will call upon women's time and energy in ways that men still escape. These patterns will continue as countries move from national to global economies and refocus labour policies to meet the knowledge needs of what is called the new economy. It is also predictable that the new economy will valorize certain skills, such as 'emotion work' (Bolton, 2000), that were traditionally seen as feminine, but appropriating and renaming them in market language, such as public relations, when opportune, while continuing to undervalue them under their old names in traditional female work sites.

Whether the concept of provisioning can create an alternative basis for legitimizing claims and entitlements people make on each other, and on the organizations and states they create on their behalf, awaits further analysis (Power, 2004). Future research and debate will determine if the concept can invite creative action towards new policies in what Beck (2000) imagines to be a 'provident state' (p. 226). Such analyses must also construct what limits can legitimately be placed on persons and groups, and how and by whom. At present, a minority in Canada, as in other countries, are using resources needed by the majority to provision. In the research that is the foundation of the analysis presented in this book we use provisioning as a conceptual tool for not only continuing the process of 'dismantling the master's house' (Lorde, 1984) but also for laying the foundation of an alternative that can shelter women, such as the participants in this study, from the social and economic storms of the twenty-first century. The data reported in the following chapters were collected just prior to the global economic storms of 2008 and the massive government financial stimulus packages for financial centres and large industries. Neither households nor community groups were bailed out. Instead they are expected to absorb a huge new wave of job losses, service cuts, and consumer tax hikes to pay for the enormous increase in public debts and market restructuring. Adding to the urgency of our concerns while writing this book is the impact of more 'efficiencies' and cuts to organizations serving women and poor communities, ostensibly launched in the fall of 2009 by governments to start paying back the recently acquired debts (e.g., Lee & Ivanova, 2009).

PART ONE

3 Provisioning Responsibilities of Women: Relationships Shape the Work

In this chapter data are presented on the provisioning work done by the individual women who participated in the study. These women all belonged to community groups that were concerned with the issues facing women marginalized by gender, income, race, and age. As noted in chapter 2, when formerly public responsibilities were off-loaded onto families and communities, the costs were disproportionately borne by those who had to cope with the consequences – primarily women in their front-line positions as family caregivers, neighbours, service providers, and community actors. This social location meant that many women experienced directly the consequences of cuts to social provisions that characterized policies of former welfare states such as Canada at the turn of the twenty-first century.

The questions posed to participants focused on the provisioning responsibilities they carried and, thus, the associated work. As anticipated, many of the provisioning relationships discussed by participants reflected responsibilities associated with family and employment. It is important to recall that, because there is less discussion of the parameters of women's lives outside of these two spheres, we particularly asked participants to elaborate on the responsibilities they carried, and the work they did, that did not fall easily into work based on kin and employment. The concept of provisioning helped to create different starting points for asking about many different types of work, including work in the local and broader community. In the pages that follow, the individual provisioning work done by the 100 women interviewed across all six research sites are summarized and discussed. Participants' characteristics, the number of women interviewed per site, and selected demographic data are summarized in table 1.1, chapter 1. Chapter 4 focuses specifically on the provisioning work of the community groups to which participants belonged.

The cross-site coding produced twenty-one categories of provisioning work that were subsequently amalgamated into twelve and organized under two major divisions: activities and strategies. The types of work associated with provisioning activities can be broadly grouped into those commonly recognized as work, and those still invisible to most as work. In analysing the data we separated activities from the different types of strategies that women described they used to fulfil their provisioning responsibilities. Some strategies seemed to be survival and coping mechanisms to address needs that had to be met, even if they were supporting the status quo and not in the participants' long-term interests. These might be thought of as the practical daily strategies referred to by Moser (1989) and Molyneux (2002). Other strategies seemed to have the potential for promoting women's interests beyond daily survival because they incorporated a consideration of structural changes. We categorize these as transformative, as they aim to create identities and envision policies and practices that dismantle gender, race, and age inequities.

Activities and strategies used by individual women are organized into categories and explicated through quotes and examples drawn from data collected at the research sites. Specific activities and strategies varied by site and participants' social location, but the categories into which they could be classified held across sites. We recognize that the subcategories, their organization, and the particular names we have given them could be challenged. However, it was agreed among the researchers that these titles did capture the content of the data. Thus we offer them as a step in 'naming' the work and contributions that women in these marginalized communities are contributing to civil society.

Throughout the chapter we attempt to link findings with theories and policy narratives that hide the extent of work that women do, that ignore the fact that provisioning responsibilities are tied to relationships and thus affect decisions about how to access resources. Such narratives oppress women through supporting myths that paid work is the most valued contribution to society.

The Complexity of the Work: Visible and Invisible Provisioning Activities[1]

Because debates about the labour market, domestic/home labour, and community engagement tend to be separate fields of inquiry, each has a theoretical presence and, thus, language and concepts that defines its existence. In documenting women's provisioning activities, however, we had to expand the boundaries of even these traditional categories in order to capture the gendered nature and structure of work at this historical moment. Among our participants, work associated with the labour market included non-voluntary 'volunteer' activities required by social assistance regulations for receiving benefits and/or curriculum volunteer hours requirements for graduating from high school. Under caring labour is found the work of older women who were provisioning for children, grandchildren, siblings, other relatives and friends, as well as aging spouses; women still in their teens who were provisioning for parents as well as boyfriends and their own infants; and women on social assistance who had complex responsibilities for a range of kin, neighbours, ex-partners, as well as their own children.

The range of responsibilities reported by participants was broad, and provisioning encompassed more than providing material resources. Thus, in addition to expanding the foregoing boundaries around material resources, we had to add categories of labour in order to catch the content that arose as participants talked about their work and responsibilities. These included descriptions of the time and effort used to sustain the health of those around them, pursuing social assistance and health officials to get the resources and follow-up appointments to which they were entitled, and calculating the costs and benefits of risky behaviours that participants deemed necessary in order to meet their provisioning responsibilities. Later in the chapter we argue that these areas are analytically important for assessing the impacts of cutbacks and other changes to social programmes for women across different social locations. They reflect important forms of inequities that in the lives of different groups of women – forms that arguably are associated with the spread of neoliberalism across policy arenas.

As table 3.1 outlines, women do *paid, domestic,* and *community work,* but traditional notions of what these encompass reveal only the tip of the iceberg. For example, young women (presented in chapter 5) were engaged in service jobs, retail, telemarketing, babysitting, and such. In addition, almost all recognized the importance of formal education, wanting to get that 'piece of paper' that would get them a 'good' job. At the same time they, along with women in other sites, enumerated 'never-ending' household duties, as well as caring for children. For example, Chantal, a nineteen-year-old Black lone mother, full-time student, and part-time telephone survey worker conveys the multi-dimensional demands on her time and energy as she combines education and employment with domestic and caring labour made possible by the uncounted contributions of work by her mother. This narrative exists alongside a dominant discourse purveying images of young women that focus on the emotional and physical challenges of developing careers and finding future life partners.

Formal community activities included such things as helping to organize the high school breakfast programme, serving on the council of a community resource centre, and volunteering in exchange for goods such as food and diapers. Life circumstances and/or social location often influenced women's decisions about where to contribute their

Table 3.1. Types of provisioning activities done by women

1. Recognized provisioning activities
    i. Engaging in formal and informal work in the labour market – Activities generally associated with jobs or careers done under market norms; contingent, casual, part-time employment; unpaid work in a family business; work placements, e.g., fulfilling community hours as a student / social assistance requirements, traditional education activities such as going to school, upgrading skills, community training programmes.
    ii. Providing caring labour in the domestic sphere – Activities centred on running the household; domestic labour, caring for children and other relatives; non-market mental, emotional, and physical caring labour for non-kin.
    iii. Undertaking commitments in the community sphere – Formal and informal volunteer activities in community organizations (including places of worship); creating and maintaining networks, visiting and organizing social gatherings.
2. Invisible provisioning activities
    i. Sustaining health – Activities associated with relationships women had with children and others who lived with disabilities, chronic conditions, or mental health issues; administrating medicines, preparing special diets; health-management tasks like scheduling, coordinating, and going to medical appointments.
    ii. Making claims – Encompasses the work of advocating for oneself and others for services and money; putting in the time learning where to look for financial assistance and other resources; learning to present oneself, dress, talk, and act in different settings; learning to make arguments with evidence and asserting one's rights; convincing family, friends, landlords, bureaucrats, professionals, and volunteers in medical, education, social, and community services that one is worthy and/or that service claims are legitimate.
    iii. Ensuring safety – Activities intended to bolster the safety of self and children. Tasks included finding safe housing and dealing with violence against themselves and others.

limited time and energy. Among our participants there was also considerable informal community managing work such as acting as the 'community babysitter' for children left unsupervised, informing other women of resources and programmes, exchanging knowledge about where to get day-old bakery products or how to obtain a season pass for children to the local swimming pool. Resource collecting and managing were time-consuming but essential activities to meet provisioning responsibilities for women who lived on very low incomes. As a member of the food cooperative notes, 'The extra clothing you get on the pick-ups, the food, the Christmas baskets, Easter stuff, all the little extra stuff; they help out. The extra food is important.'

In addition to this visible work, participants talked about the range and types of work they did in areas that we classify as invisible forms of labour. Three major areas were: *sustaining the health* of those around them, *making claims*, and *ensuring safety*. Our findings about the work entailed in sustaining the health of those for whom women were responsible echoes research on kin care documenting how families have assumed increasing labour costs as health-care priorities and budgets have changed (Armstrong & Armstrong, 2003; Aronson & Neysmith, 2006; Dyck, Kontos, Angus, & McKeever, 2005; Light, 2001). Women could not always meet the health-care needs of those around them, for lack of resources or other obligations. However, for many the mental and emotional work of dealing with substantial health issues and health-related concerns frequently shaped their lives. For instance, Gina, who manages on a very low income, does health work for her ex-partner, as well as her current husband and one of his friends:

Re: *husband*: He doesn't like to push the wheelchair by himself because he tipped over one time. So when he has a doctor's appointment or something like that, he usually takes the taxi, and I'll meet him at where he's going, and I push him to the appointment, and then I put him back on the taxi.

Re: *ex-partner*: I was doing a lot for him, filling out forms, following him to doctors because he . . . stutters when he talks. He gets nervous and he can't talk, so usually I go to the doctor's with him.

Gina also accompanies her husband's friend, who is illiterate, to his medical appointments.

For low-income women, the time and energy consumed by having to make and remake claims were enormous. On the one hand, it could be argued that women have always had to establish entitlement to services, and provide evidence of and fight for services. On the other hand, participants like Ina, mother of a five-year-old, from an employ-ment-readiness programme for women who have been abused, were not alone in feeling that the amount of this work had escalated in recent years as welfare entitlements and programmes were slashed:

> It's changed. I'm afraid to be a single mom and scared to death that what they expect from me isn't what I'll be able to deliver, and then I'm screwed. If I were to go out and get a job right now, I really don't believe that I would hold it down. I think that I still have things that I need to work through, and they don't care about that. They don't care if I fail. 'You have to do this and this' is what they say, and it's your responsibility if you fail. I'm willing to take on that responsibility, but they won't support me in that. And because you're only allowed welfare two years – or is it three years out of five? – I've used that up.

The third area of invisible labour, ensuring safety from intimates and strangers, is often depicted in the media as a problem of rising crime rates or neighbourhood youth violence. Suggested policy responses, whether 'saying no to racism' campaigns or increasing community policing, miss the emotional and daily struggle to keep oneself safe, reduce potential abuse to children, or promote pride in one's age or cul-ture. These public proposals also seldom mention the increased work borne by, or the costs to, women in local neighbourhoods. It is they who monitor themselves and 'walk on eggs' in daily encounters with potential and real abuse from partners, strangers, and even profession-als representing hurtful welfare rules (Mosher, Evans, & Little, 2004), or police investigations that cannot protect community members from retaliatory gang killings. It is the hidden, invisible work of women that keeps places safe, advocates for more safety, evaluates alternative strat-egies, and develops ways of containing, if not eliminating, the violence that surrounds their lives. Sonya provides a graphic illustration of this work:

> I walk up and down my street. I'm picking syringes off the ground. My daughter was outside and she found three of them. She knows not to touch them. And she asked me, 'Mommy, can you call the cops to come get

these?' So, for her concern, okay, you know. I phoned up the police and I asked – told them my daughter found three syringes outside. 'Is there any way you can have somebody come dispose of them?' And he told me, 'Oh, that's not my job.' I just simply lost it, you know: 'My daughter is asking for a police officer here, for a little bit of help to get rid of this dangerous stuff around our home and you're gonna tell her that's not your job!'

The Hidden Mountain of Strategizing Work: Practical and Transformative Strategies

Permeating the previous list of provisioning activities is the cognitive and emotional attention, conscious or not, that participants used to knit together, to defend, to balance and to change burdens of responsibilities that women marginalized by race, income, and age encounter. At first we just named 'strategizing' as a type of provisioning in the list of naming all the visible and invisible work that women do. However, the interviews revealed different types of strategizing; a single category seemed to hide rather than explicate the dimensions of this work. This led to the decision to develop a separate strategies chart that more accurately captured the multi-dimensionality of the strategizing that participants did. Hence, table 3.2 lays out some of the practical strategies used by women in their daily efforts to provide for themselves and others. It also organizes the less visible work associated with trying to take control of and trying to change some of the conditions that shaped participants' lives. As the following quotes show, strategies were used intentionally. However, this strategizing, this negotiating work, itself was not negotiable – given the asymmetrical and involuntary conditions that marginalize women through racism, ageism, and poverty, especially in times of heightened insecurities and depletion of public resources. Nevertheless, even in the presence of these pressures, we see women trying to use agency in tight spaces to survive in the present, to plan for the future, to refuse some responsibilities and defend others, and to create community spaces that help.

The first set of strategies documents how women dealt with the exigencies of today, using tactics available to them; strategies that reflected participants' histories of coping but also shaped and limited their futures. Such strategies had associated costs but varied in how effectively they enabled women to meet and sustain their provisioning responsibilities. Participants engaged in practical daily strategies of survival that involved not only *acquiring* but also *managing resources*.

Table 3.2. Types of provisioning strategies women used

1. Practical daily strategies
    i.   Creating and managing resources – These are ways women deal with the
         exigencies of daily living. Included are approaches to managing and gathering
         resources to make ends meet, such as exchanges, saving, selling items,
         strategic budgeting, juggling bills and priorities, making sacrifices, going without
         luxuries, cutting back.
    ii. Engaging in risky behaviours – These are ways that women respond to and
         anticipate uncertain futures with the resources at hand. They often involve
         short-term/long-term trade-offs or appear to be risky behaviours, such as going
         without food, getting behind in the rent in order to pay other bills, returning to
         violent relationships for economic reasons.
2. Transformative strategies
    i.   Recreating identity – These are ways that women take time to care for
         themselves; to do activities that they find meaningful, such as doing exercises,
         pursuing spiritual, leisure, social, and non-formal learning opportunities.
    ii. Resisting stereotypes and stigma – These are ways that women reclaim
         status, redefine and take up administrative and ideological categories imposed
         upon them. At times they strategically claim identities (e.g., client) to access
         resources; at other times they challenge stereotypes and assumptions that
         define them in ways with which they do not identify, such as youth, being poor.
    iii. Negotiating boundaries of responsibilities – These are ways women direct / take
         control of / strategically manipulate their relationships of responsibilities. They
         generally negotiate these boundaries by distributing their work across market,
         home/domestic, and community lives; developing new or setting limits on
         existing relationships with friends, families, acquaintances, and networks that
         challenge boundaries around their work.
    iv. Envisioning a future – These are efforts to define and envision how one might
         provision in the future. Activities range from making concrete timelines and
         outlining specific tasks, to more general articulations by participants of how
         they would like to experience their future lives. Included here are women's
         descriptions of what is imagined, limits to imaginings, and how futures are
         imagined.

These resonated with findings of other researchers who have focused
on women living on low incomes (e.g., Edin & Lein, 1996; Moser,
1989). Our participants named activities such as buying in bulk or
doing one's own electrical repairs. Many engaged in casual exchanges
of goods and services. Women had limited control over the amount
and kinds of resources available to them for carrying out their responsibilities; the circumstances in which they found themselves limited

possibilities for action. Thus, strategies for managing resources all too frequently are associated with *taking risks*. One participant from Cascade said, 'I pay whoever sends me a notice first; who will cut you off the fastest?' Another spoke of the work of negotiating relationships that accompany this strategy: 'Sometimes I juggle bills; go by order of importance: no cable; must pay at least part of hydro and phone and Internet; can let taxes slide 'cause if you call they're pretty good.'

Hannah and Carrie, two overburdened mothers, describe respectively how they assess the cost-benefit balance of risky behaviours:

HANNAH. I survive on four to five hours of sleep; lately I've been doing it. Is it a life-threatening approach? I've eaten a meal a day for a long, long time just so that the kids would have enough to eat, and I'll drink coffee instead of juice so that, you know, coffee is a lot cheaper than juice, so my health is affected by it.

CARRIE. I haven't done anything risky to get by, but I've been tempted. You think about the drug business, and I don't agree with drugs, but you know, the thought has crossed my mind – easy money. It's a tempting thought at times when you're down and out.

Transformative strategies are shaped by multiple and intersecting discourses about what it means to be female, elderly, young, poor, racialized, or homeless, but they also reflect some of the ways in which participants are redefining themselves and their relationships to others. The transformative strategies section of table 3.2 starts with *recreating identity*, which is a product of social interaction. A considerable body of research has examined the symbols and communication strategies people use to construct meaning and identity. These are conceptually diverse and include such activities as storytelling, cultural narratives, political ideologies, roles, and body attributes, such as gender, race, and age. They exist as part of approaches deployed to accomplish social objectives (for a review of this literature, see Callero, 2003). One arm of this tradition concentrates on how cognitive processes work to align behaviour, meaning, and identity, thus offering an explanation of how and why identities can change. The dynamic relationship between meaningful activity and identity is caught in a reflection by Clara, a long-time participant in the food cooperative, who lives with her teenage daughter – and who certainly could not be accused of bowling alone (Putnam, 2000)! Through provisioning in particular ways, her identity is shaped to move beyond one of client or volunteer to co-worker and friend.

> The food bank [has helped me out]. It's not so much the food as the emotional support. Since I'm a volunteer there, I've become like part of the family there, been ten years at this one place, made a lot of friends there. We do Christmases together. My Christmas party of the year is with the volunteers there. We have picnics in the summer. We have social events where we go out bowling together, so they've become friends and not just co-workers.

Participants frequently found themselves caught in policy discourses with negative definitions of differences that stigmatized them for being poor, Native, aging, or on social assistance. *Stereotypes* associated with being 'on welfare' were something that Echo, a woman from the employment programme for women leaving abuse, felt influenced how the legal system named who her family is and how she should look. Echo resisted being told how to dress for court; she also risked losing her social assistance and place in the programme when she refused to attack her son's father, as she still felt he was part of the family, for whom she had a relationship of responsibility. Her work of creating her own identity and resisting the labels of the court also included specific tasks, such as writing a letter to name the provisioning work of her ex-husband. He, like many other men who are performing valuable, but invisible, work essential to the well-being of children, could not escape the gendered consequences of traditional female work:

> They [social assistance officials] also told me what I should wear when I attend this court hearing and I'm like, 'No way! I've had enough, you know. You're attacking my son's dad.' I said, 'That's going to mess things up for my son.' You know, they're interfering, and I don't like it. Well, they're [welfare] going to cut me off anyway 'cause I'm not attending the court hearing that they've set up for taking him to court. So, I'm writing a letter to support him. Just because we're not together, we're still a family, and that's where my heart is.

Affecting all the strategies and activities was the key task of *negotiating boundaries* around for whom participants would be responsible and how. Sometimes these relationships were reluctantly assumed or a burden. However, no matter what the basis for the relationships, if participants had resources and adequate personal health, the burdens could be assumed more freely. For instance, while participants took steps to engage in activities that helped to re-energize their minds and bodies and break their isolation, these activities also enabled them (physically and mentally) to sustain the responsibilities they carried. Boundaries delimiting for whom they were responsible were repeatedly negotiated, as Bunny from the older women's group, who appears in chapter 8, explained:

> So, for example, this sister who has needed a lot of help, she lives far away. I would go there a few times a year, and I was talking to her every day, and I was strategizing about all her problems. I finally had to say to her, 'I can't do this anymore. You're going to use the sources of professional help that you and I have talked about and I'll call you. We'll be sisters, and that's it.' And she was happy about that, so I mean it's worked out well. So this is a fairly serious attempt to take care of myself and let me do some more of those things that really interest me.

Throughout the data, we saw women speaking about how community sites helped them meet their provisioning responsibilities, and also support the work of *envisioning a future* and negotiating new boundaries of responsibilities and possibilities. Vivian and Melissa, two participants from Hands On, verbalize this about the work they do at their family resource centre:

MELISSA. If you start drilling it into people – 'Look, this is how we can live. This is what your housing, your community – whatever – can look like, can be like,' people are going to start to keep it that way.
VIVIAN. EXACTLY!
MELISSA. BECAUSE ONE PERSON CAN'T DO IT ALL BY THEMSELVES.
VIVIAN. No!
MELISSA. You need the help and you need money to do it, so you get somebody to back the money on it, and everybody else is going to start helping and pitching in 'cause they're going to want it to stay that way.

Cuts to programmes and shrinking of community programmes sometimes provoked the redoubling of women's volunteering hours to save groups, adding to the women's workload. Conversely, at other times, there was withdrawal, a reduction of responsibility for and contributions to neighbourhoods and organizations. Costs to individual women, their children, órganizations, and society increase when community spaces disappear. The following chapter details some of the work and myriad costs involved in trying to save an organization.

Developing Theory That Connects the Dots of Responsibilities, Work, Relationships, and Costs

We have presented a schema, consistent with the work of feminist scholars such as Edin and Lein (1996), Molyneux (1998, 2002), and Moser (1989), that tries to capture and name the multi-dimensionality of the work that women do. We used the concept of provisioning, as developed by feminist economists such as Barker (2005), Nelson (2006), Power (2004), and Taylor (2004), because it allowed us to explore work and the forms it took, without being impeded by conceptual barriers of public and private spheres that interrupt and thus hide the extent of the work. Furthermore, the concept explicitly ties work to the relationship-based responsibilities that women carry. Several analytical themes emerge from these data that have implications for what a changed discourse on work needs to include, if it is to reflect the lived realities of women such as those who participated in this study.

First, our data are consistent with research showing that provisioning responsibilities are rooted in relationships that do not fit neatly into public and private notions of space (Adkins, 2005; Misztal, 2005). In addition, these data highlight the range of persons in different spaces for whom women provision: themselves, members of extended households, and family who may live elsewhere, including ex-partners and persons in community groups, as discussed in more detail in chapter 4. Furthermore, the boundaries of women's provisioning responsibilities shift – they are not static – and are seen by participants as changing over the years. The contours they take are shaped by the social context within which women take on, or withdraw from, relationships, along with their associated provisioning responsibilities. Women meet their responsibilities by employing a range of activities and strategies. These data suggest that the range of activities and strategies holds across groups of women living in diverse social locations. It is not confined, for instance, to young mothers on social assistance. As the following chapters show, while differences in income, geography, age, race, and access to non-monetary resources influenced the particulars of provisioning, variation was in the specific form that these took, not their existence. Finally, relationships of responsibility are both voluntary and imposed; their existence is a constant in women's lives, and so are their consequences; relationships, responsibilities, and the associated work are not transferable – at least, not in the short term. When these dimensions are hidden in discourses such as those found in discussions of work–life balance, seemingly family-friendly policies can oppress women by denying the provisioning demands of relationships that affect the employment decisions that they make. The overall effect is that women who have financial and/or familial resources can use the labour of other women to meet their provisioning responsibilities and thus have access to employment-related benefits unavailable to those who do not have such resources. Thus, the privileged position of market work is reproduced and reinforced.

Second, at the time of the study, public policies were undermining women's efforts to provision adequately for themselves and others. This resulted in women personally bearing the costs of such responsibilities. When their efforts failed it was they, not the policies, who were deemed inadequate. This dynamic can be seen in the ways that social-programme assumptions about lifestyle, consumption, and choice are frequently linked to notions of persons who are deemed at-risk (Elliott, 2002). In particular, the hybridization of 'risk' and 'need' in assessments can have significant consequences (Hannah-Moffat, 2002). Women who have backgrounds characterized by abuse, mental-health problems, and drug use often find that their 'needs' are reconstructed as 'risks' through these assessment procedures (Swift & Callahan, 2009). This is most marked when an individual's lifestyle is considered deviant (Douglas, 1992). The respectable victim is expected to engage with services, not challenge them, although the latter is what some of our study participants used as a provisioning strategy. Failure to cooperate is interpreted as a refusal to accept help, reinforcing a portrayal of deviance. The contradictory outcome is that women, such as those quoted in this chapter, spend energy justifying the work they do in the community, household, and market, why they do it, and for whom. Justifying how they conduct their provisioning responsibilities becomes another work demand. Justifying the value of their labour is seldom demanded of those who are employed – the exchange of work for money is deemed a sufficient signifier of worth.

Third, participants in this study drew wide boundaries around whom they included in their circles of relationships, along with their associated responsibilities. However, the resources women had at their disposal to meet the needs of those so included were limited. The relationships that participants had with others were often critical to the strategies developed for survival today and negotiating future possibilities. However, maintaining those relationships took resources, and for most participants, money was not available. Instead personal help, energy, and time were the coinage of exchange. These are resources that women who are poor can muster – at a cost. For example, participants spent lots of time walking because they could not afford transportation. They spent extra time volunteering as a way to gain access to food. Such resources are limited, however, and are not easily substituted or increased, as they are for those with financial assets. Using such options affected the quality of participants' lives, as help from others also brought other responsibilities. For instance, although data were not gathered systematically on participants' health, the transcripts were riddled with comments attesting to how accumulated pressures and stresses took their toll on participants' own health. The possibilities of meeting their provisioning responsibilities satisfactorily for themselves and others increased if women could negotiate resources through non-kin relationships, not only with neighbours and friends, but also with civil servants, health workers, social service providers, and volunteers in organizations.

Concluding Comment

The existence of non-kin and non-employment based provisioning responsibilities was revealed because the sample was drawn from community groups. Exploring relationships with provisioning responsibilities outside of the two familiar spheres of household and market was not familiar turf for participants and may well have been impossible to do if the community group had not been there for them to reference. Even so, we suspect that we only scratched the surface. Not revealing these connections allows programmes to be cut because the costs to women remain invisible or categorized as unfortunate side effects, the equivalent of collateral damage. Prominent in the lives of participants in this project were ministries of housing and social welfare. As social assistance became more restrictive, the borders for inclusion were policed more closely for signs of possible fraud; regulations for access to food became more stringent; and certain kinds of assistance available only in exchange for volunteer hours were strictly monitored. The harmful effects of programme regulations interlock with a social policy discourse that denies the existence of many of the provisioning responsibilities that women carry. These responsibilities do not shift as resources are withdrawn. Unlike the provisioning boundaries defined by participants, the policy borders that define work, social identity, and entitlements are regulated through institutional practices that make assumptions about valued and devalued work. Thus, benefits accrue to those who can capitalize on narrow definitions of what is valued work.

What we categorized as invisible provisioning activities are, for the most part, absent from social policy. When they do appear, they are clothed in their neoliberal discourse of health-care costs (versus sustaining health); risk management (versus ensuring safety); and welfare fraud (versus making claims). Likewise, strategies for transforming social identities are individualized through discourses of lifestyle choices; the resistance and creative potential of envisioning alternatives, while enmeshed in the exigencies of the present, are reframed as issues of time management or maintaining a work–life balance (see Odih, 2003; Thompson & Bunderson, 2001). This is the context within which the complex contours of women's provisioning responsibilities are negotiated. Understanding why so much of this work is rendered invisible and devalued is one of the tasks to be addressed. One aspect of this task is trying to identify how privilege is maintained by dominant understandings of work.

The broad domain of civil society engagement, with its attendant responsibilities and work, is rendered invisible if analysts attempt to encompass these activities by retaining the categories but expanding the boundaries of family and employment; likewise, they are devalued when they are put into residual categories of non-work, leisure, or volunteer activities. One result of such classifications is that the substantial work of building and maintaining networks that sustains women – and make demands of them – disappears from public accounts and is not documented, and what is not written down need not be taken up. Recently this space has been referred to as civil society (Howell & Mulligan, 2005; Jaggar, 2005). The term *civil society* was not part of the vocabulary of participants, so instead we asked them to talk about the work they did in their communities. We recognize that the term *community* is vague, its meaning contested by many writers (McBride, 2005).

Nevertheless, it was a familiar term to participants, allowing us to explore with them a range of provisioning responsibilities without the conversation being stopped at conceptual border crossings that might, for example, differentiate established NGOs from neighbourhood associations. Chapter 4 focuses on the provisioning done by community groups and organizations in the project. They are of particular interest because they can be sites for developing relationships that foster alternative identities.

4 Collective Provisioning: Naming the Work of Vital Spaces

This chapter presents the complex ways in which women name and value their collective work in diverse contemporary groups. A cardinal feature of the groups selected for study is the egalitarian participation they worked to foster in their members, thereby enhancing the possibility of exploring how transformative practices and policies are constructed in marginalized communities. Subsequent chapters examine, in more depth, how participants negotiate provisioning work in their specific communities. Chapter 9 takes up the distortions introduced by neoliberal pressures into provisioning responsibilities across the sites, as well as the persistent attempts by members to use collective spaces to create claims for social citizenship.

Our interest in collective provisioning is prompted by questioning how women work together to meet responsibilities and maintain relationships in the community – an arena outside the usual focus of policy-making related to the household, market, or state service bureaucracies. In the community, we find small and large collectivities ranging from neighbourhood and mutual aid groups to religious institutions, electronic cultural networks and non-governmental organizations (NGOs) with charitable status, estimated as including 161,000 in Canada (Statistics Canada, 2005a). As mentioned in the introductory chapter, the data on women's collective work were gathered just prior to the global economic storms of 2008 and the massive government financial stimulus packages for financial centres and large industries. Households and community groups were expected to absorb a huge new wave of job losses, service reductions, and consumer tax hikes to pay for the increase in public debts and market restructuring. The likely intensification of problems from these recent 'efficiencies' and additional cuts to organizations serving women and poor communities (e.g., Lee & Ivanova, 2009) adds to the urgency of concern that prompted the writing of this book. Unless the contours of women's collective work are understood, and the value of different types of their organizational work is accurately assessed, we will not know what has been restructured or destroyed. Thus, our research addresses the question of what is lost when collectivities serving the growing number of marginalized persons and communities shrink or disappear.

Approach to Analysis of the Varieties of Collective Provisioning

The concept of collective provisioning focuses on the totality of work women do together in informal groups and formal organizations, and the value that they give to this labour. Data sources for parsing the range of collective activities are similar to those in the preceding chapter: 100 women interviewees, 138 participants in focus groups and key informant discussions, and the field notes of researchers who developed close relationships with the six project sites – a food cooperative, an employability programme for women leaving abuse, an older women's network, a multicultural neighbourhood centre, a small tenants' group of immigrant women living in a large housing complex, and an established employment and housing programme for racialized young women.

In contrast to the focus on individual provisioning responsibilities in previous chapters, in this chapter we emphasized the labour of collectivities, analysing responses to questions asking for whom the sites and organizations provide and how, and what helps or constrains their work. Women's stories and reflections were explored to probe the visible activities and subtle negotiations in which women engage collectively as they construct what they value about their organizational labours while under constraints of systemic forces and ideas (Gunn, 2006). Because women were prompted to speak about a wide-ranging set of activities in individual interviews and focus groups, we were able to develop a nuanced understanding of activities that are formally produced by organizations, as well as those less visible ways in which the groups conduct their day-to-day operations. Under the supervision of one researcher, we engaged in an iterative analysis to examine emerg-

Table 4.1. The varieties of collective provisioning

Crafting valued goods and services
Providing material resources
Creating cultures of support
Generating knowledges
Networking connections
Constituting collectivities
Mapping common visions
Sustaining group places
Contesting differences and boundaries
Constructing alternative possibilities
Exploring new spaces and identities
Resisting injustices
Countering dominant discourses

ing concepts and themes, and to code specific categories of collective provisioning responsibilities. There were four rounds of analysis to ensure saturation and validity of categories. Each round ended with memos and papers that were discussed in site and cross-site research meetings (Boeije, 2002).[1]

In working through the analyses, we created ten categories of collective provisioning that we judged to have captured the participants' sense of their work. These categories were grouped into three variations: 'Crafting valued goods and services,' 'Constituting collectivities,' and 'Constructing alternative possibilities' (see table 4.1). Throughout this book, the aim is to bring to the surface a rich variety of theoretically promising concepts from pooled data, not to compare perceptions of women according to their social location or differences between groups. Specific manifestations of organizational work could vary by site and will be explored in more detail in chapters 5 through 8. In this chapter, we argue that the wealth of research data and the analytical processes of coding to the point of saturation support robust categories of collective provisioning that held across sites, and provide intriguing concepts for further theorizing and policy exploration. A central theme is that all these forms of collective provisioning operate simultaneously to support the survival and well-being of women in marginalized locations. In the discussion we examine the contribution of this theme to understanding the vital nature of collective spaces.

Crafting Valued Goods and Services:
'If I am not supported, I cannot give'

The women collectively undertake a wealth of complex activities to craft valued goods and services, with categories under this variation of collective provisioning named as 'Providing material resources,' 'Creating cultures of support,' 'Generating knowledges,' and 'Networking connections.' These activities are all essential to helping women and their kin survive, and retain their capacity to contribute to neighbourhoods and communities, as the quote in the subtitle suggests. The most visible work of the organizations is *providing material resources*. Food, childcare, housing, transportation, training, and employment were referred to as key material resources provided by the sites that contribute to the daily survival of their members and the economic health of the community. The importance of women-led organizations in providing material resources essential to the livelihood of members, their families, and the local economy of rural and poor neighbourhoods has been noted elsewhere (e.g., Baker Collins, Neysmith, Porter, & Reitsma-Street, 2009; Edin & Lein, 1998; Petrzelka & Mannon, 2006).

Try as they did, these sites could not provide adequate employment for their members, who had to endure cuts in pay and jobs during the study period. In each site women spoke of using the collective strength of the organization to support the efforts of members to obtain more material resources through pensions, education, employability training, employment support, and childcare and social assistance. Advocacy for individual benefits is an aspect of collective provisioning that can also serve as an impetus for efforts to change policies and practices for more women, which is a variety of work presented later in this chapter under the category of 'constructing alternatives.' The importance of collectively struggling for individual benefits is expanded in chapter 8, in which we analyse how the press for market citizenship is countered by valuing women's solidarity and challenging the state's limited definition of rights and benefits.

During the years under study, women encountered expanding household obligations, insecure incomes, and sometimes high levels of community distrust or interpersonal violence. All the organizations connected to the study were struggling to keep their doors open, and in fact the tenant group discussed in chapter 6 no longer exists. These precarious conditions are similar to what NGOs in other marginalized communities have encountered (e.g., Hanlon, Rosenberg & Clasby, 2007; Murray, Low, & Waite, 2006; Silliman, 1999). 'Rules change all the time' was a refrain that echoed throughout the sites, accompanied by fears that sharp funding cuts and policy changes distort and shift what the women valued about their collective work.

In the midst of these difficult times, women spoke of the importance of taking time and energy to work together to cultivate environments that are respectful, caring, friendly, fun, and cooperative. *Creating supportive cultures* is a highly valued aspect of women's collective work (Martin, 1990) but is invisible to outsiders. The supportive cultures created by women vary, yet are similar in their attempts to push back against the isolating problems of competition, stress, loneliness, and violence by fostering the positive atmospheres women say they need and desire (Dominelli, 2006; Gittell, Ortega-Bustamante, & Steffy, 2000; Taylor, 1999). One woman spoke about the support she felt in 'the freedom to be heard' in the community centre, calling it a rare gift: 'Knowing you were given that gift – which is a gift, because not too many organizations will ever give you that – is having a voice, having any kind of power, ownership, and trust.'

In the next quote, an elaboration of the subtitle for this section, a woman in the employability site for those leaving abusive relationships argued that the presence of a supportive culture of women's groups was requisite for creating healthy spaces within households and community: 'If I am not supported, I cannot give. If I have support and a safe place, I can give. In the past there was not support. At our organization, we learn this support . . . so the support and the dialogue moves into the community.'

In a similar vein, a member of the food cooperative spoke of the need to find support from others and a positive space that makes it possible to not only receive, but also to give to others: 'A lot of people don't have the support. They may not have family around, and when you feel isolated, it's nice to get out, of you know . . . you know where I am coming from? They are coming and participating and giving something back. And it does, it makes them feel a lot better.'

Generating knowledges is another component of crafting valued goods and services. This kind of collective activity entails not only learning what others, or the experts, know. Rather, participants in the study sites learn that they already have important types of knowledge. To support generation of one's own knowledge, for example, a policy was instituted in the food cooperative that the time spent learning together could be counted as hours of volunteering. Volunteer hours were turned into points that could be cashed in for food or goods. When asked how this policy worked to generate knowledge, a woman said,

> Oh, if somebody has an interest and has a particular skill, they would come to me and book a class. So, it could be . . . we have canning; we do our canning. So they'll come in and demonstrate and show people how to can, and the recipes and, they hold the class and they . . . it's really, it is really neat, like . . . the girl wanted to do a scrapbook, so we went out and bought the materials, and they did all photographs, and it was amazing, like most people wouldn't know how to put it all together, and she showed them different ways, and they have little stickers [with] sayings. It turned out really well.

Sharing knowledge promotes personal confidence and is linked to creating and sustaining a supportive culture in which to learn more. The young women in the multi-racial employability and housing programme, for example, spoke of the value of connecting to other young parents. One said she was learning from those who 'have gone through a lot of problems, worse situations than other people, so it's good to talk to other people than to be home alone.'

Another concluded that the learning experience was positive because others listened to the story she wanted to tell. She said they all learned that 'everyone has a story, everyone has an experience.' In addition, women learned the possibility of experimenting and learning from personal mistakes while being supported to explore new knowledges and identities. According to one participant in the multicultural community centre, 'Knowing even if you made a mistake, there were people there to guide you into making [a decision] richer and bigger, because they gave you that sense of power.'

The women desired 'real' knowledge, not like 'those Mickey Mouse courses that go nowhere' or training for 'any job as if it is better than no job,' as several women argued in the employability programme for women leaving abuse. Rather, the focus in this and other sites was on transformative learning that prioritized safety, independence, enjoyment, change, and new possibilities. Learning in the sites occurred through meeting new people and participating in literacy training, high school or college courses, and workshops on myriad concerns about racism and multiculturalism, nutritious food preparation, pension reform, creative writing, safe sex, and less harmful use of drugs.

Women reported that the sites also strategized how to generate knowledge that educates government, funders, the next generation of women organizers, and the public about the nature of women's interests and need for collective action. The employability programme, for example, developed an internationally recognized curriculum for employment training for women leaving abusive relationships. The older women's group in our study developed research expertise on the economic insecurity of older women and met with provincial agencies to discuss policy implications of the research.

Networking connections constitutes an important type of collective agency identified by Mason (2007) in her study of seventy-four Australian women-specific rural services. Networking became essential to the survival of the Canadian groups we studied, as it did for the Australian services when faced with serious funding cuts and negative changes in state policy. The manager in the young women's site that is part of a larger NGO spoke about the time and energy put into activities such as going to meetings, strategizing with other agencies, and writing funding proposals. She argued that a key reason for participating in many networks was to ensure the survival and promotion of women's interests in her own organization, and in the larger community.

This giving of energy and skills through networking is not only for visible collective campaigns, lobbying, joint proposals, and protests on a particular issue, such as welfare reform, but also for building relationships that connect women within the sites and their communities. Without a collective space, this is difficult to do. A young woman spoke of how important it was to 'find some space from your family' as a step to creating community networks. Echoes of the following quote from the older women's network are found throughout the data, as women look for connections to groups that could be part of their lives, providing solace and solidarity around common values: 'What I was really trying to do was to connect with women who would be part of the next phase of my life. I think I was looking for a group who would be my life as an older woman.'

The work of networking and connecting is linked to the previous categories of collective provisioning – 'Creating supportive cultures' and 'Generating new knowledges.' Knitting together knowledges from different members clarifies what the valued services and goods are in a particular community, and identifies what hinders women's capacity to meet their provisioning responsibilities. Providing supportive cultures, knowledge generation, and networking activities of organizations are valued services in their own right. They are also foundational to the collective work undertaken to resist blaming or shaming individuals for difficulties rooted in economic, gendered, and racial inequities – and to construct alternatives – the final category of collective provisioning described later in this chapter.

Constituting Collectivities: 'This is what we can do as a group'

While crafting goods and services is the collective work of providing for individual members, the labour of constituting collectivities – the plural noun we use in this book to name the diverse organizations – refers to provisioning for the group. We conceptualize 'constituting the collective' as taking three distinct forms: mapping a mission premised on shared values, sustaining group places and spaces, and contesting differences about what is important. Much of this labour is performed backstage, out of public view, in the proverbial kitchens of the groups and community, and in boardrooms. It determines 'this is what we can do as a group,' as one participant concluded. Other researchers have noted the considerable effort that goes into writing mission statements and maintaining the activism of women's organizations (e.g., Blackstone, 2004; Gittell, Ortega-Bustamante, & Steffy, 2000). Our data highlight the important emphasis associated with the relational work in constituting collectivities. This work is often unfunded and not visible to those outside the organization, yet necessary to articulate the collective responsibilities of women in marginalised locations, and to make visible the contesting of boundaries about who groups provide for and how, especially in times of constraints and increased demands.

Mapping a common vision is the behind-the-scenes analytical work of defining publicly the purposes and identity of a collectivity, thereby signalling sufficient agreement on values, priorities, and relational responsibilities. In the words of a participant in the community centre, this category captures the work of engaging with others to 'create an understanding of where we come from and what are our issues.' The older women's network was most explicit in arguing the need to establish a feminist vision. One member underlined the need for 'a collective voice . . . as this is particularly important right now because gender equality has been losing ground.'

Defining and supporting this collective voice are not finite tasks. Members spoke of the repetitive labour required to articulate and explicate the common vision of a site to its own members and to others. Research participants also spoke of the difficult conversations that occurred when sites considered changing priorities, relinquishing responsibilities, or taking on new ones. Conversations on new visions are most problematic when groups are pressured to respond to externally imposed constraints such as loss of staff, individualizing discourses, funding cuts, or introduction of performance outcome measures that do not respond to the central purpose of a group (Lowen & Reitsma-Street, 2006; Masson, 2000; Silliman, 1999).

The activity of *sustaining group spaces* refers to the familiar, yet complex processes of translating a mission statement or set of principles into practices and services. This collective work uses the paid and unpaid labour of its members, performed regularly and continuously, throughout times of stability, but even more so in times of change and crisis. It includes hiring and laying off staff and recruiting board members, ensuring members are well informed and training volunteers, managing conflict between members, negotiating responsibilities between paid staff and volunteers, writing funding proposals and accounting for services, and organizing social events for members and volunteers.

Less visible is the shadow work needed to sustain groups. One member of the older women's network defined this type of work as 'the steps that I have to do before I even get here.' She is referring to the cognitive, practical, and emotional costs associated with finding time and energy, amid busy days, to prepare for a meeting, including travelling. Such work is difficult for women in the groups we studied, since they may be volunteering many hours because of their commitment to the organization, and possibly other causes in the community as well, while at the same time working in various low-paying jobs to make a living or caring full-time for their own aging or ill bodies or other family members who are young or ill.

A significant type of labour involved in constituting collectivities is *contesting differences and boundaries*. This is the work of recognizing conflicts and responding to varying ideas about what the group can and cannot do, especially in times of crisis or serious differences in members' interpretations of priorities (San Martin & Barnoff, 2004). All the study sites encountered difficulties in responding adequately to the diverse needs of past, present, and future members and their families. Each faced agonizing decisions about what and how the site could provide, and how it could do so and still sustain itself as a group. Disputes about membership criteria, for example, and eligibility for services for families living in poor neighbourhoods adjacent to, but outside, the boundaries originally established by the community centre necessitated figuring out anew what were the core values of the organization, what diversities were to be encouraged, and what compromises were unacceptable.

Making boundaries around responsibilities requires conscious attention to seeing differences, in addition to commonalities, and deciding who does not recognize or affirm the group purposes, and how to deal with them. Jaggar (1998) argues that women's groups ceaselessly patrol their boundaries to decide what behaviours and attitudes signal inclusion and exclusion, and to negotiate exceptions and revisions to responsibilities and privileges of members and 'outsiders.' How sites react to funding decisions that can change the service that is offered and to whom, and who has responsibility to make these decisions, is intensive work, requiring substantial cognitive, interpersonal, and emotional labour, particularly challenging when resources are severely limited or change rapidly. A key informant in the employability programme for women surviving abuse spoke about the rapid cycle of endings and extensions in their contracts, adding her assessment of the toll this takes on staff and members: 'It is very, very draining; we worry about the service. Don't know what to say to recruits.'

Another student in that site expressed her anger at the changes in boundaries that determine who gets services, not only for herself but also future students who may not get the necessary education to stop violence in their lives.

> I'm really angry, and my class is really angry that we have to play this waiting game, 'cause I would say that I would come back for the next class, but we don't know if that's for sure [if the programme will continue to be funded]. I'd love to be able to finish, because it's done so much for me. And it's not knowing that's an anxiety to bear. This place has been successful for me so far, and it's scary and sad, because women who are abused need to come and be around women who have been abused.

Contesting differences is fraught with contradictory possibilities that challenge core values of an organization and its members. This is especially the case when consequences are negative or unknown. In one site, for example, there were difficult meetings and disrupted relationships as members grappled with the implications of seeking official status as a charitable organization. This change could have opened up funding opportunities, but at the same time it limited their capacity to resist injustice and counter dominant discourse – varieties of collective provisioning we take up in a subsequent section.

Another site grappled with the consequences of new restrictive provincial social assistance and employment laws on its values and services. As the following quote from a member in the young woman's employability and housing programme suggests, keeping a common vision provoked tensions about how to navigate differences in responsibilities during times of constraint.

> When the changes to Ontario Works [the social assistance laws] came, we had major discussions. Some aspects, mandatory reporting – we didn't want to be part of that. The only part we thought we could be a part of was support services for women. We feel we haven't compromised our values; we're not turning women in, because that was not the way we want to work. We could've been part of all of it; we chose not. There were values we want to hold that are dear to us. We want to have programmes that encourage and promote and give women options to take care of themselves, not to spy on them, absolutely not.

Not reporting the volunteering contributions of women could threaten their individual eligibility for social assistance or employment services, as well as funding for the organization. However, reporting women to the authorities threatened the group's values and magnified small differences in behaviour that could turn women into welfare defrauders, or criminals. Thus, the collective tasks of mapping a common vision, sustaining the group, and contesting boundaries entail the nuanced work of defining and supporting 'this is what we can do as a group' while negotiating what decisions are possible, such as obviating the mandatory reporting that reinforces the distrust of young women or welfare recipients by 'spying on them.'

Constructing Alternative Possibilities: 'If it wasn't for the cooperative . . . I wouldn't have been able to take on City Hall'

In this third aspect of collective provisioning, the focus moves away from constituting the organization and serving members in the present, to the categories of work required to construct alternative policies and practices, including exploring new spaces and identities, resisting injustices, and countering dominant discourse. Originally the groups, networks, and organizations in the research began as sites of social justice struggles within marginalized communities. We found that participants developed a set of organized strategies to construct alternative possibilities, premised, in part, on 'political essentialism' (Lind, 2005, p. 10). This refers to the experience of groups of women who, despite their differences, unify purposively for a time around particular experiences in order to overturn injustices or claim rights to resources.

The initial purpose in coming together requires continued reworking. The cultures of support that reflect or intend to respect the ethnic and age diversities in a site can become seedbeds for change. In the next quote from a member of the fledging tenants' group, there are hints of the analytical labours that depend and build on these positive, friendly cultures to explore new spaces and identities. Given pervasive racism, sexism, and violence, women need spaces to come together and find a bond without forcing it, in order to sort out concerns and 'do their thing' – a mantra repeated throughout the quote. The supportive culture of an organization serves as an alternative space in which women can enjoy and build collective energy, knowing their children are not in danger on the streets. Here they can begin to imagine what 'their thing' might be, both personal and common issues:

> I think it helps because it brings everyone together, and it makes people . . . it gives people a chance to resolve their issues, and come together and kind of bond together more, you know . . . Like, you know, we have our [name of cultural, religious group] community, and if they can come in and have a chance where they can get together and do their thing, and the kids, different age groups, can come and we don't have to worry about the kids being on the street, you know, maybe dealing some drugs or trying to act cool.

Despite women's desires for supportive cultures, conflict is inevitable in the pursuit of exploring alternatives. Within the previous quote, there is an assumption that not everyone would get along and issues needed to be resolved. Bonding and togetherness have to be actively constructed, or agreed to for a time, so that tensions about issues can be safely addressed. The need for spaces that encompass these tensions is captured in the words of a woman who joined the older woman's network. She spoke of the importance of women finding times and avenues to argue about new ideas, recognizing that these discussions could provoke disagreements and difficulties, and concluding that 'conflicts need a space to be heard and discussed.'

Collective spaces are needed to imagine other futures. 'To bring together women is really, really important,' concluded a participant in the employability site for women leaving abuse, so that a woman can begin 'to start to trust others, and trust yourself,' and proceed to name what is wrong and fight for their concerns and desires. What is wrong is every form of abuse. The message that it is unacceptable needs to be stated clearly over and over, to the women themselves, and to the public, as concludes another woman in that site: 'There is clear communication, and caring people who are together themselves . . . really amazing, positive, healthy role models. They don't teach "It's your karma to live with abuse, go back to him or learn from abuse," as some people say, and as I used to think.'

Constructing alternatives not only supports women to come together to invent new identities and possible futures for themselves. It is also the work of building alternative organizations. For example, two study sites worked to buy or build buildings so they could create new types of spaces that, in turn, could foster alternative relationships, identities, and ways of living. The affordable housing cooperative built by the older women's network and the community resource centre for marginalized, multicultural neighbourhoods became concrete representations of new places that signalled the importance of collective connections. As a staff member of the community resource centre proudly concluded when their plan to purchase the community centre building came to fruition, 'We will be visible . . . like a statue in the community . . . saying, you know, this is going to be a community centre.'

Resisting injustice is the bedrock work of global feminist movements and as well as local daily protests. This category of collective provisioning speaks truth to the problematic practices and policies that unfairly distribute the costs and benefits of wealth creation and social reproduction (Miles, 2004–5; Mohanty, 2003; Ricciutelli, Miles, & McFadden, 2004). Resisting injustices were manifested in our study sites in campaigns to repeal the two-year limits on social assistance in one province, for example, and challenging onerous requirements to establish social assistance eligibility in both provinces. Other examples included building a housing cooperative for older women, despite strong political opposition, and fighting against unsafe neighbourhoods, as captured in the story of a woman from the food cooperative:

On my street, in less than a year and a half, I had three murders on my street; there's prostitutes on my street constantly. I had to clean my back-yard of drug paraphernalia because there's a church next door to me where the hookers do their thing . . . before my son can go outside . . . [Now] we have police presences on the streets almost all of the time. There have been two major drug busts since last December . . . And, I [wouldn't] have been able to do it if this person wouldn't have been able to put me in touch with this regional counsellor. If it wasn't for the cooperative, I wouldn't have been able to pay to go to school, to take these courses, to take on City Hall last year.

The concluding phrase 'to take on City Hall,' used in the subtitle of this section, aptly summarizes the visible aspect of resisting unjust practices and policies. It is through such testimonials that we see how the visible work of naming the violence and getting City Hall authori-ties to use more street policing to increase community safety is linked to the less visible collective provisioning work of crafting valued goods and services of a food cooperative. The otherwise hidden relationships of women are crucial to their successes, as in this instance, the provi-sioning of food, clothing, support, and connections helped the woman to name the dangers in her neighbourhood, pay for some education, connect her to politicians, and join others for policy changes.

In addition to openly resisting injustices in the sites, there is the subtle strategic collective work of *countering dominant discourses* (Car-roll & Ratner, 1996; Gunn, 2006). What differentiates this category from the previous one is recognition of the additional work required to disrupt assumptions about what women do or want. To ensure that the issues of women with insecure incomes or difficult backgrounds are not forgotten, this work of countering dominant discourse neces-sitates repetition and creatively reworking messages for different au-diences. A staff in the employability programme for women leaving abuse argued that their key message for their members, and the public at large, is that violence is hurtful, and no violence is to be tolerated. She added, 'It is a constant job. That message is getting out, but it is a regular piece of work.' The women in this site also pointed to the more subtle aspect of countering dominant discourses by daily modelling peaceful language and behaviours. A board member summed up this work as follows: 'We are role model[s] for ourselves and each other. How we work together, how we communicate with each other, how we solve problems in the teaching, is a role model for the students, for their children, and beyond. Also [we are] a role model for other agencies.'

The complex labour required to challenge misconceptions about violence, poverty, dependency in aging or youth, and to contest untruthful explanations of their causes needs to be made visible. If not named or counted, this aspect of collective provisioning work is not recognized as valuable or deemed relevant to policy or practice (Power, 2004; Waring, 1988). The older women's network explicitly named itself a feminist site with a mission to counter stereotypes of older women as dependent burdens. The site members boldly spoke of the significant economic and social contributions older women continue to make to society – a theme taken up in chapter 7. The older women argued that it was not age or health that marginalizes women, but sexism and economic systems. Said a focus group participant, 'I think the stereotype of older women is all wrong, so I want my voice to be heard out there, and I think that people should know that we're sitting on various committees. We're involved in intersecting committees. When they're talking about stuff, we can pipe up and say, "Hey, yeah, but how's that going to affect me as an older woman? You've forgotten that whole issue."'

Collectivity as Vital Space

This chapter has described the work that women do together as collective provisioning that is embedded in their relationships and in what they value about the purpose and practices of their organizational labours. The categories and varieties were presented separately, so we could explicate their dynamic and relational complexity beyond the usual description of services, advocacy, and organizational maintenance. Yet the types of collective provisioning – named as crafting valued goods and services, constituting collectivities, and constructing alternative possibilities – are interrelated and are all needed to respond adequately to the practical immediate needs and the long-term strategic interests of communities marginalized by age, race, and poverty.

Without public appreciation of the holistic nature and interdependence of the components of collective provisioning, women's groups and organizations will have even more difficulty than they already do in responding to limited resources and restrictive laws. A narrow focus on organizational services for immediate physical needs, for example, reduces attention to the supportive cultures that women crave, and it misses the collective work required to attend to other responsibilities, such as resisting stereotypes and racialization. Delivering only material resources funded by short-term performance-based contracts, institutionalized by neoliberal policies (e.g., Cohen & Brodie, 2007), masks the realities of negotiating changing responsibilities associated with collective work and holding to the perceptions of what women value as important. Conversely, understanding the range and interdependence of collective provisioning activities promotes the possibility of a more accurate analysis and adequate responses to the tensions, burdens, and costs of what women value in the work they do together.

The activities identified in this chapter are primarily non-material and invisible to the outside observer. These less visible activities nourish relationships and clarify values that are central to collective provisioning. The extensive and mostly unpaid emotional, social, cognitive, and political collective provisioning that generates new knowledges, maps group visions, and sustains the daily life of the organization provides the substrata in which the crafting of valued services and goods are rooted. Were it not for the contesting boundaries of responsibilities and challenging the political acceptability of writing off some communities as unworthy, individual women bear the brunt of blaming for provisioning failures (Lind, 2005). Asking members for whom organizations provide, and how, brought into the open the extensiveness of the efforts required to protect supportive spaces situated in places away from dangerous streets or violent relationships.

The participants in our study clearly identified the many ways in which provisioning a social space is one of the groups' key accomplishments. Within this space, women aim to work together in integrated ways to establish the values of the group and define boundaries for collective responsibilities. Here members determine the central 'values we want to hold that are dear to us' and map the vision that constitutes the group. The relational aspects of the work form part of all that is undertaken: from effecting values, making decisions, and delivering services, to negotiating conflicts that address material matters affecting bodily, economic, and relational well-being. Establishing a vision is hard work that involves debates about priorities and new provisioning responsibilities made more difficult by imposed constraints. The emotional work involved in envisioning collective activities is largely invisible, to outsiders and even to members themselves until asked to examine how they accomplish their activities. Yet the relational activities of labouring bodies (Franzway, 2001) is essential to transforming the 'details of life and ways of being' (Aptheker, 1989, pp. 183–4).

Beyond those deliberate activities that develop a collective voice is the use of the social space as a place where personal troubles are shared and commonalities can be seen. One of the strongest themes permeating the interviews and group conversations is the value women give to meeting 'others in the same situation.' The commonalities women discover in reflecting on the conditions of their lives begin to shift an individualized explanation of those troubles to a more structural one (Erbaugh, 2002; Finn, 2002; Lind, 1997; Reid, Allison & Frisby, 2006; Susser, 1988). The values of equality and non-hierarchy that are the hallmarks of women's organizations shape interactions within the collective social space (Rebick, 2005; Weeks, 1994). Such values promote a non-linear process of support that allows individuals to see others and themselves as whole people within their self-defined circle of relationships and responsibilities: women can be validated and valued in their own right.

What is sought is dialogue and understanding, even in the presence of different points of view and turbulent controversy (San Martin & Barnoff, 2004). This is especially important for women who have experienced stigma and oppression, whether of racism, sexism, ageism, or the stereotypical views of women in poverty. The stigma of being visible minority mothers in poverty is intensified in a neoliberal era, as they are vilified in the media and by social assistance programmes that ignore their provisioning responsibilities to others (e.g., Piven, Acker, Hallock, & Morgen, 2002). Responding strategically to provisioning responsibilities amid negative experiences of poverty and racism is taken up in chapters 5 and 6 on young and older mothers of diverse cultures living in a large city, and in chapter 8 on poor women from three sites in mid-size cities.

The collective provisioning that takes place in the social space of organizations goes beyond Band-Aid solutions to problems facing marginalized women. As Howell (2005) has argued, women's movements, community organizations, and informal groups give women 'a space for association, for the articulation of interests, for ideological contestation' (p. 5). Women's hopes for a better world are turned into realities through the working of collectivities to help women address gender and material concerns – not only by liberating constructions of masculinity and femininity, pursuing equality, and opposing sexism, but also through constructing sustained access to adequate food, education, housing, employment, and recreation. At the same time, women are offered a space in which they can practise building peaceful words and worlds, and collectively challenge the arbitrary limits in social assistance laws or unravel the damaging messages of 'at risk' young mother or 'dependent senior,' as these are taken up in more detail in chapters 5 and 7.

To provision collectively is not to sell services to customers or clients but to offer public services for the needs and desires of citizens that go beyond technical solutions. At the most activist end of the continuum, this space can offer transformational possibilities for women to explore identities that defy stereotypes. A collective space validates and values women in the present, in their own right, and the provisioning responsibilities they name as important to take up. This vital collective space also serves as the crucible out of which women imagine and practise citizenship claims for themselves and for others – an argument developed in the last two chapters of the book.

PART TWO

5 Producing Racial Knowledge in Community Programmes for 'At Risk' Young Women

SANDRA TAM

In chapter 3 the provisioning responsibilities and associated work done by individual women across all the research sites was examined and organized into broad categories. In chapter 4 a parallel analysis was presented that outlined the responsibilities and associated work done within collectivities. Both chapters included data from participants at Gen-Y – the site that is the focus of analysis in this chapter. In the following pages I try to unravel how individual and collective provisioning responsibilities and work come to take the shape that they do for racialized[1] women in community programmes for 'at risk' young women. I aim to show how particular forms of racial knowledge are produced at the site of a community programme where young racialized women make career decisions, and youth workers help them to do so. My observations reveal that the young women between sixteen and twenty-four years old made educational and career decisions with limited reference to racial impacts. In contrast, workers in the programmes provided advice that acknowledged the racial barriers and discrimination faced by their young clients. However, their advice appeared to be tied to institutional processes and practices related to professional obligations and organizational mandates that reinforced rather than challenged social inequalities. I argue that in these community programmes, the production of racial knowledge occurs through young women's decision-making and youth workers advice and work processes as they enact anti-discrimination and diversity policies in the organization.

Studying Young and Racialized Women's Working Lives

Although women face challenges in their working lives based on their gender, it is generally acknowledged that racialized women experience specific disadvantages in the labour market. According to Statistics Canada (2005c), both visible minority women and non-visible minority women tended to be employed in traditional female-dominated jobs like administration, clerical, sales, and services jobs. Both groups of women were also more likely to work part-time than their male counterparts. However, visible minority women are less likely than non-visible minority women to be employed, and more likely to experience higher unemployment rates and lower average annual employment earnings (Statistics Canada, 2005c). In addition, care responsibilities may be more onerous for recent immigrant women without family or other social support networks (chapter 6, this volume; George, 1998; Grahame, 2003).

Studies of younger women of all racial backgrounds have tended to focus on problems such as teen pregnancy, body image, girl culture and identity, sexuality, girl gangs, and violence (Brown, 2003; Chesney-Lind & Irwin, 2008; Frost, 2001; Gonick, 2003; Kaplan, 1997; White, 2002). Some critical ethnographers have included problems of work in their investigations of young women's identity formation and educational experiences (Bettie, 2003; Mirza, 1992), although more often than not young women are studied with reference to reproduction. Very rarely does work or employment feature as a problem in studies of young women in the way that it does for young men (see McDowell, 2002). This research on young women's provisioning experiences is meant to fill knowledge gaps in understanding what gives rise to women's racialized experiences of work.

Critical Perspective on Race and Racism

This analysis uses the conceptualization of race from critical race theories (Delgado & Stefancic, 2001; Essed & Goldberg, 2002) to understand the impacts of racism and racial inequality on young women's working lives. The strength of these theories is their assumption that race is an organizing principle in society and that racialization is a process. The critical tradition is concerned generally with the construction, perpetuation, and dynamics of social realities and inequities.

By focusing on race as a socially constructed, relational category (rather than a fixed, biological one) that intersects with other dimensions of social identity like gender and class, studies of working racialized women aim at gaining insight into the formation of race in specific social contexts. For example, historical and contemporary research on racialized women's work experiences has demonstrated various and specific manifestations of racist sexism (or sexist racism) in occupations where women predominate, such as nursing, domestic work, technical work, and call-centre work (Calliste, 2000; Collins, 2000; Ehrenreich & Hochschild, 2003; Freeman, 2000; Glenn, 2002; Mirchandani, 2006). Much of this labour reveals subtle forms of racism and racial subtexts infused into ordinary and daily social interactions.

Studies that apply critical perspectives on race and racism have tended to examine the social and economic conditions that give rise to racial inequalities. Researchers often consider how people's experiences are shaped by the larger context of globalized economies and labour markets. For example, Ng (2002) argued, on the basis of her study of globalized restructuring in the garment industry, that immigrant women who expressed a preference for work at home because of responsibility for domestic work (even though they were paid low piece rates) contributed to the perpetuation of racial inequalities through a 'self-regulated' form of colonization. Mirza (1992) found from her school-based ethnography that Black teenage girls were attempting to achieve upward social and occupational mobility by entering traditional female occupations like social work, nursing, and teaching. Their career strategy was seen by the researcher as a rational choice based on the young women's own assessment of job opportunities that were acceptable and accessible to them under the severe economic constraints of a racially and sexually segregated labour market in the 1980s in Britain.

In a U.S.-based study of the racial-ethnic organization of dietary and nutritional science, DeVault (1995) observed that the operating framework of cultural differences approach to nutritional counselling failed to account for how African American nutritionists utilized their ethno-specific knowledge to address cultural and ethnic issues in their daily work. Neither was the cultural context of race and ethnicity in which their work was performed adequately referenced. In a study of a local welfare-to-work programme, Solomon (2003) described how the enactment of 'mothering' and 'sistering' discourses by a White, middle-class trainer and poor, African American, and Latin American trainees effectively processed an administrative logic that articulated the need of the medical industry for low-wage workers. A few institutional ethnographers have been particularly interested in examining the professional work conditions of Canadian community and social programmes as local sites of racial knowledge production (Ng, 1996; Parada, 2004; Swift, 1995). In an earlier study, Ng (1981) challenged the notion of ethnicity as essentially associated with the presence of 'cultural traits' by examining ethnicity as a social relation from the perspective of Canadian immigrant women's lives and their relationship to the labour force, systems of service delivery, and other members of society.

Methodology for Revealing the Ruling Social Relation of Race

The data in this chapter come from a study of young women's working lives in the context of global labour markets and welfare state restructuring. Dorothy Smith's (1987) institutional ethnography (IE) was used to reveal racialization processes. Like other types of ethnography, IE is a qualitative research methodology used to study social settings and interactions in everyday life. In contrast to more traditional ethnographies that primarily describe people's experiences and settings, IE seeks to explicate the social relations of power that organize local settings and conditions under which people's experiences arise (Campbell & Gregor, 2002; Smith, 1987). Ruling relations are a particular type of social relation that concern the institutional ethnographer; they are socially organized exercises of power: 'They are those forms that we know as bureaucracy, administration, management, professional organisation, and the media. They include also the complex set of discourses, scientific, technical, and cultural, that intersect, interpenetrate, and coordinate the multiple sites of ruling' (Smith, 1990, p. 6). Here I use IE to explicate the ruling relation of race, which is seen to operate through the courses of action taken by young women and youth workers in their community programmes.

The research was conducted at a well-established women's social services organization, which will be referred to as Gen-Y, in a large Canadian city from 2005 to 2006. The agency was selected for its long-term commitment, expertise, and history of working with young women. Fifteen women between the ages of sixteen and twenty-four who were deemed 'at risk' youth were recruited for individual, face-to-face interviews. The participants took part in housing (a women's shelter), employment, young mothers', and girls' programmes. The interviews were arranged with the help of programme staff, who told the women about the project during their regular group sessions. The women were also told that they would receive an honorarium for participating in the study, and if they were interested, they should contact the researcher directly. The interviews lasted approximately an hour and they took place at the programme site for the convenience of the study participants.

One-third of the young women were working part-time or on a casual basis; one-third were full-time students; one-third had completed some post-secondary education; and one young woman was a university graduate. All but one of the group were members of racialized groups (from African, Jamaican/Caribbean, and South and South-East Asian backgrounds). Seven were lone mothers, the majority of whom had one toddler; one woman had two children. All of the women had either low incomes or were from working-class families. As in the other research sites, the young women were asked open-ended questions about how they provided for themselves and others they felt responsible for. They were also asked about their involvement in paid employment, secondary or post-secondary education, and community programmes.

In addition to young women, ten key informants, including frontline youth workers and administrative and management staff from the programmes identified above, were interviewed. Most of the key informants were white women, while two were from racialized groups. They were invited to participate on the basis of their interest in the research, but they had to have had experience working in social services programmes that support 'at risk' young women. Youth workers were asked about their programmes and how they do their work with young women clients. As well as interview data, field observations of young women's and youth workers' interactions in programme settings and programme documents were collected for analysis.

The analysis focused on how the young women talked about race and racism in relation to their education and career decisions and how youth workers saw racial issues affecting their clients. By juxtaposing young women's accounts to those of the youth workers in field observations and descriptions of activities, the results map out how racial knowledge is produced through the workers' assessment of the needs of young women clients in relation to institutionally based programme goals (Tam, 2007).

Juggling Family Caregiving, School, Volunteering, and Paid Work

The main provisioning activities of Gen-Y young women involved juggling family, caregiving, school, volunteering, and paid work responsibilities. Many of the young mothers were performing household work (laundry, cooking, cleaning, and grocery shopping), trying to continue their education while child-rearing (doing homework), doing paid work to put food on the table, and making choices about future job possibilities. Chantal, who worked part-time conducting telephone surveys, explained how she manages her workload and cares for her toddler:

> I have time when he's sleeping to get everything done, and while he's at my mom's house, I'd be working. From there, my mom would drop him home. Everything's basically done when he's sleeping. I make food the night before so the next day food would be prepared for him. I can't cook while he's around, because my child likes to run into the kitchen and I don't have a gate to put there. He doesn't like to be in his playpen; he starts screaming. He likes a lot of attention, and nobody's there to watch him. I try to get work done – I do homework – but sometimes I get in at midnight and I just want to go to sleep. Sometimes I do a little studying or I get up early in the morning to study. When I tell [people] I go to work, they think, 'How could you do that? You go to school, and you have a son to take care of. Isn't it hard?' It's hard, but I have to do it for my son, not for me – for my son. [But then] it's not that hard, 'cause I have family to watch him, and I only work on weekends and his father is there to help me. (Chantal, Black-Canadian, nineteen-year-old lone mother and full-time secondary school student)

Given their circumstances and the responsibilities that the young women carried, some of them distinguish themselves from other young people. As Chantal said, 'I don't think about going to parties and stuff like that. Like when you have a child, you don't think about that anymore, you just want to be home with your child. Be there for him. That [going out] doesn't even concern me.' For Melissa, because of her duties at her family's bakery and her health-care activities for her father and brother at home, there is simply no time to watch television, play video games, or surf the net – activities one might expect younger people to be doing.

This group of young women used a variety of provisioning strategies. Even though the young women were generally keen to work, they had to consider childcare, housing, and transportation. When asked whether she takes extra shifts at her telephone survey job, Chantal responded, 'No, not really, not until school is done, because I want to be with my son. If I go to work, he hardly sees me. I don't want that.' Rather than cutting back on paid work, other young women prioritized employment in the short term to achieve long-term economic independence. Keesha, who was job searching while living with her mother, wanted to be a nurse, but enrolling in a post-secondary nursing programme was not immediately possible because of her financial situation.

The Gen-Y women were resourceful to the extent that they were able to draw on different sources of support. However, the resources available to them were limited to a handful of community and government income-support programmes and private familial arrangements. Furthermore, in doing what they had to, to attend school, care for their children, and earn a living, the young women did not appear to be typical, carefree youth.

Provisioning in the Present Jeopardizes the Future

The young women were interested in occupations such as nurse, teacher, childcare worker or social worker, cosmetologist, dental assistant, law clerk, real estate agent, lawyer, and doctor. Just about all of the young women, regardless of whether they were students in secondary education or university graduates, mentioned that they wanted to pursue some sort of post-secondary education, upgrading, or training as a way of provisioning for themselves and their families. However, most of the Gen-Y women expressed reluctance to apply for student loans to finance their post-secondary education. The lone mothers were especially concerned that the burden of debt would prevent them from being able to support their families in the future. Some had plans to earn their tuition by getting a job and saving money.

It is notable that the young women talked about their career decisions without reference to racial barriers that might have an effect on their access to jobs or education. The young women had clearly defined career goals, but their actual options were likely restricted as a result of their race, low incomes, or working-class status. Realistically, these young women needed jobs with good wages to support their families. Working in low-end youth jobs in the short term seems to be a risky choice for these young women, because it could take a long time to save enough for tuition fees. By working to meet present needs, these young women may be jeopardizing their future ability to achieve long term economic independence and well-being.

In the title of this chapter, the expression *at risk* was used to describe the young women who participated in Gen-Y programmes. This professional descriptor is often used to portray individuals and groups who seem to be living in precarious circumstances. Although Ulrich

Beck is credited with introducing the modern debate on risk when he published *Risk Society: Towards a New Modernity* (1992), neither the concept of risk nor its primarily negative overtones are limited to his work. The history of the concept is rich, but two particular threads are pertinent to this chapter (for a detailed discussion of the concept, see Swift & Callahan, 2009). The first, developed in the work of both Beck (1992) and Giddens (1994), focuses on the changing policy discourse in European societies when former welfare states shifted their efforts to cushion the inequalities of market economies by redistributing goods and services, to the containment, or management, of the fallout from global market forces over which individual nation states had limited control. The second thread focuses on how, under ensuing neoliberal regimes, individuals were positioned as being proactive citizens, assuming responsibility for making choices, which included an assessment of the risks involved. This construction has contradictory outcomes for both individuals and service providers such as those at Gen-Y. For example, empowerment theories and associated interventions can help women take control of some aspects of their lives, such as asserting independence in abusive relationships and making plans for the future, rather than 'leaving it to fate.' On the other hand, making choices now means assuming responsibility for them – and the associated risks. When actions don't work out as planned, the individual woman not only suffers the consequences, but responsibility for the failure falls primarily on her shoulders – policies and programmes manage to escape much of the blame. Thus risky behaviour refers to individuals, not policies.

Racism and Racial Impacts on Career Decisions: 'It Never happened to me Personally . . .'

At about the period when the interviews were conducted, *racial profiling* was a term used in the local media to describe how Black youth were targeted by police for criminal activity. Yet when the young women were asked about racial profiling or racial discrimination, they did not deny that racism occurs in general; however, they did not see it as something they faced in their school or career goals. Michelle confirmed,

> No, I couldn't say I have experienced it [racial profiling] myself. I'm trying to think back if I've ever seen it, but I haven't [been able to] process it. Sometimes you see things and you don't really know what's going on. So

if someone explains, 'Okay, if this and this and this happened, that means you were a victim of it,' it clicks in your mind, 'Oh yeah, something like that happened.' In terms of myself, it [racial profiling] never happened to me personally – I'm trying to think back a bit. No, just the typical things you see on the news. (Michelle, nineteen-year-old, Black-Canadian, lone mother, and secondary school student)

None of the young women said that their racial or cultural background directly influenced their career choices.

I don't really think about it [racial discrimination]. You know when you're interacting with someone, you don't really think that because I'm Asian they're treating me in a certain way. I recognize that discrimination is out there, but for me, my experience, I don't really find that affected my schooling or work. I don't think people treat me any differently because I'm Chinese or I look a certain way. (Melissa, Chinese-Canadian, twenty-four-year-old university graduate looking for employment)

While the young women did not see racism as having any effect on the career decisions they made, their provisioning experiences were nevertheless influenced by racial inequalities. Melissa, who was from a Chinese immigrant family, was job searching and helping out in the family bakery and deciding whether to apply to graduate school. In her case, the historical racial inequities and exclusions in the labour market are manifested in self-employment, which is one of the strategies immigrant families use to overcome employment barriers. The family owned a small business with high employee turnover. In the interview, Melissa reported that family members were not advising her either to pursue particular career opportunities or to continue the business. Even so, her future career prospects and provisioning activities and strategies were influenced by her family's need for her to work in the family business, even though she was making career decisions and struggling to find her own way.

When the young women raised the issue of culture, it was in relation to their families and church communities as sources of support that they drew on for strength and motivation in difficult times. Some mentioned the positive influence of a mother, grandmother, or other female relative on their career choices. For others, family influence did not take the form of direct advice on what career to pursue. Instead, racialized family members seemed to subtly and indirectly shape how the young women approached their career decisions. Nadine spoke about the influence of her Jamaican immigrant mother, who was terminally ill at the time of the interview: 'Having an ill parent helps me focus a lot. I think about the sacrifices my mom made to come to Canada from Jamaica, and it keeps me focused every day . . . It helps me motivate myself to be stronger and to focus on my goals and to complete my education and be the best possible person I can be and help other people' (Nadine, Black Canadian, twenty-five-year-old homeless, postsecondary student).

Eve (an eighteen-year-old homeless, Jamaican Canadian) chatted about how she enjoyed going to church as a child and the importance of the church as a place where she experienced Jamaican culture:

EVE. There was church dinner on Sunday, and stuff, and communion; it was very fun. [We had] dinner, and because I'm from a Jamaican background, there's a lot of Jamaican cooking, Jamaican talking, Jamaican culture, so you go back to your roots every Sunday.
INTERVIEWER. Why was that [attending church] important?
EVE. Because it teaches you not to forget where you came from and emphasizes that you could have a lot of problems in the future, but as a community we're strong together.

Annie (a South Asian teenager and secondary school student) said that she would be interested in joining an ethno-specific group when she started university.

INTERVIEWER. How come you're going to check out the Sri Lankan students at university?
ANNIE. It would be fun to join in where you can relate and share things about your background.

Gen-Y women's comments indicated that they found strength in and had a desire to connect with their own ethno-racial and cultural group in times of stress and uncertainty. These young women's accounts of their decision-making revealed how culture acted as a kind of emotional security. It provided the grounding they needed to make life decisions that would allow them to support their families and make career decisions. Some of the women volunteered in these cultural spaces where they could both provide for themselves and their families by gaining material resources and develop a sense of community belonging and support. For example, several of the young Black women (Eve, Michelle, Keesha, and Nadia) spoke about going to church and involvement with their church community, which from their descriptions were ethno-specific cultural spaces.

In describing their provisioning experiences, the Gen-Y women portrayed themselves as responsible individuals making what most people would consider reasonable career and educational choices. In the process of doing so, they had to attend school, care for their children, and earn a living. Although the work and responsibilities seemed daunting, these young women did not appear to acknowledge the presence of racial barriers on their working lives. However, once they entered the community programmes, they encountered reactions to racial issues in their interactions with youth workers and counsellors.

Addressing Individual Acts of Discrimination in Programmes

Focusing on individual acts of discrimination through the workers' actions and interactions with clients was a key way in which racial knowledge was produced. Counsellors generally made well-intended efforts to help their clients strategize the everyday sexism and racism they encountered while in the programme. Workers immediately addressed oppressive acts that occurred among clients. Two situations illustrate what counsellors dealt with.

In the first example, a casual conversation among a few young mothers and the counsellor was overheard during a field observation session. The clients were sitting around in the programme area before the formal group session began. In their discussion, one young woman used a derogatory term to refer to a classmate from Trinidad and Tobago. When the counsellor gently but firmly reprimanded her for using a racist term, the young women did not see their use of the slang as problematic. They accepted the counsellor's alternative terminology in what appeared to be a good-humoured, light-hearted exchange (field note, May 2005).

In another example, a programme worker described the shelter's anti-discrimination policy in her interview with pride. She explained,

PROGRAMME WORKER. There's an anti-discriminatory agreement that
  women have to sign when they come in . . . We talk about discrimination,
  cooperative living, [and] what it looks like. Both staff and resident sign
  [the agreement]: 'We are going to try not to be discriminatory while we

live here.' So that opens women's eyes up for the first time to homophobia or issues of racism. A lot of different women are coming from different places; they may not have encountered a gay/lesbian person in their
lives . . .

INTERVIEWER. How do you introduce that form?

PROGRAMME WORKER. It's part of intake. It says all women have the right to be
treated with respect; everyone has the right to be here . . . Yeah, there's all
sorts of examples of discrimination, from transgenderism, to homophobia,
to racism, to ageism, to lookism. We even made up some names ourselves
for what it is, like it's not okay to make fun of people for who they are, how
they look, what they say, how they dress, what they eat – anything like that.
So that's laid out right at the beginning. I don't think a lot of them have
considered that before in their lives. It's something to call them on, to
bring them back to should they be behaving in a way that's not okay, you
know . . . You [the client] could get a serious warning for being seriously
discriminatory, or you may get an exemption, depending on the situation,
what was said, how it was said, if you can own it, if you can recognize it
and have a conversation about it and take a step back and say, 'Oops, I
shouldn't have said that. That was a really dumb-ass thing for me to have
said,' that might be an exemption. If it's an outright, 'I know what I said,
I'm glad I said it,' that's a serious warning. There's all kinds of room to do
education around the issue.

It is the approach that workers take in these situations that serves as
the main point of analysis. The workers' responses might have been
different if they had located the young women's racist remarks and
potentially racist actions within the context of their clients' lives. In
the first case, the young women were using racial slurs without thinking about their meaning. They appeared to be using the term descrip-
tively, not maliciously, but as part of typical, jovial youth-speak with
friends. In the second case of potentially disruptive behaviour in the
shelter, it is understandable that women who are living with strangers in close quarters at a time of crisis feel vulnerable and scared, and
might lash out at each other in racial terms. This, of course, is not to
say that name-calling and other manifestations of 'isms' should be
tolerated. But with a focus on social contextual factors, the worker
might have critically reflected on how racism manifests as individual
conflict across different situations and what specific structural arrangements facilitated the racial dynamics playing out in the local
setting.

Executing Professional Obligations and Organizational Mandates

The youth workers' professional obligations and organizational mandates may be what draw their attention away from seeing how individual racist acts are connected to broader social contextual factors and processes. First of all, providing career choices and supportive career counselling is well within the youth workers' professional role. While they might have suspected that their advice would not necessarily promote social change, given the difficult life situations and gender and racial inequalities in the labour market that their clients faced, at the very least, they were meeting their professional obligation to support and empower their clients to make choices.

The theme of providing choices to clients ran through the programmes. One programme worker claimed that they try to offer clients 'anything they want' in the programme. About the programme choices, she said, 'It's fun. It's educational stuff. A lot of it is free stuff.' When asked how she decided what to do, she replied, 'It comes from them, it comes from me, from the community, what ends up on our doorstep.' She said that over the years she had drawn on some 'pretty standard stuff.' She named a few activities that she had organized in the past: workshops on self-defence, alcohol and drug awareness, sexuality and birth control, employment services, and rights in the workplace.

The individualistic nature of choices was emphasized by the centrality of life-skills training in all of the programmes. This common programme component introduced useful strategies for everyday living; however, the focus on individual choices often comes at the expense of underestimating how young women's choices are structured by labour, social assistance, housing, and education policies that fail to produce conditions whereby this group of 'at risk' young women – some of whom are homeless or lone mothers – can acquire secure and affordable housing, access post-secondary education, meet their caregiving responsibilities, and achieve economic well-being. The equal opportunity structure of choice within programmes is clearly not connected to the unequal opportunity structure of choices outside of them, so that even when young women make appropriate career choices, they experience the real, inequitable conditions of labour markets and impediments that line the pathway to economic success. In a way, an over-emphasis on individualized choice-making practices potentially set these young women up for failure.

The workers also viewed educating clients on anti-discrimination as part of their professional responsibility ('There's all kinds of room to do education around the issue'). In practice, the shelter worker executed the anti-discrimination policy by focusing on the micro-level manifestations of discrimination, in the form of name-calling and personally harassing behaviour. From the shelter worker's ever-expanding list of 'isms,' she seemed to be using diversity language to mean 'Be nice to each other.' Note her comment that 'it's not okay to make fun of people.' In some ways, the worker was relying on anti-discriminatory policy to maintain order in the group programme or shelter. Appropriate behaviour and conduct of clients is an institutional priority. The shelter worker said, 'We are going to try not to be discriminatory while we live here.' In other words, the shelter residents were expected to abide by the anti-discriminatory policy in particular while they were living at the shelter. Since the worker introduces the policy along with other house rules during the intake process, there is nothing that distinguishes racist acts from other disruptive or disrespectful behaviours like rowdiness or theft.

To regulate individual racist and sexist behaviour, the production of racial knowledge in these programmes takes on a form that is distinct and separate from the systemic barriers young women face outside the programme. The manifestation of racist acts is not linked, for example, to the lack of culturally sensitive housing options for racialized women experiencing abuse. That young women in the shelter feel stressed and act out is due at least partially to the circumstances of gendered violence that led them to the shelter in the first place. As it turns out, emphasizing racism as individual acts allows workers to accomplish their professional and institutional responsibilities. It enables clients to participate in programmes in supportive environments of mutual respect and free of harassment. These benefits, however, come at a price. Clients learn skills for handling racism at the level of individual actions, but at the same time there is little space for analysis and for practising skills necessary for connecting these acts to institutional structures.

Counselling Young Women to Overcome Racial Barriers

In contrast to the young women, the youth workers acknowledged that the young women in their programmes face systemic racial inequality and discrimination. In one example, a worker recognized that Muslim young women who wear hijabs (headscarfs) may face discrimination during a job interview, but she admitted that she did not know how her colleague in employment programmes advised these clients about employer expectations and the various types of discriminatory practices that occur before, during, and after job interviews. A counsellor from another programme reported the intersecting forms of gender, race, and age discrimination: 'They [clients] face a lot of discrimination. I have one girl who pretends her child is her little sister. She took her to a job interview, and they [the interviewer] asked, "Is that your kid?" She said, "No it's my sister; I have to babysit her today." Same thing with housing: I've had girls who go to apartments, and it's illegal [for landlords] to ask if she's on welfare or a single mom. But the girls don't know; they don't know the route to take to sort that out.'

Even though the workers saw systemic racial, gender, and class issues affecting their clients, they provided counselling and career advice that casts racial and gender barriers to employment as individual barriers that could be overcome by young women who take personal risks associated with making the right education and career choices. In a motivational talk organized by the agency, the guest speaker, the director of a community-based legal clinic, shared her career path and journey with a room full of programme participants. When the audience asked for suggestions on how to overcome obstacles, she answered, 'Just clench yourself up and send the nervousness to other parts of your body, like your knees.' She said that one has to find a way around, over, or under the obstacle. At one point in her talk, she said, 'It may sound corny, but if you're determined, you'll find a way to do what you want.' At another point, she said, 'It's always scary, even though I might seem confident. Speak your mind, even if your voice is shaky.' However, the speaker did acknowledge that she came from a white, middle-class family, and that some women may encounter barriers beyond their control in pursuing their dreams.

There were no obvious signs that the counsellors' career advice differed for racialized and for non-racialized clients. It is not the advice per se that is of issue here: there is nothing wrong about advising young women to pursue college or to follow their career dreams. What is remarkable is how the notion of making appropriate career choices dominated the discussions. The focus on individual decision-making seemed to prevent workers from considering why Gen-Y young women, who are already disadvantaged in labour markets stratified by gender, race, and age, and who may be responsible for substantial caregiving, were being asked to make choices that involve taking on personal risks, given that the margins for economic success are narrow.

Programme Funding Aligns Youth Work Practices to Tackle Individual Acts of Racism

It is within the organization's programmes, during interactions between youth workers and their clients, that racial knowledge is produced. The youth workers point out that programme funding, or lack
of it, shapes the context and the quality of their work with young
women. But funding can indirectly influence counsellors' assessment
of racial issues in their programmes as primarily individual racist acts.
It would take considerably more effort to develop and launch a sustained and comprehensive approach based on an analysis of systemic
racism. Some counsellors may be aware of systemic issues, although
they must struggle amid time and energy demands to advocate with
clients for social change, while others seem not to be cognisant of systemic barriers, preserving the position that individuals are responsible for their own fate. The bottom line is that counsellors are dealing
with high workloads, high-needs clients, and crises in their day-to-day
work. What counsellors can do is coach young women to stand up for
their individual rights, and they can advocate on their clients' behalf
to social workers, doctors / medical professionals, or police officers /
legal professionals at an individual level.

The agency's response to diversity and representation is another way
that funding affects racial knowledge production. It was observed that
funding guidelines facilitate a view of racism as a lack of diversity and
access to programmes and services. Often, major funding agencies like
the United Way require, as a condition of funding, that organizations
adopt an anti-discrimination policy and address barriers to access to
programmes. The guideline under the criterion of accessibility states,
'Agency uses its multicultural/anti-racism policy to systematically address barriers to participation' (United Way of Toronto, 2007, p. 7). And
the standard is elaborated: 'Agency works to broaden access to diverse
groups in its community, including racial and cultural groups, men and
women, people with disabilities, people with different sexual orienta-
tions and people in varying economic circumstances' (p. 7).

An examination of several of the agency's official documents suggests
that their response to the call for diversity was to incorporate access and
equity goals into their programme planning. For the youth employment
programme, the goal was to increase contacts to ethnic media for outreach purposes; for the shelter programme, find renovation solutions
to accommodate women with disabilities; and for the young mothers

programme, outreach to Aboriginal and Asian young mothers. Aside from the fact that no reason was given for the proposed outreach to Aboriginal and Asian groups specifically, this last goal was most peculiar, since almost three-quarters of the young mothers served by the programme that year were already identified as members of racialized communities. In the case of this young mothers programme, the problem was not one of access for racialized young mothers; the problem is indicated by their over-representation in the programme. The institutional uptake of the funding guidelines for diversity, equity, and access has occurred in a way that is actually counterproductive for examining how racism can be manifested through over-, rather than under-, representation in programmes such as those at Gen-Y.

These observations do not deny that racist acts and diversity need to be tackled through policies based on access and equity principles. The problem is that racism has been associated primarily with individual racist acts and the lack of organizational diversity, instead of the embeddedness of the relations of race in the everyday institutional processes and practices in the agency. An accurate depiction of how race as a ruling relation is organizing and connecting practices inside the agency in response to outside funding pressures would be required in order to address the racial inequalities experienced by young women in these programmes.

The Dynamics of Racial Knowledge in 'At Risk' Young Women's Programmes

This chapter set out to reveal how racial knowledge is produced as a form of ruling that occurs in a local community setting of youth employment and women's programmes. The analysis brought into focus the dynamic effects of institutional processes and social contexts on different actors in programmes serving 'at risk' young women. It was discovered that the young women did not refer directly to racial impacts on their career decisions and advice, even though they were influenced by their ethno-cultural heritage, and youth workers acknowledged systemic forms of racial inequality. The young women's and youth workers' concerted efforts to reinforce the individualistic choices framework within the programmes made it difficult to see that the young women's ability to exercise their career choices outside the programmes would require more financial and caregiving support than what was available through their student loans or social assistance benefits.

Individualized forms of racist acts and discrimination emerged as the dominant form of racial knowledge at the local programme site. The youth workers' professional obligation to educate and empower young women on racial discrimination, and to meet programme goals with limited resources and funds, directed them to attend primarily to racism as individual acts of discrimination instead of systemic manifestations of racial inequalities. This parallels neoliberal understandings of who is 'at risk' and how to intervene. If the active citizen is one who exercises choice and assumes the costs of any associated risks, there is little room to explore how these definitions reproduce the very conditions that counsellors were trying to change. The effect of the youth workers' professional activities was to cast the problem of race as individual, overt acts of racism; this occurred at the expense of seeing race functioning as a social relation organizing professional, anti-discrimination, and diversity practices in response to funding pressures and organizational mandates.

By focusing on the operation of specific, historically located forms of power tied to social institutional processes that extend beyond the local setting, this institutional ethnography – guided analysis revealed the disjuncture between individual and systemic manifestations of the racial phenomenon as it was constituted through young women's provisioning experiences. The investigation intended to determine and account for how policies and institutional structures shape people's experiential accounts and understanding of racial phenomena. Thus the study has methodological implications. In examining ruling practices at the local level of community programmes, this research used worker accounts, field observations, and programme documents, as well as interviews with young women. Because multiple actors at the site produce the ruling relations through their work, researchers need not rely only on poor or otherwise marginalized people to tell their stories (which may be emotionally draining or traumatizing) in order to understand how oppression is reproduced.

What can be said about formation of race in young women's provisioning experiences? Whereas racial differences and racial inequalities are relatively easy to measure and monitor, articulating the phenomenon of race requires careful consideration of racialization processes. Examining Gen-Y women's provisioning provides a localized understanding of how racialization occurs. The Gen-Y women are a group of racialized youth whose provisioning entailed juggling present futures: they were trying to provide for themselves and others by making future career and education decisions that made sense in light of the resources and strength they drew from the relationships they had with loved ones, influential families, and youth workers. While they do not claim that these decisions are specific to their racial background or racism, their experiences are nevertheless shaped by racialized labour markets and youth programmes to the extent that these programmes over-represent racialized youth.

This analysis suggests that that race is not absent in individualized choice structures and that workers acknowledge race in how they present choices to the programme participants. These understandings come together when the young women make decisions and the youth workers engage in professional work, including the local administration of anti-discrimination, diversity, and access and equity policies. An important implication of this analysis is that the potential of community programmes for 'at risk' youth and equity policies for eliminating social inequalities cannot be taken for granted, because programmes and policies operate locally, and the dynamics influencing their implementation are specific to the site. In other words, it is not enough to simply have anti-racist programmes and policies in place. It is necessary to investigate how anti-racism translates into everyday practices, how power permeates and is manifested through institutional practices.

6 Provisioning for Children in a Low-Income Community

JUDY CERNY

This chapter presents interview data from a site where most of the women were low-income urban immigrant or refugee mothers. As is evident throughout this book, all low-income mothers perform a wide range of provisioning work to sustain their lives and those of their children. I argue that as a result of living within a specific area of the city, and the fact that most were relatively recent immigrants to Canada whose first language was not English, the participants in this site faced a particularly challenging set of barriers, most of which were beyond their control. The chapter begins with a brief description of the neighbourhood in which the study was conducted and the women who participated in the research. Next is a portrayal of what provisioning looks like in the lives of these low-income women whom I will often refer to as mothers because the responsibilities they shouldered in this area dominated our conversations. This happened because their mothering work occurred in one of the poorest, most unsafe neighbourhoods in the city. In addition, one focus of this particular set of interviews was the availability of childcare, or more accurately, the lack thereof. The chapter ends with a consideration of how community organizations can assist women such as these participants in analysing the causes and consequences of the provisioning responsibilities that they carry.

A Priority Neighbourhood

Low income is a risk factor for a range of social problems facing children and their parents. Children growing up in poverty encounter many obstacles, as highlighted in a report by UNICEF: 'It is a consistent finding of research, in many different countries, that poverty in childhood is associated with negative outcomes in adolescence and adult life. More than any other variable, it is low family income that is the most reliable predictor of educational, psychological, and behavioural problems' (UNICEF, 2008, p. 28).

A Statistics Canada (2009d) report showed that, in comparison to their higher-income counterparts, low-income families have fewer resources with which to cope and mitigate the negative effects of stressors, such as marital conflict, living in a neighbourhood that requires heightened vigilance because of crime, or inadequate resources to meet the demands of work and life (Orpana, Lemyre, & Gravel, 2009). Mothers living on low incomes routinely make personal sacrifices for the well-being of their children, such as compromising their nutrition to feed their children (McIntyre, Glanville, Raine, Dayle, Anderson, & Battaglia, 2003). Mothers on social assistance often depend on multiple government programmes; thus, they have to undertake additional tasks in order to deal with the reporting obligations and at times contradictory programme requirements of a range of programmes (Cumming & Cooke, 2009).

Having a low income makes the daily tasks of survival arduous and stressful, leaving little time and energy for anything else. Thus it can be isolating. External barriers such as a lack of transportation prevent members of low-income families from participating in economic and social activities (Jones, Graham, & Shier, 2008). Furthermore, low-income families in Canada have limited access to formal childcare services, and children from less privileged families are less likely than their more affluent counterparts to access childcare services (Japel, Tremblay, & Côté, 2005; Prentice, 2007).

Low-income mothers living in urban settings provision for their children under relentless constraints and numerous barriers. At the core, these constraints include a continuous shortage of money and childcare issues. In this study community, almost one-quarter of the families depended on government transfers such as social assistance (Cerny, 2009, p. 89). The social assistance income for a lone parent with one child in 2008 was $16,683 and $21,215 for a couple with two children – an income that fell well below the Statistics Canada Low Income Cut-off (before tax) of $27,601 and $41,198 respectively for families living in large cities (National Council of Welfare, 2010, p. 1; Statistics Canada, 2009d, p. 25). Women's lives in this particular neighbourhood were constrained by isolation resulting from having few family or friends in Canada to call upon for support. Data on the provisioning activities and strategies of many study participants show how limited English-language skills and the challenges of adapting to a new country made daily life an ongoing struggle. In this community, more than half the population was not born in Canada (Cerny, 2009, p. 89).

The women described in this chapter lived in a predominantly low-income urban area that is designated as one of the city's 'priority' areas. Priority areas are identified communities where households have persistently low incomes, there is a high proportion of new immigrants, and there is an unequal distribution of services and facilities (City of Toronto, 2005, p. 3). Nearly one-third of the households were headed by a lone parent; one-third of the residents had not completed high school; and almost one-quarter of the families depended on government transfers such as social assistance (Cerny, 2009, p. 89). Compared to the rest of the city, the area had a large proportion (more than half) of residents born outside of Canada and depended to a greater extent on precarious, low-wage, blue-collar occupations in manufacturing. There were few opportunities for employment in the area, and the neighbourhood had high levels of gun violence and criminal gang involvement, with the highest homicide and violent crime rate in the city in 2007 (Toronto Police Service, 2007), the time during which many of these data were collected.

Eight of the women interviewed belonged to a public housing tenants group called Jane's House. These data are combined with interviews with an additional twenty women in the same community who were affiliated with a voluntary social service agency called Riverview.[1] Of the twenty-eight women who participated in the research, eighteen were lone parents and ten were married/common-law. Fifteen of the mothers had three or more children, eight had two children, and five had one child. Most of the women (nineteen) were on social assistance, six depended on their husband's employment income, and three survived on their own employment income. Nearly three-quarters of the women in the study lived in public housing. Twenty of the women were immigrants from Africa, Asia, the Caribbean, and Central or South America, with the remainder being Canadian-born. This demographic fact shaped the lives of this particular group of low-income women. The neighbourhood was not a desirable place to live because of violence and drug-related gangs. However, both of these visible phenomena are underlain by racist, anti-immigrant sentiments that exist along with Canada's discourse of multiculturalism (see Bannerji, 2000; Dua, Razack, & Warner, 2005).

Provisioning Activities

In seeking to understand what types of childcare arrangements would be useful to women tackling the challenges faced by the study participants, the provisioning that low-income mothers carry out specifically for their children emerged loud and clear. As in other chapters, some of this work done by participants is familiar and visible, such as providing familial caring labour, doing some paid work, and volunteering at Riverview or at the local community centre. Then there were the less visible tasks, such as sustaining health, ensuring safety, and making claims and asserting rights. However, for those women who had young children, providing caring labour consumed the bulk of their time and energy. As will become evident, the lack of suitable childcare arrangements virtually excluded most participants from the labour market. Supporting previous work, mothers in this study resisted social assistance requirements that privilege paid work over time spent caring for children (Hennessy, 2009).

The intricacies of dealing with government agencies and social service organizations are convoluted for the general public. For low-income women, thy are even more so, because of the other constraints and barriers in their lives, such as limited language and literacy skills and lack of transportation to get to health and social services. Low-income mothers engage in vast amounts and different kinds of provisioning work. These activities, linked to relationships of responsibilities, are interconnected and thus the stress quickly escalates.

SANDRA. My children are my world. If something hurts them, it hurts me, and I want to go deal with it.
JOCELYN. [My grandchildren] usually come to my house. It's much better because they get to sleep on a proper bed, and they get to eat and eat. And they always want to come to Grandma because they have food to eat. Don't ask me where I get the food, but I always manage.
MARRIBA. I always wish to do something for my sister and my nephews [back home] . . . I was always thinking if I got a chance, if I am in a position, I do something for them.

Women have multiple relationships of responsibility. They care for their own children while provisioning for other relationships of responsibility, including adult children, elderly parents, or youth living in the community. Some of the women in this study had family living nearby, while others were alone in Canada, with many relatives still in their country of origin. Provisioning for extended family might include supervising nieces, nephews, stepchildren, or grandchildren; grocery shopping for their elderly parents; or sending money 'back home' to take care of family members there.

Providing Caring Labour in the Household

Activities carried out by women include managing the household, caring for children, and doing general household work. Aside from physical work, these activities include the mental and emotional work that is part of caring labour.

MAXINE. If I am going upstairs, [my twin sons] would follow me upstairs. If I'm downstairs, they come downstairs. I don't leave them. I won't leave them upstairs by themselves or leave them downstairs by themselves.

MARIAN. Now [my daughter] is so active, and up and about, it's so hard. Sometimes she wouldn't stay still. She always keeps moving. I always have to watch her 24/7 because she always keeps putting things in her mouth.

Maxine's and Marian's descriptions of the intensity of their monitoring activities would sound familiar to many mothers of young children. Caring labour also includes taking children to the library and to the park several times a week – activities that almost all of the mothers in the study talked about doing regularly. It was common for mothers to spend fifteen hours each day on provisioning for their children. However, for women with few resources, the expenditure of time and energy was greater. For instance, walking children to and from school frequently consumed up to two hours daily. A trip to the grocery store meant walking with shopping buggies or taking the bus with young children in strollers, which limited the items they could bring home on their trip.

While it is difficult physically, the mental process of trying to decide what one can afford to buy on a low income adds to the challenge. Children's requests for items that mothers cannot afford make the task emotionally draining. Cathy, a mother of three, described the mental and emotional work that accompanied trying to provide for her children while on social assistance:

I don't even have a bedroom set. I sleep actually on the floor. It's ridiculous. I try to work it out to get the things that are necessary in terms of health and comfort, like to get little blankets [for the children] and their beds. I've gotten their beds, so that was a big relief. But it was very stressful for a long time . . . no money, and I don't like to take charity from people. I know they say beggars can't be choosers, but . . . it's just a hassle knowing that your kids are doing without. It's very stressful.

For those who came to Canada as adults and had limited English-language skills, mothers had difficulty navigating the school system, and helping their children with homework caused them tremendous concern. Doreen devoted considerable time each day to her children's homework and to overseeing their home responsibilities: 'Even when he doesn't have homework, I still give him homework. We study our times tables.'

Participants gave as well as received support from their families. For instance, Jocelyn has two school-aged children and eleven grandchildren. Her three adult daughters live on their own, yet she is committed to providing financial support to them so that they will not have to struggle in the same way she did: 'I just want to do something else, you know, where I know I'm going to be making some money to help my kids out, because my daughters, like, I know they're trying, but I don't want them struggling like how I struggle . . . So I want to be able to like help them along the way.'

In addition to their own children and grandchildren, these low-income mothers frequently had provisioning responsibilities for their parents and other relatives. Doreen has two children and also takes care of her mother who has arthritis: 'I clean because she can't bend. So I help her clean her house at least twice a week and on the weekend. I'll go sometimes in the middle of the week when the kids are in school.'

Sending money 'back home' to help out family members still in their country of origin was a common priority for many of the immigrant mothers. When they were unable to send money, they felt that they were shirking their responsibilities in that sacrifices had been made by others so that they could come to Canada, but they were not able to reciprocate.

While most of the women in the study did not engage in the labour market at the time of the research, the need and desire to do paid work was a major concern for them. Each of the full-time caregivers – whether they were on social assistance or had employment income from their husbands – talked about a desire to upgrade their education and get a job once their children were in school.

Engaging in Formal and Informal Work in the Labour Market

Engaging in the labour market is more complicated than simply getting a job or going to school. The degree to which mothers could take up paid work was, to a great extent, related to the childcare options available to them. Furthermore, the types of jobs open to participants were frequently casual, part-time, or low-wage work, as Jocelyn's experience shows: 'I'll work three, four jobs just to take care of my kids. People do not understand. They say, "Why do you need two, three jobs?" I said, "Because one pays for the babysitter, one pays the rent, and the other one buys some food and stuff for me and the kids to eat."'

The majority of participants had been in the labour market, most earning minimum wage, and intended to return to employment as soon as their children were older. Jocelyn, one of the older women in the study, exemplified the fluidity of mothers' lives as they move in and out of different roles, alternating between employment and full-time child rearing. She was employed just before her son was born, then stayed home until he was six, and then returned to the labour market. When her daughter was born, Jocelyn stayed home for three years, and then returned to employment again, but as she notes, 'Can you believe [it]! Every cent I worked, I had to pay a babysitter with it.'

Magdalena was one of only a few mothers who worked full-time and whose source of income was her own wages. 'I have to work. I can't stay home because it's the only money I earn. I start at 8:00 but when I leave home it's 6:00 in the morning because I can't afford twenty-five dollars a cab to bring me here.'

Five mornings each week, Magdalena would leave home before 6:30 with her daughter and walk several blocks to the before-school childcare programme. She needed to arrive there by 7:00 in order to catch the two buses that would get her to work by 8:00. At the end of the day, Magdalena picked up her daughter at 5:30 from the after-school childcare programme.

Most of the women volunteered each week in community programmes. Occasionally, women were able to get limited paid work, but these opportunities were dependent largely on project funding received by community agencies. Bahati worked one day per week on an eight-week government-funded project, and she received forty dollars for each day she worked, but when the project ended, so did her pay. The sense of being self-sufficient was desirable, even though it was simply a trade-off between relying on social assistance and surviving on a series of low-wage jobs, such as Jocelyn and Magdalena were.

Many low-income women try to upgrade their education by enrolling in training programmes or completing high school equivalency, as was the case for those educated outside of Canada. For women who had received post-secondary education outside of Canada, the requirement to complete a high school education can be discouraging and demeaning. Eshe, a refugee from Nigeria and mother of a six-month-old baby, had been educated as a teacher in her country of origin. Like many other mothers on social assistance, Eshe was being encouraged by her social assistance worker to become a personal support worker (PSW): 'That's the only thing the government wants to pay. I wanted to go in for nursing. At first they said I can't go for nursing. I said, "Okay, what about public work, public services?" They said, "It's only PSW they pay for or I could go back to – go back to high school." I told them, "High school? I don't think I want to go back to high school, but maybe I will think about public health and the PSW thing."'

There is a constant demand for personal support workers, often attributed to the aging of the Canadian population. However, there are very high turnover rates in this occupation due to low wages and often poor working conditions. As is the case with women who work as nannies, it is ironic that these women are being trained to care for the children and frail elderly relatives of others – and they cannot get childcare for their own children. This dynamic goes well beyond the local situation and is now referred to as the 'global care chain.' Women from poor countries leave the care of their dependents to other family members as they migrate to richer countries to take up jobs as nannies and personal support workers (Browne & Braun, 2008; Cohen, 2000; Hochschild, 2000a). In Canada, these types of jobs are offered on a casual or part-time basis and often involve shift work, making childcare arrangements even more difficult. Camila, who had been in Canada only three years, was completing her PSW training and had been offered a position at a nursing home. Her shift would be from 6 am to 2 pm, three or four days per week. She wanted full-time employment, so when she finished her regular shift, Camila got extra hours of work through one of the many for-profit agencies in the city that hires PSWs to work privately in people's homes.

Undertaking Commitments in the Community

'When I take care of my community, I think I'm taking care of myself, too. It helps me' (Jocelyn).

For low-income mothers, formal and informal volunteer activities can range from helping out in community programmes to 'looking after' or mentoring youth in the community. Participants often volunteered in the community: some as part of their social assistance requirements, others because they enjoy the opportunity to socialize and to develop new skills. As discussed in chapter 3, social assistance regulations that require volunteering as a condition of payment have been divisive among community-based agencies. Not only is forced volunteering an oxymoron, but it artificially divides people along the lines of their reasons for doing so. It sets up a false dichotomy, suggesting there are good and bad motives for volunteering. Research shows that people volunteer for many reasons and derive a range of benefits from their involvement (Statistics Canada, 2009a; Williams, 2008). For instance, Marriba hoped that volunteering would help her find a job: 'I wish I could become an accountant but, in the meanwhile, I'm trying to do something in the community. Maybe if I do my contributions on the community work, maybe I get a job. I'm not able to do job in the factory, because I've got arthritis and I don't want to lose my health right now.'

Cathy talked about the consequences of the volunteer requirements under social assistance guidelines. In her case it became similar to a shadow job, with a coercive edge to it: 'You only have to volunteer a few hours. But when you're actually there, you're not going to say "I'm coming for one hour a month." No. They're not going to allow that. And then you end up dedicating all this time, or else you just look like a goof with the agency. And then what kind of reference are you going to get? So I'm giving them at least twenty hours a month, which doesn't seem like a lot but it's a lot with three kids.' Yet she also felt a sense of responsibility for her community: 'I volunteered to be the youth coordinator last year and, along with my school and raising my own kids, and my sister, I dedicated a lot of time to the Theatre in the Park and going to all these meetings, trying to get money. What we're trying to do also is make things better for the kids in our community – right? – so it takes a lot of time and dedication.'

Courtney, who had her first child at eighteen, cared especially about the girls in her neighbourhood: 'If they're into trouble, they'll come and they'll talk to me . . . especially the young girls in my neighbourhood . . . Some parents, when their kids are in trouble . . . they'll be coming to me . . . to just talk to them . . . I guess it's because, you know, I was kind of a troubled child.' She was proud to have been able to help out on the advisory committee of a local programme for young mothers:

'It just started out as just an idea on a piece of paper and now it's actually on its way . . . young women who are on the system and want to get off and work and don't know how to help. And we actually created it. It's amazing.'

Faith was one of the older women in the study and had been undertaking commitments in the community for over two decades. She initiated programmes for children and helped her neighbours with writing letters and preparing résumés, often using her own computer for those who didn't have home computers. Following a gun shooting in the community, Faith organized a prayer service.

Sustaining Health

Sustaining their own health and that of their children was difficult for these mothers, for a lack of money, transportation, and health benefits. Many of the mothers were newcomers to Canada, so their children had, in a sense, special needs because they faced social and language barriers.

Health-related work increased if children had significant health problems, and these had a profound impact on their mothers' lives. Women talked about dealing with a range of conditions including visual impairment, asthma, attention deficit hyperactivity disorder, depression, and anxiety. The work included scheduling, coordinating and going to medical appointments, as well as administering medicines or adhering to special diets. Mothers' primary concerns were for the health of their children. For instance, Magdalena took her daughter to see the psychologist once a month. Although she felt that a monthly visit was insufficient, she could not afford to pay for additional sessions.

Several of the women in the study had their own health problems – some more severe than others – but they could not always attend to the, for lack of resources or other obligations. As a result, the diets of some were inadequate and many went without proper dental or vision care. Bahati, for example, had a serious vision problem for which she had frequent medical appointments and reluctantly took strong medication. Because there was no one to look after her son if she was delayed, she often took him along – at a cost to him: 'They said we don't have a choice, we have to give you that. So they gave me. I'm taking the medication, but every two weeks, three weeks, to go there means crossing the streets downtown. I took the little one with me but to go and come back, it takes time. So he's absent in the class.'

Ensuring Safety

Ensuring safety emerged as a major provisioning responsibility for the women who were interviewed at this site. Participants were very conscious of the environment within which they were raising their children and tried diligently to ensure their children's safety. However, low-income urban mothers face numerous threats to the safety of their children, most of which they could do little to ameliorate. These ranged from a lack of supervised play/recreational facilities to the very real daily dangers of living in an area classified as a priority neighbourhood. Some safety issues mentioned by participants were:

- a shortage of safe, licensed childcare arrangements;
- a lack of affordable, extracurricular, recreational programmes;
- peer pressure at school and in the community;
- unsupervised computer use; and
- gun violence, illegal drugs, and related criminal activity in the community.

Mothers addressed these concerns in a variety ways, including, as mentioned earlier, caring for their very young children full-time and being reluctant to have anyone else care for them. If they had to turn to non-parental childcare, mothers would get to know the childcare provider personally. Leena, however, did not feel secure in leaving her child in anyone else's care: 'I never trust. Actually, there's a lot of people from my country. Good people. But I never trust to leave her.'

Many participants forbade their children to play outside without supervision. Children were encouraged to be independent thinkers and to make appropriate decisions. At times, mothers even had to remind their children not to put anything into their mouths at school because illegal drugs were prevalent, or warn them to avoid laundry rooms in their buildings. Mothers would invite their children's friends to their homes rather than have them hang around outside. Some mothers had to place restraining orders on their former partners or fathers of their children; a few were forced to move to a different neighbourhood.

Some effects of this constant safety work on the quality of participants' lives are revealed in excerpts from several interviews. Bahati, who lived in a townhouse, would have her tea beside the window and watch her children playing in their yard. She did not allow them to go to the nearby park alone. For other women, such as Camila and

Amisi, who lived in high-rise apartment buildings, there was no option to watch their children through a window. Camila would not let her eight-year-old son play outside alone, but she would go with him to the park and watch while he rode his bike. Likewise, Amisi did not allow her youngest son, aged nine, to play basketball outside in the community courts because of the high levels of crime and violence in the neighbourhood, and therefore he was never allowed to be alone outside. She wished she could enrol him in an after-school basketball programme, but the subsidized programme was full and the cost of other programmes was too high. Sara tried to find extracurricular activities for her children to keep them safe and provide healthy activities: 'If they come home and have dinner, and then go [to a programme] and, you know, they wouldn't be hanging out with their friends or causing trouble, especially I find when they . . . they're at this transition period when they're in middle school or in high school. They need a lot more community centres to be offering more programmes.' Each morning when she walked her daughter to school, with her younger twins in tow, Sandra would wait with her until the school bell rang, before leaving the schoolyard to go back home.

Living in the neighbourhood that they did, concerns for their children's safety was especially grave for mothers of older children whom they could no longer supervise at all times. Many noted that it was important that they be available and that they be at home after school and in the evening. Jocelyn talked about her son, who had experienced violence in the community basketball courts, and the need for her to be there for him. '[My son] used to play basketball and he stopped because he'd get into fights because of basketball. And he says he doesn't want to get into a fight, so he stopped playing basketball . . . He got robbed already by gunpoint . . . in the middle of the basketball court. So I have to make sure I am home. When I used to go to work, he wouldn't sleep until I came home at midnight.'

Making Claims

One of the less visible provisioning activities on which poor women spend a lot of time and energy is advocating for themselves and their children for benefits to which they are entitled, such as social assistance, child support, legal aid, public housing, day-care fee subsidies, and programmes for their children who have special needs or developmental disabilities. This means that they often must deal with multiple government ministries, departments, and agencies, each with its own requirements. These organizations include the social assistance bureaucracy, public housing authorities, the court system, the education and health-care sectors, the immigration department, child protection agencies, crisis intervention services, and food banks – to name those regularly mentioned by participants.

The impacts of social assistance access on lone mothers have been well documented in the literature (Caragata, 2009; Evans, 2007; Little, 1998). Lone mothers on social assistance have a particularly difficult task in managing the various and at times contradictory guidelines of multiple government programmes from which they receive support (Breitkreuz, 2005). This is one aspect of women's provisioning that we are only starting to understand. In their study looking at the work demands of lone mothers managing multiple state-provided benefits, Cumming and Cooke (2009) note that 'there has been little attention paid to how these programmes interact to form a web of rules and obligations for recipients' (p. 75).

Learning where to look for information before one can even begin to advocate for services is a separate and often difficult task. Access to service information is a challenge for most poor women, but it is especially so for women who have limited English-language skills. Even Courtney, whose first language is English, tried in vain to get information about whether her needed dental work would be covered under social assistance: 'I'm still trying to find out – I have a problem with my teeth since I've had my kids. I can't pay $100, and it's like $180 just for a check-up. Welfare pays for children and emergencies for us – I don't know what an emergency is and nobody will tell me what stands for an emergency. So I pretty much got to suffer now because I don't have the money for it.'

However, the work of acquiring information about day-care fee subsidies was even more difficult for Tuyen: 'I don't know English much, so I ask someone help me, but I try, you know, I try and try. So I go to day care, I ask them, and they told me . . . like this you have to do. I try by myself and I got [the subsidy]; my God, I was so happy.'

Sandra had to make claims regularly, to multiple organizations:

• for her daughter with special needs: 'I can't send [my daughter] to any regular programme because they're going to complain that she's not listening . . . and I never know when she's going to have an outburst . . . It's hard, but I finally found somebody said that that there's a programme for kids like her.'

- for child support: 'You go to the courts . . . first of all, you've got to go down [to the courthouse], fill out your papers, see duty counsel, then come back and then wait for your court case. All for what – an extra $100! I don't have it in me . . . I don't have the time. I don't have the money.'

The need to make claims for child support affects most lone mothers and is particularly onerous. Some of the mothers dealt directly with the fathers, while others dealt with provincial government agencies responsible for overseeing child support payments. Mothers on social assistance have the amount of their child support payments deducted from their assistance cheques, regardless of whether they are, in fact, receiving the set payments. This was Bahati's situation. She was uncomfortable and felt shy about pursuing this discrepancy with her social assistance worker. Bahati wished she could get a job so she wouldn't have to rely on assistance or support payments from her husband that seldom arrived: 'Child support he start, he give me every month $200 and now – three months, four months – he still don't give money. The social assistance, they don't give me because they think he's going to give me . . . We went to the court. He started to give me, again he stopped.'

A Word on Having a Space to Develop Voice

The women who provided the data for this chapter were not randomly selected from an urban 'priority neighbourhood.' They belonged to two community groups in the area. These two spaces – Jane's House and Riverview – were critical in facilitating women's provisioning work. Their presence is relatively invisible in the foregoing analysis, which centred on the provisioning of individual women – especially in their childcare responsibilities. However, it is highly unlikely that I would have been able to talk with these women if they had not been members of these groups. Not only did their involvement in these groups allow me to access them as potential study participants but, as in the other research sites, their membership facilitated starting the conversation about provisioning responsibilities that are not discussed, and thus go unanalysed. Once again, the presence of physical spaces that do collective provisioning is essential if poor women are to analyse, as well as grapple with, the myriad barriers and constraints they face. It should be noted that Jane's House and Riverview were two quite different types of organizations: they had different histories, structures, mandates, and activities. However, both provided critical supports and did important collective provisioning work for and among their members.

Riverview was an established community-based organization serving low-income families in the area for many years with programmes such as family resource services, settlement services for immigrants, and a variety of community supports and leadership development programmes. It also provided opportunities for participants to volunteer. As a tenant organization with no paid staff members, Jane's House depended on a voluntary steering committee. It had a grassroots structure, having been started by one of the mothers in the study who originally spent her own money on organizing a neighbours night out rather than on the hearing aid that she needed. The group members were mostly lone mothers who came together around the safety and recreational needs of the community. There were approximately twenty-five regular members who met weekly to discuss issues of concern, to plan actions on advocating for their needs as a community, and to organize activities such as social events (e.g., movie nights, Bingo), an after-school homework club for children, music lessons, and fundraising events (e.g., lawn sales). The women coalesced as a group only when they successfully advocated for a physical space (a community office) and it became available. The work of this tenants group reveals some of the costs, as well as the benefits, of grassroots organizations.

The space was needed and welcomed, yet presented a challenge because the distrust and frustrations of living in a 'priority neighbourhood' marked by poverty and violence created animosity among neighbours, which at times carried over into the tenants group. The formation of the group provided mothers with opportunities for information sharing and advocating, such as writing letters to government departments about social assistance, housing, or immigration, and arranging meetings with local agencies and government representatives. The women were provisioning for the community in other ways, such as accompanying drivers to pick up items that were needed by / donated to the group, setting up for community events, and contributing to community potluck dinners.

Doreen, a lone mother of two children under the age of ten, became involved in Jane's House because she 'liked to know what's going on in my neighbourhood and liked to know what they have to offer here and what's going on with all the other kids.' Cathy described the importance of having a space in which collective provisioning can take place:

I think it helps because it brings everyone together, and it gives people a chance to resolve their issues, and come together and bond. Not everybody is going to get along with everybody. You can't force them. But at least if you're providing a place where people can come together as a group and do their things . . . and we don't have to worry about the kids being on the street, maybe dealing some drugs or trying to act cool. They have a place where they can come, chill with each other, do their thing. You know what I mean? I think that that's important. They need that space.

This quote resonates with findings underscoring the fact that for women living in the circumstances of these participants, their responsibilities as mothers shaped their participation in community groups. In fact, Osborne, Baum, and Ziersch (2009) found that when women participated in groups that did not recognize the responsibilities they carried as mothers, their mental health actually deteriorated.

There are multiple discourses about poor mothers. Discourses of resistance may be available, but they can go unrecognized if women are isolated geographically in surroundings where the only ones available tend to blame the victim rather than offer systemic explanations about the causes of oppression. For instance, McCormick (2004), comparing urban and small-town mothers on social assistance in the United States, found that despite the many challenges of living in a high-poverty urban area, the women felt less stigma because the visible markers of being on social assistance, such as using food stamps, were a common condition in the area. Of interest here is that McCormick noted that no women in her sample belonged to organized groups such as those represented in the research sites discussed in this book. Nevertheless, the urban participants in her study seemed to understand the structural basis of poverty that the small-town residents, who were a numerical minority in their communities, did not. Specifically, the urban women saw themselves and their neighbours as born into a certain stratum of society, while the small-town mothers had more individual explanations of their situation.

Implications for Poor Women

The greater the number of barriers and constraints facing women, the fewer the options available to them. The mothers in this study had limited choices and used a variety of strategies to counter barriers – except that the strategies cost them in time and health, as well as physical, mental, and emotional energy. Government assistance does not provide enough money for families to get by, but neither does minimum wage employment (Weigt, 2006). Poor women understand this reality; they daily experience the demands of caring for children; they see the shortage of jobs, the impossibility of survival on a low-wage job while attempting to pay for rent and childcare. And yet even they seem to endorse the moral superiority of paid work. The dominant Canadian neoliberal discourse means that this contradiction will continue to shape low-income mothers' lives in the foreseeable future.

However, the study findings point to some interventions that can at least cushion, if they cannot resolve, the contradiction for those women who bear the brunt of current neoliberal policies. Chief among these is the need for both income and community support programmes to help low-income mothers in their provisioning, including flexible childcare and a range of supports for families with children. Campbell (2006) argues that a national childcare system must be premised on a 'new way of envisioning family relationships and responsibilities, work and child care' (p. 171), and that a successful childcare policy gives thoughtful consideration to the role and value of women's work. Childcare policy should communicate the fact that caring for children is demanding, requires skill and knowledge, and deserves appropriate compensation. Investments in a range of community supports in low-income neighbourhoods are essential. The mothers in this study lived in a neighbourhood that was disadvantaged when measured by prevailing economic and community standards, placing considerable demands on already limited social and community services. All nations, including Canada, rely on the work of social reproduction that women do. A mix of income programmes and community supports would reflect recognition of the provisioning responsibilities that mothers carry. Year after year, mothers will continue to do this work, as described by Jocelyn, a mother of five and grandmother of eleven: 'Over the years I don't think anything will change that much, because none of us has won the lottery, and we don't have no big inheritance to get something [*laughs*]. So I'll be still taking care of them. I still help them. I still have to help my daughters with my grandkids . . . I don't have no food – but they won't go to the food bank, so I'll go.'

A society in which Jocelyn's daughters and granddaughters would be appropriately supported in their provisioning responsibilities is possible (Gurstein & Vilches, 2009). However, to do so would require major changes in the neoliberal political economy that now defines the Canadian state.

7 Revealing Older Women's Provisioning Responsibilities[1]

The theoretical analyses of older women's provisioning in this chapter are situated within debates at the intersection of feminist theory and critical gerontology. They document the range of personal and social responsibilities carried by a group of older women. The intent is to challenge discourses that position older women as potential consumers of services or a caring problem-in-the-making that will tax health-care budgets, as well as the younger working population. A projected demographic tsunami scenario obscures the value of the contributions that older women make in their families and communities, while allowing the costly effects of current patterns of health-care funding and organization to fade into the background.

Against this discursive account, with its age, gender, and class assumptions, data from in-depth interviews with older women reveal just how extensively they provide for those around them. Before presenting data on the different types of work done by older women, we examine the caring literature, concluding that aspects of it need to be reconceptualized if they are to be useful for rethinking the work done by older women and its implications for theory and social policy. We then argue that the concept of provisioning has potential for revealing the multiple dimensions of older women's social contributions. After presenting the data, several theoretical and policy implications are considered.

The Context of Older Women's Lives

Descriptions of women's work outside the paid labour force are frequently captured under the term *caring labour*. As noted in previous chapters, there are a number of streams in this now substantial body of literature. However, in this chapter we focus on how older women are positioned in caring debates. Studies of care patterns show that family members continue to provide over 80 per cent of the labour needed to support elderly persons living in the community, whether or not formal services are used (Glendinning & Means, 2004; Scourfield, 2006). Policy responses such as carers' allowances, paid volunteering, and direct payments to care users to buy help are used to varying degrees in different countries (Rummery, 2009; Timonen, Convery, & Cahill, 2006; Ungerson, 2004; Ungerson & Yeandle, 2007). However, the dollar value attributed to informal caring labour does not reflect the amount of work entailed, and thus there are always questions about the adequacy of the help provided and/or the competence of those doing the work.

Another stream of analysis has focused on gender differences in the types and amount of informal caring work done by women and men (Olson, 2002; Statistics Canada, 2005c). It shows that both older women and men do caring labour, but its focus and meaning varies by gender. As the result of differences in life expectancies and the fact that women tend to marry older men, more women provide care for longer periods of time – seldom under circumstances of their own choosing. Furthermore, taking on this work earlier in the life cycle affects women's options in the labour force, their resultant meagre pension entitlements, and the toll it takes on their own health.

Parallel to this social science and health policy literature, theories about the ethics of care have been developed (Clement, 1996; Ellis, 2004; Gilligan, 1982; Hankivsky, 2004; Koehn, 1998; Nelson & England, 2002; Tronto, 1993) that challenges individualized concepts of justice and rights. Of interest here is the focus in this literature on how relationships that underlie and shape women's responsibilities influence what are considered to be ethical choices. Taken together, this body of scholarship problematizes the fact that social conditions such as need, labour such as unpaid work, and statuses such as being a recipient and provider of care are not attached to social entitlements. Ensuing debates have attempted to reconcile the apparently oppositional approaches of care and justice ethics so that policies promoting the well-being of marginalized groups, such as older women, can be developed (see, for example, Sevenhuijsen, 2004).

Finally, research on caring labour often implicitly categorizes women as receivers or providers of care, thus invoking the neoliberal underlying dualism of dependent/independent discussed in chapter 1. There are differentiations made between spousal carers (noting how they are often elderly themselves) and children (usually daughters). In addition, there is recognition of the particular challenges facing 'young carers,' as well as the aging mothers of adults with disabilities. The more recent literature on grandmothers (Callahan, Brown, MacKenzie, & Whittington, 2004; Dolbin-MacNab, 2006; Goodman & Silverstein, 2006; Minkler, 1999) also highlights the caring work of older women. This research notwithstanding, the significance of the work is seldom interrogated as a challenge to assumptions about the contributions, and thus citizenship claims, of older women.[2] One argument developed in this chapter is that the multiple relationships of older women, and their attendant responsibilities with their associated work, remain largely invisible because the persons involved are older women. Who does what work affects its value.

The relational aspect of the concept of provisioning is particularly useful in an analysis of the provisioning responsibilities carried by older women, because it does not link work to the paid/unpaid labour dichotomy and moves beyond the implicit dichotomy embedded in care-giving and care-receiving debates. The challenge of valuing older women's work entails attention to interpreting and counting it. Valuing work varies by age and intersects systematically with gender, class, and race to produce inequitable outcomes. The work of older women, and its related claims, is routinely undervalued and/or obscured. The critical gerontology literature underlines the contribution of feminism to the field but notes that aging has not been a central theme in feminist theory. One reason posited is that members of the women's movement have not yet moved into old age (Biggs, 2004). If this is the case, then the aging of baby boomers suggests that this should soon change. However, at this historical moment ageism reigns. The cultural turn in gerontology is now producing a richer understanding of identity, but a citizenship model built on the social contributions of older women has yet to take hold. In the following pages, provisioning is used as a conceptual entry point to explore these contributions and challenge discourses that render them invisible.

A Sample of Feminist Older Women

'Older women' is a social category that derives meaning only when it is set within specific social historical contexts. In the site being reported here, called Heracane, participants were women who consciously took up the identity of 'older women.' All participants self-identified as belonging to a group that had as its stated goals to promote public discussion on issues relating to security and justice for older women; to advocate for policies to address these issues; to campaign for greater representation by women on government and community decision-making bodies; and, to challenge stereotypes and support positive portrayals of older women. Total organizational membership was approximately three hundred. Members' energies were focused upon a half dozen areas deemed critical to the quality of life of older women. All defined themselves as feminists, although the term had different meanings for different participants.

In the older women research site, twenty-nine women volunteered to participate in eighteen qualitative interviews and two focus groups. The quotes in this chapter are primarily from the interviews, except where explicitly noted. The validity of the findings was strengthened by subsequent analyses of the focus group data, which had been directed at the work and relationships in the organization, and the reactions of fifty-five women who came to a feedback session where preliminary results were presented. The latter entailed a very lively discussion!

Participants' ages ranged from early sixties to mid-eighties. Even though there was some diversity in race, ethnicity, and sexual orientation, participants were primarily white, and most had some post-secondary education. Household income varied, but no participant was living in poverty. At a minimum, all had sufficient resources to allow them the time and space to actively engage in the organization's work. One-third lived with their spouses, while two-thirds of the participants were single at the time of interviewing; of those single, about 20 per cent had never married, another 20 per cent were widowed, while the rest were separated or divorced.

Ageism also influences what is told and what is heard (Ray & Chandler, 2001–2). Thus one of the authors who identifies as an older woman did all the interviewing for this group. In addition, her background in social work and women's studies allowed her to make use of feminist theory to listen for silences, what was absent from the conversation, and what was articulated. Probes explored hesitancies, responses that seemed ambiguous, where responsibilities and their associated relationships and boundaries were implied or questioned, and when ideas about what constituted community engagement were raised.[3]

Provisioning Activities: 'How do I continue to service all those people?'

Our data reveal a range of responsibilities carried by older women. Like their younger counterparts in the other research sites, older women were engaged in various types of recognized or publicly visible work, as outlined in table 3.1 in chapter 3. Several were employed full-time or part-time (some by choice, others as the result of necessity); many engaged in formal and informal educational pursuits, and all gave hours of unpaid community work to voluntary organizations, churches, and informal networks. Consider Ginger, who lives alone but is involved in the lives of others who form the communities of which she is a part. Since formally retiring, she has become a catalyst for bringing people together around shared interests. She organizes Cool Chat for girls in their early teens, an arena where they can informally discuss topics important to them; Tomorrow's Leaders, a support group for adult women experiencing difficulties; and Share a Story, a reading group for young children. We return to Ginger later when discussing how older women's relationships of responsibility cross traditional kin and community boundaries.

Older women provided caring labour to family, friends, and neighbours. As noted above, in the North American literature there is now a body of research examining the responsibilities that grandmothers carry. Goodman and Silverstein (2006) conclude in their study comparing African American, Latina, and white grandmothers that across ethnicities there was a strong commitment to family survival and continuity.

Many participants in the study were still providing financial and emotional support to their adult children and grandchildren, supporting findings from other research (Gibson, 1999; Plaza, 2000). For instance, Sweety, at seventy-nine, lives with a spouse five years older who is beginning to develop serious health problems. They have four grown children, one of whom continues to consume financial as well as emotional resources. Sweety states, 'Fortunately three of the kids are okay . . . but every step of the way, Mother gets called, and it all gets dumped on my doorstep.'

Participants' circles of provisioning responsibilities included siblings and other relatives. Mary, now in her early seventies, was divorced over a decade ago, after her children grew up. She lives alone, and one grown daughter lives in the same city, but Mary's caring responsibilities are focused on the older generation: 'Then there is Auntie – Auntie is 102. I do her laundry here every Monday; I go to visit her every Friday; plus about two hours a week, you know, I have power of attorney, so I look after all her business affairs as well. So I would say probably on average it's about six hours a week.'

In addition, friends are getting older and need help. Says Bea, 'I have a friend who had a hip-replacement operation and her friends are taking turns looking after her – aftercare!' Rose, in her mid-seventies, poses a question, the implications of which are discussed later: 'I'm getting older, so this is for me becoming an emotional problem. How do I continue to service all these people who are getting older and older and needier and needier?' Shannon, who retired several years earlier, reflects on how things are not quite working out as she had anticipated. Time has always been a scarce resource for her. She divorced while her son was still quite young and raised him alone. There were some difficult years, but now he seems launched. She was expecting to have time to be involved in organizations to which she could bring some of the skills she has acquired over her years in the education system. However, although she does some of this, she finds herself assuming unanticipated hands-on caring responsibilities for older kin: 'It was one of those unplanned things, but also it was the sort of thing that – I don't know – maybe it's the thing to do in the later years of your life that people used to do. They used to take it for granted that they had to spend their time caring for older family members.'

Later in the interview, when asked to elaborate on how this unforeseen responsibility arose, she observed that she now had time. Shannon resented being expected to help her sister, but for an elderly aunt and uncle, it was something she assumed willingly and 'got a lot out of.' All participants provided support – physical and emotional – to friends as well as neighbours who were shut-ins. The majority of participants saw this work increasing in the next three to five years, although for some, the focus of and the people involved in this caring labour will be changing.

In this sample of older women, some of the provisioning activities listed in table 3.1 are more visible than others. Among the invisible ones that emerged in the larger study there were three: sustaining health, making claims, and ensuring safety. Although older women did extensive health work for others, the aspect of this category that is highlighted here is the work of assuming personal responsibility for maintaining their own health. Older women do self-health work, both physical and psychological, knowing that their continuing independence is dependent on it. Commenting on findings from her study of the health-care practices of women who belong to different ethnic groups, Wray (2003) notes that across groups, older women are concerned about maintaining their mobility rather than their appearance, focusing on what they can do, rather than what they cannot. Fitness regimes were not a focus in the interviews, but they emerged in all but five conversations as part of a broader discussion about the need to prioritize time and energy – which participants see as becoming increasingly scarce resources (a theme taken up later in the chapter). Veronica explained why she withdrew from certain activities: 'I was interested in putting my own priorities of exercise (yoga, swimming, walking) in there. Starting at that point, then I looked at what extra time I had left. So I reversed the order of what was important and what was going to get attention first.'

Ensuring safety for self and others was not as present in older women's stories as it was among participants in some of the other sites. In their seniors' apartment, several participants had a buddy system, but safety work for most participants focused on mounting public campaigns, such as improving accessible transportation and changing emergency room procedures to ensure that home-care arrangements were in place before rather than after seniors were discharged. Making claims was central to the mission of Heracane, and thus was picked up in the interviews as requiring a lot of work but best approached as a collective rather than individual responsibility. One focus group member said, 'I want my voice to be heard out there, and I think that people should know that we're sitting on various committees. We're involved in intersecting committees. When they're talking about stuff, we can pipe up and say, "Hey, yeah, but how's that going to affect me as an older woman? You've forgotten that whole issue."'

Provisioning Strategies: 'Some things have got to go'

Older women use practical daily strategies to create and manage resources to meet their provisioning responsibilities, such as arranging for heavy groceries to be delivered, organizing activities so that two afternoons are available each week to look after a grandchild, and exchanging services with neighbours. The older women interviewed did not seem to engage in personally risky behaviour – at least not at the time of the interviews. Many had done so earlier in their lives, such as staying in an abusive relationship because of the financial consequences of leaving. However, given our interest in developing alternative discourses about older women, it is the transformative strategies employed by participants that are highlighted here.

Meeting new demands associated with non-kin responsibilities often involved deciding to change behaviour. For instance, Anne recalled, 'I sort of decided when I retired to make some choices in my life, and one of them was that I would no longer continue to have friends that upset

me.' Another strategy was freeing up time and emotional space by taking steps to control family expectations about participants' availability.
Bunny, whom we briefly met in chapter 3, is seventy and married, with
grown children, as well as several siblings. Her reflections capture the
work involved in setting the boundaries necessary for creating space
for change:

> It was something that was brewing anyway, but then I got sick, and that
> really was the impetus . . . In fact, if I were to die now, I would be pretty
> mad, because I didn't finish all the things I want to finish. So I've got to
> look at things and some things have got to go . . . So it was a fairly deliber-
> ate thing. But more importantly, I think if I'm not careful I could fall into
> what is sort of a life-long pattern of mine, which is being pulled in many
> different directions and finding it difficult to say no to some things. In fact,
> for a lot of older women that's fairly common.

Dealing proactively with stereotypes, and the associated stigma that
older women experience, is part of the everyday work of participants.
Della defines the problem:

> We can't just sit around putting up with this little old lady attitude, you
> know, this patronization. I think there's a certain amount of attitude to-
> wards older people, especially older women. I know there is. I know
> I look like probably a typical middle-class, you know, kind of person, and
> I know there's attitude! There are expectations of what you . . . of what
> you are, you know, what you're supposed to be. I think we pick up it up,
> you know. I used to think, 'How does a person become old? How do you
> learn to be old?' Well, the same way you learn everything else. You just
> watch what other people are doing. You know, if everybody around is like
> the media and other big . . . [*here words fail her as Della's voice trails off and
> she shakes her head*].

Participants' efforts to build new capacities, to articulate alternatives,
mean constantly confronting sexist and ageist assumptions that perme-
ate a society that does not recognize the priorities and work of older
women.

A theme in the older women's data that did not emerge in the other
sites was the challenge of integrating an aging body into a changing
identity. The aging body, particularly when it's female, is the site of contradictory discourses. On the one hand, it is routinely presented as failing and thus the object of health-care interventions. On the other hand,

there are images of successful aging that portray the body as indefinitely robust – if one only exercises responsible choices about lifestyle (Rudiman, 2006). Rebuttals to both discourses have not diminished their force. Theory needs to reflect the realities of the physical capacities of an aging body but not do so in ways that diminish the agency of the individual who inhabits it. During the feedback session where we presented preliminary data results to members of the site, one woman put it this way: 'I see a major problem being lack of energy. People ask why you cannot do things; physical capabilities are limited; expectations are there, but so is the denial. People don't want to see us age.'

Another identity dimension is cultural – articulating meaningful social engagement that defines older women as valued contributors to their communities and to the broader society. As noted earlier, a substantive body of research shows the variety of ways that grandparents contribute to the well-being of their grandchildren. Our data support these findings, but rather than seeing them only as indicators of family support or intergenerational solidarity, we consider them within the pressing need to build multi-dimensional theory that centres on older women. Older people can provide valuable resources that the middle generation cannot, sometimes as the result of time constraints, but also because they do not have access to the requisite knowledge. Shirley shows how she structures identity formation among her grandchildren in a way that roots them in their community:

SHIRLEY. I feel more responsible to my grandchildren than I do to my children who are now adults. And when I say to my grandchildren, I mean that I like to be centre focused in their lives so that what I do is help them have a foundation. I know their mom and their dad are – they feel responsible for certain things. But I feel . . . as Grandma I like to make sure that a stick-to-it-iveness is there for them, in relation to them. Like growing up, you know, as strong adults and maybe having a history of their . . . from where they came like from, surrounding their mom and dad and myself, you know – and their grandfather.

INTERVIEWER. Um hum.

SHIRLEY. That kind of thing. So I feel responsibility that way, and so I guess in providing an education for them – an education as to their background and to give them that strong stability to where they have . . . where their family has come from, I guess, yeah.

INTERVIEWER. You seem to be talking about a sense of identity.

SHIRLEY. Yeah, that's a good descriptive word. I like that . . . for the children to have that identity. Yes.

Neither Shirley nor the interviewer verbalizes that she was teaching her grandchildren how to survive as Black teenagers in a metropolitan area marked by racial tensions, where Black youth experience high levels of unemployment, where rival gangs struggle for 'turf' in poor neighbourhoods, and where encounters with the police bear high costs for non-whites who are in the wrong place at the wrong time.[4]

We introduced Ginger earlier, commenting on her extensive and expanding visible contributions to community. Ginger negotiates her responsibilities within a web of many different types of relationships, most of which cross traditional notions of familial, community, employment, or political social networks. She seemed almost unaware of such boundaries; her networks intertwine. Similarly, her provisioning activities and strategies are at all levels – from the most concrete, such as securing accommodation for someone, to the most abstract, such as helping others through the groups she organized to develop visions of possibilities.

Envisioning a future may be a key strategy for transformation, but for the older women members of Heracane it necessitated a constant rebalancing of problems, possibilities, and probabilities. For some participants, kinship ties were seen as becoming more complex in the years ahead. Veronica captures the competing claims older women face, and their effects, as she negotiates her own possibilities over the next few years:

VERONICA. Change could be more responsibility in terms of my granddaughter, if the marriage [of her son] breaks down. And I . . . I'm never quite sure, you know, but I think that that's possible, especially given the odds today, but also it's possible looking at certain things. So I could have more responsibility, more support will be needed for my granddaughter and also to her parents. I have concerns about my sister. She's okay now, but she's a person who my brothers and I think is somewhat frail, and if she were to become needy, even though she has children, I would want to spend more time with her and also see what, you know, what we could do to help – so that's a possibility. In the immediate five years from now, I'm actually hoping to step up 'non-responsibility' just to . . . just in case that happens, right? I have a strong sense of really just wanting to . . . to wander and, you know, to focus on living in the moment kind of thing.

INTERVIEWER. Um hum. I get from your tone that you want to focus on living in the moment now because you do see some changes coming in five years that may close off some of those . . . those options.

VERONICA. Yeah, absolutely, that's what I'm saying, yeah. And then you never know – your own health either. I have terrific health so far, but you never know.

This segment of the interview was filled with a sense of the present being a hiatus, a pause pregnant with possibilities, and the yearning to 'wander,' but there was also a feeling that it was the calm between two storms of provisioning responsibilities – one more or less completed but another on the horizon.

Participants from Heracane engaged in a critical analysis of their situation – an analysis that incorporated the personal with the political, as they envisioned their own futures and contemplated the options available to older women in general. At the individual level, Rose articulates the ambiguities of trying to envision meaningful personal relationships when there are no guideposts, no scripts, only images of dependency. Later, she reflected on how she is building a new relationship with someone who has a terminal illness: 'Neither of us can quite believe that this is happening; both of us had to come to terms with our situation. We've resolved whatever conflicts we've had. We've accepted our life situation, and yet this is because we know it's temporary and know we're both old; life is temporary. Our physical disabilities are going to increase. We don't know how long we've got, so there's a bittersweet aspect to this that intensifies the beauty of our relationship because there are no hidden agendas here.'

Strongly evident in these excerpts, and present in most interviews, is participants' realization that time increasingly shapes how they weigh their options and consider their futures. Conflicts over the very meaning of time and the interpretation of events within it are important (Everingham, 2002). 'Disparate understandings of time are reflected in struggles over collective perceptions, memories and modes of reflections and self descriptions' (Fitzpatrick, 2004, p. 201). Thus older women understand and assess the impact of their provisioning responsibilities within a time framework that is not employed by younger cohorts in a society where death remains a taboo subject.

Implications for Theory: Back to the Future

Anne observed, 'An older society will be a society of older women. Maybe that's one reason why it's greeted with such an "Oh my God, we're an aging society; there'll be more women," you know! More of the poor elderly are women definitely, and they are poor because of a lifetime of sexism.'

In the foregoing section, we examined activities and strategies separately to reveal their existence and impact on the lives of participants. In fact, activities and strategies operate together, revealing more about the social context of older women's lives than they do about the particular women who participated in the study. The emphasis in this section suggests theoretical domains that need exploration if dominant ideas of the lives that older women lead are to be successfully challenged and alternatives articulated. Images of lifestyle choices that emphasize activity and leisure, on the one hand, while portraying aging women as heavy users of health-care services on the other, are both stereotypes. The women present in this chapter belonged to an organization focused on challenging stereotypes of older women. Women who belonged to Heracane could exercise some control over the amount of provisioning they did, for whom, and how they carried out their relationship-based responsibilities. Members were not poor, but even in a country where minimum pensions and basic health-care guarantees are available, many older women still are. Thus, understanding the impact that provisioning responsibilities have on this relatively privileged group will undoubtedly underestimate the direct and indirect costs borne by women with fewer resources.

A caveat is in order before proceeding. The focus in this analysis on the provisioning responsibilities carried by older women is not meant to deny that they are also the recipients of provisioning by others. Rather, the research focus was designed to challenge discourses that deflect attention from the contributions that older women make to their families, and the broader community. Using the concept of provisioning helped us to open up the dichotomies that have crept into how we think about work, care, and community engagement. Older women do work, but most of this occurs outside of the formal labour force.

Participants' responses support other research showing the ongoing responsibilities that older women continue to carry for their kin. The data suggest that it is the magnitude of the work, not its occurrence, that participants had not anticipated. Older women are not shirking their multiple familial provisioning responsibilities, but the amount of work this entails is considerable, and putting boundaries around kin claims has to be negotiated, as noted in the previous section. When participants are asked to envision what the future might hold, these responsibilities are frequently cited as variables that have to be factored into any equation. Options available to older women seem to be shaped by their awareness of the present and future implications of these provisioning responsibilities. This interpretation was underscored in comments made during the feedback session: 'What gets missed [in many debates] is the role of grandmothers – men [fathers] are not carrying their share, so mothers turn to their mothers.' 'The wedge of taking care is getting wider – it is happening in our individual lives and organizations such as this one.'

Theoretically, we would argue, this happens because the work and the actors are not seen. There is no public arena in which this work is tracked. The amount of unpaid domestic and caring labour of younger women has slowly been exposed over the years, but this has not been the case for older women. We suggest there is an assumption that the load becomes less as one ages – thus the 'shock' experienced by some participants as they examined their situation. Even more concerning is how it left them with a sense of restricted futures and threatened their health – and these are findings from a relatively fortunate group of older women. Shannon was expected to do work that she had not anticipated; Veronica hoped she could just be free for a few years. This silence is costly to women, reinforcing privilege structures and weakening older women's claims. The silence becomes another mechanism whereby social inequities are reproduced.

One very real shadow on the horizon for all participants is the implications of an aging body (Twigg, 2004). How to theoretically factor in physical limitations while avoiding ageism is the conundrum. If one starts from the premise that language delineates relationships within which meaning is produced, that knowledge is power-laden and power-producing (Barker, 2005), developing alternative discourses about the aging female body will require new language. The knot that has to be untied is once again the tendency in European thought to organize concepts by their polarities. In this case, the youthful body portrayed as the consumer in the market is juxtaposed to the decaying body presented as the object of the health-care system. Neither really exists, but both are powerful, because they are associated with concepts that reinforce the dualism – youth/old age, independence/dependence, healthy/sick. These are the dubious conceptual tools available to older women as they struggle to develop transformative strategies that reposition them as citizens carrying provisioning responsibilities and making social contributions to their communities.

Another dimension in the older women's data is time. A keen sense that time is a diminishing finite resource – so well captured by Veronica – was reinforced in the feedback session. Time is determined by culture, the structure of a society, and individuals' abilities to control the use of time in their lives. Western societies use time designations to mark boundaries between spheres of activities, to create expectations about the use of time, and create hierarchical rankings of the value of the time, work, and persons involved (Thomas, 1996). Research on paid work documents the emergence of an understanding of time that might be called an 'extended present.' Work is experienced as being speeded up, with multitasking being a skill required to get the work done. Using time to plan for the future or connecting relationships to tasks is not part of such a work model. Instead, work is developed to fit an 'expanded present,' in which the future never arrives. The inability of these work models to incorporate the future impedes building theories that reflect the finite nature of time in everyone's life, not just that of the older woman. The meaning of time within a finite lifespan was very real to participants, even if culturally denied in a society in which people live in an 'extended present,' a state of being in which 'there is no time in the present to plan for the future' (Brannen, 2005, p. 114).

A time dimension that was meaningful to participants is that of a lifespan. A lifetime is finite. One contribution of these conversations with older women to theorizing is their challenging us to consider how much an extended present is a mirage that does not correspond to their need to carefully weigh what responsibilities must go, what needs to be renegotiated, and what is important to expand during their remaining years. Insisting that a finite future be inserted into theories of the present acknowledges their understanding that time is limited. Present priorities and relationship dynamics are shaped when an aging body reminds one that death is on the horizon. Insisting that discussions of provisioning responsibilities be placed within the time frame of a human lifespan challenges the denial of death that lies behind notions of the extended present. As such, older women are learning, engaging, and communicating to those with whom they interact, another way of doing aging.

Conclusion

Data from this sample of older women vividly testify to the fact that older women shoulder many of the provisioning responsibilities carried by other groups in our study. The major difference lies in how they are performed and valued. The representation of who does work is a powerful determinant of its value. Theorizing embodied difference is central to a feminist analysis (Barker, 2005) but equally importantly, we argue, is its potential to provide new knowledge about the reality of older women's lives – knowledge that can move social policy beyond coping with caregiving to the more pressing need to reconceptualize what constitute contributions to society. Citizenship claims associated with these contributions lie less in arguments about whether or not work in the domestic sphere is a form of civic participation (Lister, 2007), than they are a response to the retreat of the state from social provisioning that has resulted in older women (and their younger sisters!) having to pick up the work. Relationship-based ethics assures that women will; market economics ensures that the costs remain invisible. In a classic sleight of hand, a public issue is transformed into private troubles.

Change is usually initiated from the bottom up, by those oppressed by prevailing hierarchies of privilege. Thus, despite the above analysis, we remain optimistic that as sectors of the feminist population age, concepts and knowledge that underpin policies and programmes will change. The actions of older women will result in policies that are less discriminatory to those who must grapple with relationship-based responsibilities that they cannot ignore, even if public policy does; who need to pace their work, commitments, and dreams to the realities of an aging body; and who belong to that segment of the population that must face the fact that a lifetime comes to an end. It is ultimately this kind of time that is the scarcest of resources. It cannot be bought or retrieved if lost, nor can it be extended.

8 Counting the Costs of Provisioning for Women Living on Low Incomes[1]

In chapters 3 and 4, the concept of provisioning helped to identify the kinds of work that are rendered invisible when the categories of paid and unpaid work are used. Using data from all study sites, that work was described for both household and collective provisioning. Chapters 5, 6, and 7 focused on specific sites, revealing how individual and collective provisioning looks somewhat different when done by women whose lives vary in class, age, and ethno-racial membership, although they all resided in a large metropolitan area. In this chapter we explore the intersection of household and collective provisioning for low-income women in three small urban areas where the impact of cutbacks in public provisioning on participants and the organizations to which they belonged was particularly acute. We first consider what the provisioning focus can contribute to this examination and then report the strategies used by women living on a low income and the importance of the collective provisioning of organizations to household well-being.

A weakness in the conventional binaries of paid/unpaid work and formal/informal economy that is of particular concern in this chapter is that they fail to address the cost of the transfer of responsibility from the market or from public provisioning to private provisioning (Beneria, 1995; Donath, 2000; Elson, 2000; Himmelweit, 2002; Pettman, 1996; Taylor, 2004). In the provinces where this study takes place, a transfer of responsibility did take place, as there were substantive cuts in funding to voluntary organizations, including women's centres and frontline neighbourhood service centres who work with the economically marginalized, at the same time as the government stepped out of the role of service provider. The result has been a reduction in the ability of organizations to deliver programmes and services at the same time that the number of potential social service users was increasing (City of Toronto, 1997; Meinhard & Foster, 1997; Peters & Kwong-Leung, 2004). Failing to address these costs can lead to the assumption that such transfers are costless or that households are bearing them without strain.

Studies of how women respond to increased responsibility with fewer resources document a number of strategies, including using extended domestic and household networks (Deere, Safa, & Antrobus, 1997; Edin & Lein, 1998; Feldman, 1992; Giri, 1995), engaging in informal economic activity such as taking in boarders or providing services on the side (Deere, Safa, & Antrobus, 1997; Pettman, 1996), and reconfiguring household membership (Deere, Safa, & Antrobus, 1997; Feldman, 1992). Some of these strategies have been made more difficult in the context of a restructured social assistance system that includes work for welfare, reductions in benefits, time limits, and complex forms of surveillance and regulation of both eligibility for and retention of income assistance. The provisioning strategies of low-income women in the context of this restructuring will be explored below.

Situating the Sites

In this chapter we examine women's individual household provisioning and how community groups contribute to that provisioning. This examination draws on interviews with individual women members and/or service users from the first three sites to join the project: Cascade – a food cooperative programme within a multi-resource centre; Pont Place – a women's society offering employability training to women who have left abusive relationships; and Hands-On – a community resource centre for families in a two poor, multicultural neighbourhoods. These interviews explored household provisioning and the role of community groups in that provisioning.[2]

As table 8.1 shows, participants (fifty-eight) varied by age range, household type, source of income, and number of children. Participants for the individual interviews reflect a diverse group of women and included women whose first language is French, First Nations women, and African, Asian, Indian, and Latin American immigrants. The individual women interviewees share a marginality of position, with the majority living on low or precarious incomes. Interviews were conducted by co-investigators and/or experienced research assistants, except in one site where the participants interviewed each other in dyads (Porter, Neysmith, Reitsma-Street, & Baker Collins, 2009).

Table 8.1. Demographic characteristics of participants

Age	Household type	Source of Income	No. of children
17% are 20–9	48% are lone parents	28% are employed	21% have no children
33% are 30–9	29% are couples with children	28% receive social assistance	22% have one child
24% are 40–9	14% are single	26% receive disability	28% have two children
20% are 50–9	9% are couples without children	8% receive other government transfer	29% have three children
6% are 60+		6% are students	
		4% receive spousal/ child support	

Provisioning Activities of Women Living on Low Incomes

As we anticipated, beginning with the question 'Who are you responsible for?' uncovered a broad range of activities that women undertake that are not part of the paid employment of the formal economy. The women we interviewed engage in many different kinds of activities in order to provision. Most women combine strategies to produce the resources needed by those for whom they are responsible. In this section we describe the activities that women undertake to supply material resources when their current source of income is insufficient to purchase all that the household needs. Some examples of this kind of provisioning that we found include the following:

- *Self-provisioning*, a term used by several authors, refers to 'the extraordinary work of producing goods and services for a family's use' (M.K. Nelson, 1999, p. 519). This work is undertaken by members of the household within the household for themselves (Pahl & Wallace, 1985). Examples of self-provisioning in our study included buying in bulk and canning or freezing, growing vegetables, doing one's own plumbing and electrical repairs, and painting.
- *Small-scale entrepreneurial activity* takes place in the form of side jobs or self-employment taken on in order to earn extra income (Deere et al., 1997; M.K. Nelson, 1999). Women in our study made extra

income by cleaning for other households, babysitting, refinishing antiques, making crafts for gifts, and repairing furniture. Women also use assets to create cash resources. Women who own cars will use them to earn extra cash by giving rides for gas money. A young mother with small children spends several hours in the evening on her computer entering contests and filling out surveys for which there is a reimbursement. In addition to the reimbursement, she has won compact discs, movies, a trip to a spa, a video game, and other items. What she cannot use, she sells, and some items become birthday or Christmas presents. She is able through this activity to make up the monthly fee for Internet service. The amount of extra income brought in through these entrepreneurial activities is meagre, but also essential to making ends meet.

- *Exchanges of goods and services* take place with members of other households in what is called the social economy (M.K. Nelson, 1999). In our study we found many examples of extended household exchange networks. One woman will take care of her friend's cat when she is away and her friend will take her for groceries and pay for them. Another woman has a good friend whom she helps with the cleaning in exchange for using her fax machine. She will also babysit her friend's children and her friend will cut and colour her hair.

- *Managing scarce resources* is another activity undertaken by economically marginalized women. There is a shared knowledge about how to manage bills when resources are insufficient to pay them all on time. Women learn how much to put down and which bills to pay first, to avoid termination of service. Frances reported, 'I pay whoever sends me a notice first, who will cut you off the fastest. Sometimes I juggle bills. I go by order of importance. No cable. I must pay at least part of hydro and phone and Internet. You can let taxes slide. If you call, they're pretty good.'

- *Community managing work* is a term we borrowed from Moser (1991) for work that women do in community to provide for their and others' households. Community managing work can happen in informal ways or through formal organizations. Some examples of informal community managing work include acting as the community babysitter for children who are left unsupervised, informing people in the community of community resource centre programmes, exchanging knowledge among women in a food cooperative about where to get day-old bakery products or how to obtain a season pass for children to the community swimming pool. More formal examples include helping organize the high school breakfast programme and serving on the council of a community resource centre.

The term *community managing work* also refers to 'the provision of items of collective consumption' (Moser, 1991, p. 86). As noted earlier, the women represented in the study were all part of formal community organizations that engage in collective provisioning. Women's connection to these community groups may be one of membership and mutual support, volunteering in order to receive services, and/or simply being provided services. When data from all six sites allowed for saturation of the categories, it became obvious that this category included many different types of work and needed to be expanded.

Provisioning Relationships across Permeable Boundaries

In addition to capturing other kinds of work, there is a concern in the literature to capture the complexity (Haylett, 2003; Naples, 1992) and the context (Naples, 1992; Oliker, 1995) in which the work is situated. Numerous authors make the case that neatly defined boundaries between the different spheres of women's work do not exist. The boundaries between formal and informal economic activity (Donath, 2000; Pettman, 1996), between self-provisioning and housework (M.K. Nelson, 1999), between activism and mothering or between family and community (Naples, 1992) are permeable and not tidy. M.K. Nelson (1999) speaks of moonlighting, casual exchanges, and self-provisioning – all supplemental economic activities. Naples (1992) notes a blurring of community work and family-based labour when persons open their homes to those in need. Discovering the links and the connections between the various forms of work is important (Beneria, 1995; Taylor, 2004).

Another concern being addressed in the push to find new language is to make visible the ways in which economic relationships are embedded in social relationships (DeVault, 1991; Mink, 1998; Oliker, 1995; Taylor, 2004; Williams & Windebank, 2003). Oliker (1995) makes the argument that one of the 'proximate contexts' in which women's work choices are made includes the 'structural patterning of personal relations and of the social relations in which they are embedded' (pp. 251–2).

In this examination of low-income women's provisioning activities, the complexity described above and the embedding in social relationships are clearly evident. In particular, the boundary between care activity (reproductive) and economic activity (productive) does not reflect the reality of low-income women's lives. Provisioning work does not separate neatly into those two categories. Our work uncovered *provisioning relationships*. In the Southern Ontario site, for example, there were a significant number of inter-generational relationships, with grandparents caring for grandchildren during the day while parents worked, and grown children visiting regularly with their families on weekends. In these situations, grandparents are providing both care and food to children and grandchildren. In most situations there was a reciprocal contribution to grandparents from their adult children in the form of providing loans in emergencies, buying them furniture, or contributing larger-cost items such as new appliances. These relationships involve both care and exchange, both care activity and economic activity. The caring work helps grandparents put food on the table. Many of the exchanges of goods and services and some of the entrepreneurial activity denoted above are also rooted in relationships between family members and/or between friends.

The *provisioning relationships* described above exist in multiple layers. Family connections of responsibility and provisioning extend beyond the members who live in the household full time. There were numerous examples among women we interviewed of family members who live in the household on a regular but part-time basis. Examples include children for whom someone in the household (the woman, her partner, or her grown children) has custody on weekends, or grown children and their families who come home regularly for weekend stays. There are also family members who do not live in the household for whom women have relationships of responsibility. One woman regularly helps her mother care for her brother who suffers from schizophrenia, while another woman's brother comes for meals when he is short of food.

It should be noted that these relationships are a complex mix of reciprocal relationships where care and provisioning are mutually exchanged and relationships where the care and provisioning is one way. The care for brothers noted above is an example of one-way provisioning. In an example of a mutual family exchange, a woman bakes for her father and in return uses his washer/dryer to do her laundry. Some of the activities noted above are based on long-standing relationships or ongoing informal contacts, while others are more episodic and unconventional, depending on opportunities and needs that arise.

The provisioning relationships described above consist not only of support but also of obligation (Stack, 1974, as cited in Oliker, 1995, p. 255). They not only provide resources but also 'exact resources' (Oliker, 1995, p. 255). One woman we spoke to is the primary caregiver for her husband, who has had a debilitating stroke and continues to live at home. Her husband's care (feeding, bathing, dressing) is a twenty-four-hour job, and she receives very little support from family and only two hours of assistance from the Red Cross each week. She indicated that her husband 'takes all his stress out on me' and gets angry frequently. This woman is in poor health herself, with chronic pain from a near-fatal accident some years ago now compounded by arthritis. She spoke repeatedly of her fatigue and her lack of energy. Her hope for the future is to rest.

Provisioning Strategies in Tough Times

In addition to activities that households undertake to supply needed material resources, some activities are undertaken when the needed material goods are insufficient. We document below the strategies that women use to provision when there are not enough resources for all the people for whom they are responsible. In a subsequent discussion we examine the long-term costs of employing these strategies.

Household Formation

First, we found that household formation itself becomes an arena for provisioning strategies. We found household boundaries to be fluid, with changing configurations of household membership such as increases in household size. According to Moser and Holland (1997), households restructure in response to external crises, such as housing problems: 'In the short term, households act as "shock absorbers," reducing vulnerability for individuals who join them' (p. 9).

There were numerous examples in our study of households acting as shock absorbers. In an example from Southern Ontario, one of the women interviewed had her niece and her three children living with her temporarily, since the niece had been evicted from her apartment. This same woman had earlier in the year lived with her sister (mother of the niece) when she lost her housing. In an example from the West Coast, a mother's pregnant daughter, who had been living on the street, came home to live with her. In Northern Ontario, a woman took in her chronically ill uncle to provide health care for him and trained her children to look after him in a caring way. In some situations, additions to the household are a drain on resources, while in others they allow for the pooling of meagre resources.

Consumption Patterns

Second, women also change their consumption patterns as a way to provision. Examples from our study included reducing consumption by not filling prescriptions for medicine that were not covered by provincial health-care plans, cancelling the newspaper subscription, shutting off cable TV, going without new clothes so that mothers can provide clothes for their children, going without haircuts, going without certain kinds of food (fruit, milk, or meat, which cannot be obtained at a food bank), or going without food so children can eat.

Households also sell items that are 'close to me' in order to pay for essential items. One woman stated, 'I don't ask for help from very many people. In the last couple of years, I think I must have sold over three thousand dollars worth of stuff just to make ends meet at different points in time.' Another woman lost her computer to the pawnshop: 'I bought a computer once, and I had to hock it to get some money, and I lost it. A thousand-dollar computer and I got 250 bucks for it and I didn't have the money to get it back.'

Another consumption strategy is to put off bill payments. One woman states (when asked whether she engaged in risky behaviour to make ends meet), 'Well, the risky thing that I did was I didn't pay my rent so I could pay my phone . . . which got me a notice that if it wasn't paid by such-and-such a date we would be evicted . . . we ended up fixing it, but that was a risky thing.' Or in the words of another participant, 'The bills aren't completely paid off, but I give them something just so I can keep my water, my electricity on, that kind of thing.'

Provisioning for Survival

We have considered in this chapter a variety of provisioning activities and strategies that the women in these low-income sites undertake in the informal economy. These activities are not necessarily unique to women or to economically marginalized groups. Studies have shown that households across income groups and men as well as women engage in informal economic activity (Jensen, Cornwell, & Findeis, 1995; Pahl & Wallace, 1985; Petrzelka & Mannon, 2006).

What is important to note is that the women in our study enter into provisioning activities for economic necessity and survival. Our study uncovered the ways in which women make up the gap in resources between those available through income support or low-paid work and those that are needed to survive. These activities bring in small, seemingly insignificant amounts of cash or other resources, and yet these resources are indispensable to survival. One woman commented on the importance to her family's survival of her relationship with an elderly woman for whom she did odd jobs for pay. She was worried that this woman might pass away: 'The only thing that would make it harder for myself is for the elderly lady I shovel for; it would make it harder financially for myself and my family if she passed on. Then I wouldn't have that extra money that I earn with shovelling her snow and cleaning her kitchen. It's small amounts of money, but it's still something that we still earn for our family, and we can buy things with it, so if she passed on, we wouldn't be able to earn that money.'

In their study of informal work among rural households, Jensen, Cornwell, and Findeis (1995) note how important for poor families are the small amounts of income added through informal work to the household's resources. 'While the reported income is modest, in many instances it is clearly perceived as critical for making ends meet' (p. 100). For women in low-income households in our study, collective provisioning around food security was especially important. For example, most of the women who belong to the food cooperative in Southern Ontario state that they could not survive with the food assistance they receive. In Northern Ontario, the community resource centre provides a breakfast programme for children that is very important to household provisioning. And on the West Coast, food assistance from the employment programme for abused women is 'what we've been living on.'

In a similar way, the relationships that the women developed with community agencies are also connected to their survival. Collective provisioning is essential to obtain needed services and/or material goods. In their study of how women living on low incomes make up the shortfall between income and expenses, Edin and Lein (1998) found that most women maintained connections with over a dozen separate community organizations in order to get the help they needed. The women in our study also use multiple agencies to meet their food needs. One woman on the West Coast reports that in light of food bank rules that limit visits to once a month, she 'goes to them all.' Another woman described how she can get nearly five free meals per week by going to a variety of different Native, church, and other programmes. It is important to recognize the work that goes into establishing and maintaining these relationships to obtain food (Edin & Lein, 1998; Oliker, 1995). It can be as time-consuming as a part-time job. One young mother in our study who had numerous exchanges of goods and physical labour stated, 'It takes years to build up all these connections.'

Participants reported that they receive significant emotional support from their connections to community groups. This emotional support is important, given their marginalized situation. It is particularly valued because of the stress and demoralization of not being able to provide for those for whom one is responsible. Stated one woman, 'Sometimes I worry about having food and the bills being paid. How am I going to make this month go? Sleepless nights, thinking about it.' Another woman expressed fear over how she would raise the funds for her daughter's high school registration: 'I don't know where I'm going to come up with the money for [high school] registration. It's $65, expensive calculator costs $140, locker $20. Don't know where I'm coming up with that. I have no idea right now where the hell I'm going to get $200.'

Even volunteering for community organizations can take on a function of helping with economic survival. The women who were part of a food cooperative in Southern Ontario volunteer extra hours in the food warehouse in order to earn 'food points' above what they would receive as co-op members. Three-quarters of the women interviewed in this site reported that they worked extra hours in the food warehouse to earn additional food points. One might call this work volunteering in order to provision – another example of permeable boundaries (Pettman, 1996) and the 'interlocking and reinforcing connections' referred to by Naples (1992, p. 442). In volunteering in order to earn extra food points, women are connecting their community managing work to their household provisioning work. It is also important to note how crucial these extra food points are to poor households. One woman stated, 'The five points are crucial to me. I really plan, but there are times when I've run out of food . . . With the five points I could get cheese and bread and have grilled cheese when the food ran out.'

Discussion

Cornwall and Gaventa (2001) note that informal and indigenous forms of civil society can be critically important to marginalized households. Informal networks and self-help groups 'are actively involved in bridging the service provision gap' (p. 14). As noted earlier, the contribution of community groups and collective provisioning is critical to the women in the study, particularly with regard to food security. As a member of the food cooperative commented, 'The extra clothing you get on the pick-ups, the food, the Christmas baskets, Easter stuff, all the little extra stuff, they help out. The extra food is important.'

Failure to recognize the importance of these informal activities can marginalize their importance in discussions of social policy (Cornwall & Gaventa, 2001), and even more concerning are the consequences of this failure: it allows policymakers to hide the true costs to households of changes in the formal economy and reductions in public provision. It is simply assumed that the transfer of provisioning responsibilities from the public sector to the private is unproblematic.

Donath (2000) points out that a reduction in services in the market economy means an increase in services provided in the informal economy. What may be passed off as increased productivity is simply a passing on of costs from the visible economy to the invisible. In a parallel argument, Pettman (1996) comments on the reduction in access to state services as a result of structural adjustment programmes: 'They effect a transfer of many social costs from public to private sectors, from state to household, and from paid to unpaid labour. These transfers are especially damaging to women' (p. 168).

To see the domestic sector as the social safety net of last resort is a one-sided view, according to Elson (2000). The domestic sector does not have an unlimited capacity to replace resources that have been taken out of the public sector: 'The domestic sector, therefore, cannot be seen as a bottomless well upon which the other sectors can draw. Unless the inputs from the public and private sector are sufficiently nourishing, human capacities and provisioning values will be depleted, they will drain away' (p. 91).

We have noted that one provisioning strategy that women in our study use is changing household formation in order to survive economically. This strategy confirms research demonstrating that in the face of cuts in public provisioning, women change the configurations of household membership (Feldman, 1992), often increasing the size of the household, and they revitalize or expand their domestic household exchange networks (Deere, Safa, & Antrobus, 1997; Giri, 1995). This strategy has long-term consequences. In a panel study that examined the impact of significant policy changes in Ontario on forty households over three years, the authors note that while family and friends provide critical assistance in times of need, these relationships are 'easily exhausted in conditions of poverty' (Neysmith, Bezanson, & O'Connell, 2005, p. 145) and are not a substitute for an adequate income or public support programmes.

It is important to note here that the fluid and changing pattern of household formation is not recognized in the rules and regulations of social programmes, where a static definition of household is required. This means that the extra resources needed to care for occasional household members are not forthcoming. More importantly, household adaptations that result in sharing resources may actually lead to penalties and reductions in income if the sharing is reported. In the West Coast example, the mother and daughter pool their resources, though they have not reported this to public officials. New regulations for social assistance in both provinces in which the study was done enable officials to reduce social assistance cheques by the amount recipients receive in aid from family/friends and to require households to charge rent to those who move in, whether or not they are able to contribute to household resources (Baker Collins, 2004).

Listening to the women in our study describe their reduction in consumption strategies should alert us to the current and future depletion of resources in the household sector. Going without food to pay for other necessities is an example of a depleting strategy: 'There are times when I can't pay the bills. Then I go without food. Happens one or two days a week.' The impact of the reduction of consumption on health is a significant and troubling finding from our interviews. When medications are not covered under provincial health-care plans, women do not take them. A woman who has spurs on her heels needs orthotic insoles. She lives in a second-floor apartment and cannot manage the stairs without pain and further injury to her feet, but she is not able to afford the insoles without foregoing something needed by her children, 'So they give to me the prescription for the insole, but it's $450, so I must pay. I don't know when I will buy . . . this is the most important, actually, for myself, but it is my three children, my son is . . . is . . . need food or something. So I don't know, I just postpone the insole.' Another woman endures chronic pain because there is no money for transportation for her to reach a hospital for pain-relief management. Her husband's income goes to trying to keep up with the mortgage payments and putting food on the table.

In their study of citizen participation in response to economic restructuring, Staeheli and Clarke (2003) make important observations that are paralleled in this study of women's provisioning. They note that in response to the retrenchment of social rights, citizens pursue two possible scenarios: they decide that political action carries very little hope for countering the impacts of economic restructuring, or they engage in political activism in order to recapture goods and services that used to be available through public provision. Social rights, according to Staeheli and Clarke, no longer *enable* citizen participation; rather, citizens participate to reclaim social rights or to compensate for their disappearance.

The same is true of women's household provisioning. In the face of significant cutbacks in public provision of goods and services, women are engaging in a complex network of activities in order to compensate through private provisioning for resources that are no longer available through public provisioning. Although the provisioning choices and strategies that women follow relate to small amounts of income or resources, those choices can carry enormous consequences. Choosing between meeting immediate housing needs or treating chronic health conditions, choosing between selling valuable household goods or not making utility payments, and reducing food consumption so children can eat are all choices that meet immediate demands but reduce well-being in the long term.

Conclusion

One premise of this chapter (and the research project) is that using the concept of provisioning to describe and understand women's work would uncover activities missed when conventional categories of paid and unpaid work are used. The variety of activities described by individual women as part of their provisioning work in this and other chapters show the promise of the concept of provisioning in documenting women's work more fully. In addition, by conceptualizing provisioning through relations of responsibility, the social embeddedness of women's work is also demonstrated.

We have also examined more closely a particular kind of provisioning activity undertaken by women living on low incomes – to privately provision for resources that in the past were publicly provided. This examination has demonstrated that women use unpaid labour, household exchange networks, connections to community groups, self-provisioning, and casual exchanges to compensate for cuts to public services. Because these activities are not part of conventional economic analysis, the assumption can be made that resource reallocation is cost-less (Elson, 1992). In fact, households do not have an endless capacity to act as 'shock absorbers' (Moser & Holland, 1997). This study has demonstrated that the starting place to document the costs of public to private resource allocation is to examine the provisioning 'choices' that women make.

The transfer of responsibility from public provisions to private means relieves the state of the costs attached to that responsibility, and the community becomes the new means for achieving social welfare (Hyatt, 2001; Ilcan & Basok, 2004). The myriad ways that women use to cover the gap must not be interpreted as proof of the capacity of the community to respond to increased need. Examining volunteer activi-ties among marginalized communities reveals 'not the absence of civil society but rather *the absence of material resources*' (Hyatt, 2001, p. 211, emphasis added).

However, we should not take the absence of material resources to mean the absence of government involvement. The state is involved in new ways. Women's provisioning responsibilities do not change with the reduction in public support for provisioning. What has changed, however, is the extent to which private choices to supple-ment declining public support are now policed by the very public system that has pulled away its support. As women seek to draw on other sources of support, their choices are delimited by the regula-tions of the income support system on which they rely. Many of the ways in which women meet these needs are contrary to the new reg-ulations. Were the exchanges, side jobs, and bartering relationships reported or discovered, this could result in a reduction in social as-sistance payments. The very complex and creative measures women take in private provisioning to make up for cuts in public provision-ing can actually place at risk their already very limited public provi-sions. The policy context both reduces public provisions and polices their private substitutes.

This contradictory nature of public policy needs to be exposed. It is our contention that the concept of provisioning has been helpful in revealing the costly consequences of this contradiction. In addition to showing the contradictions, we must also shift our gaze from the indi-vidual choices that women make to the risky public policies that en-danger women and the persons for whom they have relationships of responsibility. One way in which to challenge such policies is to find new language that situates economic activity and decision-making in its proximate contexts, which recognizes its social embeddedness and acknowledges human provisioning as legitimate economic activity. This should make sense even to policymakers who have designed the welfare regime. It is ineffectual to expect the domestic and community sectors to take on more responsibility while administering policies that threaten disintegration in these very sectors.

PART THREE

9 Collective Spaces as Incubators of Citizenship[1]

This chapter is focused on the work of women's organizations as it relates to their collective provisioning under the constraints of neoliberal policies. Three of the organizations we studied espoused overtly feminist goals (Heracane, an advocacy group for and by older women; Pont Place, an employability and counselling programme for abused women; and Gen-Y, serving the housing, employment, and parenting needs of young women), but all three incorporated material bases for women's existence as well. Other groups, using feminist principles, focused more directly on supporting the social and material provisioning responsibilities of women (Cascade Co-op, a food cooperative; Hands On, a community resource centre for families; and Jane's House, a tenants' self-help and advocacy group).

All of the organizations in the study operated within the public arena to provide for their members (both staff and clients) in ways that de-emphasized hierarchy and supported holistically the wide-ranging provisioning responsibilities that women undertake. As such, we argue, they provided a space for women to challenge market citizenship – the predominant model for social policy formation in Canada since the 1990s (Crouch, Eder, & Tambini, 2001). In the following pages we examine the ways in which conceptualizing the work of women's community organizations as collective provisioning spaces allows us to see linkages between women's material and strategic interests that keep alive feminist struggles in the face of the political and economic challenges of the twenty-first century.

In our examination of the obstacles facing women's collective work in a neoliberal era, we challenge narrow interpretations of Molyneux's (1998) original discussion of strategic principles for feminist organizing in making the case for a more inclusive view of citizenship. It is clear that women's groups have suffered in many ways from reductions in social spending that have squeezed their resources while increasing the number of women needing help. Yet we argue that this is only part of the story. What we have also seen are signs that these organizations try to keep alive, albeit under difficult circumstances and in vitiated form, a vital social space that serves as a catalyst for resisting an individualized citizenship.

Neoliberal Pressures on Women's Collective Provisioning

While T.H. Marshall's notions of social citizenship rights may have been too idealistic (Crouch, Eder, & Tambini, 2001), during the post–Second World War period the Canadian welfare state did manage to achieve social rights through public provision of health, social, and educational resources that were seen as enabling citizenship. Social rights language provided an opportunity 'for the systematically disadvantaged to talk back to the welfare state, and to make claims as citizens who had been actively denied its promise of equality, redress and progress' (Brodie, 2008, p. 151). It was through the equality discourse of social rights that women's groups were afforded space to make claims on the state on women's behalf (Dobrowolsky & Jenson, 2004).

By the turn of the twenty-first century, citizenship discourse had shifted from a vision of social citizenship guaranteeing social entitlements to one that promotes market citizenship (Crouch, Eder, & Tambini, 2001; Dobrowolsky, 2008; Jenson & Phillips, 2001; Schild, 2000). In the latter citizenship regime, social policies are directed at market interests that encourage 'flexible' forms of employment and free trade practices instead of investment in policies that promote community development and equitable distribution of employment and family responsibilities (Frazer, 2005; Standing, 1999; Stratigaki, 2004). The market citizen is an autonomous individual whose receipt of short-term assistance is expected to lead to self-sufficiency. Access to social provisions is channelled through the market, and citizens are now considered to be individuals with specific interests, rather than members of collectives (Ilcan & Basok, 2004). Commenting on the rules attached to income assistance in British Columbia, one participant pointed to ways in which market citizenship violates the tenets of social citizenship: 'If this happened to me now, I'd take their asses to court, and I bet you ten dollars that I would have won, because there's nowhere on that paper that says when you go in there, that if you win the lottery or if you get whatever, you have to pay them back. There's nothing that says that. *As my right as a Canadian, these things, social services, are out there, and I'm sorry that I'm whatever to society, a burden to society.* It's not like I haven't tried.'

The juxtaposition of social citizenship ('my right as a Canadian') and a marketized, individualized citizenship ('a burden to society') in this one statement illustrates the contradictory forces facing women in need of social services.

The market-oriented citizenship discourse has grown with neoliberal policies enacted since the watershed federal budget of 1995. These policies have both worsened the socio-economic realities of individual women and reduced the resources that women's organizations require to support women's needs (Cohen & Brodie, 2007). Hallmarks of the neoliberal mindset that has overtaken government budgeting and policymaking include (1) cutbacks in government spending; (2) a narrowing of eligibility requirements for programme participation; (3) an all-encompassing emphasis on paid work as a means to responsible behaviour; and (4) a much more regulatory presence in the lives of citizens (Bashevkin, 2002). Women, especially low-income mothers, have borne a disproportionate share of the impact of reduced income support programmes, an increasingly work-tested policy environment, and minimal childcare provisions (Bashevkin, 2002; Dobrowolsky, 2008; Gaszo, 2009). At the same time, public funding for housing, childcare, and food security is shrinking, the burden of caring work is expanding, and surveillance and punishment for women who need social assistance, use drugs, or break criminal and refugee laws are increasing (Chunn & Gavigan, 2004; Hermer & Mosher, 2002). The preceding chapters have documented the particular forms these took for our study participants.

Under the neoliberal agenda, the claims-making of organizations representing marginalized groups, including women's groups, has been effectively de-legitimated by cuts in funding and changes in funding regimes (Brodie, 2002; Ilcan & Basok, 2004; Jenson & Phillips, 2001).[2] Since the turn of the twenty-first century, direct funding for women's organizations and issues has been reduced or eliminated in Ontario and BC (Creese & Strong-Boag, 2005) – the two Canadian provinces that, together, encompass our six study sites. Government policy structures supporting women's equality have also been eliminated or weakened. The innovative Ministry of Women's Equality in BC was disbanded in 2001 (Teghtsoonian, 2003) while pursuit of equality was dropped from the goals of the Status of Women Canada, the one remaining Canadian federal agency dedicated to women's groups, research, and policy[3] (Drevlend, 2007; Hanlon, Rosenberg, & Clasby, 2007; Tang & Peters, 2006).

The market fundamentalism of neoliberal regimes is squeezing women's organizations by increasing expectations that they provide even more for families and communities while it has reduced their resources and restricted their autonomy (Molyneux, 2002; Naples, 1998). Consequently, community organizations, including women's groups, have become more focused on direct service, with less time and fewer resources for meeting strategic goals through community-based research, policy analysis, advocacy, community development, and promotion of social citizenship (Arai & Reid, 2003; Ilcan & Basok, 2004; Richmond & Shields, 2005). The business logic of a piece-work payment system for service organizations means that organizations are paid only if they produce certain predetermined outcomes within a rigid accountability system.

Increasing reliance on volunteer labour to meet service demands under budgetary constraints has led to the hijacking of organizational resources into providing employability training for volunteers, further diverting the organizations' scarce resources into the service of market citizenship. As funding requirements force the voluntary sector to comply, it then participates in shaping public understanding of poverty toward an impoverished view of citizenship, one that demands employment rather than providing rights (Hyatt, 2001). Thus, community agencies can unwittingly become training grounds for fulfilling these employability obligations.

Groups of women who have organized to make history that is attentive to both gender and material matters have been severely challenged. In the face of shrinking social services, increased social need, and new demands on service provision, women's community work faces a central dilemma: the work of collectively meeting increased needs takes energy and resources away from the strategic work of challenging a re-privatization of what women have fought to make public. If we judge, as does Barrig (1994), that organizations choosing to place scarce resources in direct services, as opposed to activism, can only entrench the status quo (or create a new market-based status quo), then meeting women's strategic needs has been effectively closed down. The question then becomes whether there can be any meaningful spaces for meeting women's strategic needs within women's organizations.

Considering women's collective work in provisioning allows us to view community organizations in ways that go beyond seeing the prevailing definition of practical (working to improve daily lives) and strategic (working to challenge the gendered relations that produce the conditions of daily living) goals in women's organizations as oppositional (Barrig, 1994; Lind, 2005). The routine collective provisioning of women's groups (see chapter 3) offers a vital social space that, we argue, is the basis for continued incubation and nurturing of women's activism in the larger socio-political arena. Nevertheless, the kinds of decisions that are required to meet the constraints of the neoliberal agenda are powerful ones that set out the conditions for survival for women's organizations in ways that paradoxically threaten to pull them apart.

Staying Alive: Struggling to Maintain the Vital Spaces of Collective Provisioning

Cuts in funding and new regulations forced all groups in our study to confront the central paradox of neoliberal changes: how to survive and change while holding values that are dear, and at what cost. Such pressures are played out in the boundary issues: the complex work of attending to conflicts and illusions about what the group can and cannot do (see chapter 3). These are decisions about whom they can provide for, and whether and how to comply with the new regulations and reshape the organization accordingly. Making each of these decisions can entail disputes about what the common values are, what differences can be encouraged, and when compromises in the operation of this vital social space will change the very nature of organizational provisioning. The time frame for these decisions is usually very short, leaving little time to consider the immensely important issues, such as the longer-term consequences of short-term rule changes.

The collective provisioning responsibilities of women's organizations in this study formed the basis for struggles to retain the integrity of their values based on collective provisioning, while struggling to survive. Women's investments in their organizations were very high, and their provisioning responsibilities crossed the boundaries of private and public; the responsibilities of the organizations reached beyond organizational working relationships. Although guided by principles of fairness and justice that opened up their organizations to both actual and potential membership, facing budgetary restrictions frequently meant increasing their workload or making painful decisions to set restrictions on membership. Such pressures on ways of working induced emotional anguish about how to keep inviolable the basic values of the organization to provide a welcoming, holistic space for women.

When, in 2002 in BC, the provincial social assistance policy and funding structure unilaterally changed the admission for employability programmes and closed down many community services to women, the situation for the organization serving women leaving abusive relationships was dire. As a consequence of funding cuts, one study site had to draw on financial reserves that had been so carefully accumulated for future endeavours, move to smaller offices, and lay off three of the eight staff in order to keep its doors open. Funding became tied not only to the admission of women barely out of their abusive contexts, but was also connected to performance: the students in the programme had to complete a rigid six-month programme for the site to be reimbursed for its costs (Lowen & Reitsma-Street, 2006). As one staff member characterized the situation, 'We are going into financial crisis because we are trying to operate under the government's rules which really limits those who are qualified to come to the programme. Therefore, minimal enrolment; therefore no funding . . . We are in an abusive relationship with the government.'

To treat women who are in abusive relationships as if they were merely needing employment-readiness training is to deny the difficulties women face if they are also travelling the long and troubled road back from physical or mental illness or poverty (Gurstein & Vilches, 2009). Lack of government funding for the sophisticated, sustained work of supporting women leaving abusive situations undermines the programme as a whole and ignores all the invisible, uncounted work that went into helping abused women become employed. In the organizations in our study, and in other organizations that respond to abuse, members value the collective, careful work required to support women leaving abuse and to take their concerns, their realities and their hopes seriously (Mason, 2007; Weldon, 2005). Staff members fought to maintain the same types of services but, by the end of the study, were forced to deliver them in a way – through Internet courses – that actually reduced the ability of the abused women to benefit from the protective social space provided by the organization.

Funding requirements threatened to alter boundary definitions in collectivities in ways that could fundamentally shift their central values. In one case, changes threatened to drive a wedge between the women most closely associated with the organization and all the other women who participated in the organization in some way. The parent organization of the food co-op set out new requirements for monthly proof of income and identification, which ended up restricting the ability of the co-op to work as a community. Because this abrupt change in boundary-setting implicitly called the members' trustworthiness into question, members felt less trusted by the organization. They were now required to become supplicants, reminded that in order to get help they needed to document their dire economic situation. The result was that women who came to the food co-op to help themselves and each other were made to feel more helpless and disempowered.

In another case, the community resource centre that defined itself as 'rooted in a neighbourhood' was required by a new funding source to expand the boundaries of service to the wider community. Recipients of services were to be defined programmatically, rather than holistically as members of a community able to participate in the day-to-day activities of the community. Some members legitimately worried that 'when the organization spreads out, it runs the risk of spreading itself too thin' and thought that it could find itself unable to address needs within the immediate neighbourhood.

To take yet another example of how sites struggled to survive while holding close to their values, this same community resource centre faced changes to a social assistance regulation that then began to mandate that volunteers be monitored. Dependent on volunteers for much of its work, the group had to make the difficult decision of whether or not to continue to have volunteers on this basis. Mandatory reporting was deemed unacceptable because it threatened the central value of the organization to provide a non-judgmental attitude toward all members involved, whether staff, parents, or volunteers.

Our findings reveal how the pushback against fiscal policy drove women's organizations to preserve their fundamental values of egalitarianism and inclusivity in order to stay alive. Despite considerable pressures to capitulate, women's organizations managed, often through volunteer work by paid staff, to find ways to maintain themselves as a social space. The collective provisioning taking place in those spaces suggests ways of revisiting the assumption that meeting practical needs within women's groups may simply reinforce pre-existing roles for women. Our findings lead us to question this conclusion and suggest that the ways of doing provisioning work in these groups meld women's practical and strategic interests and overcome the seeming paradox.

Collective Spaces Incubate the Seeds of Citizenship

Distinctions among women's groups that sort some into more progressive, strategic organizations placed to transform politics, and others into service organizations that acquiesce to neoliberal demands are likely to be ultimately self-defeating, because they are not based on the way women actually work (Molyneux, 1998). For Molyneux, it is the anchoring of activities in women's everyday lives that makes these organizations responsive to the needs of women – women who, correlatively, are willing to give back to the organizations.[4] Despite considerable diversity in scope, size, and sources of funding, all the women's organizations we studied were engaged in quality-of-life matters related to good schools, neighbourhood safety, education, childcare, food security, housing, and adequate health care (Acklesberg,1988; Barrig, 1994; Susser, 1988; Taylor, 1999). As such, the data analyses from these groups support the finding of others, showing that in general, the boundaries dividing family, community, and society are routinely transgressed when women work together (Jaggar, 2005; Staeheli, 2004).

In our conceptualization of women's groups as arenas of collective provisioning, we see this linkage between practical and strategic purposes as crucial for members to develop a critical response to the severe testing they receive in a neoliberal political regime. In particular, it is the way in which collective provisioning is done, how it connects practical and strategic interests, and the social spaces in which it is done, that are important. To see meeting women's immediate needs through collective provisioning as primarily serving practical interests overlooks the many ways in which the social space of the collective offers ways of working that nurture women's strategic interests. Moreover, our analyses show that organizational engagement in political advocacy serves women's strategic interests primarily when it helps women build confidence in their abilities and sense of self-worth. Direct service and strategic goals can be organically interrelated and they, in turn, can be seen as involved in the local practice of social citizenship.

The concept of citizenship is increasingly being redrawn in more inclusive ways that reach beyond the private/public dichotomy. For instance, Lister (2007) argues that work done in the domestic sphere contributes to social well-being and thus serves as a basis for citizenship claims. Similarly, Kershaw (2006) locates the roots of political citizenship within caregiving in domestic spaces. Desforges, Jones, and Woods (2005) underline the need to study citizenship as it is 'enacted in everyday life in a variety of contexts' (p. 448). Relational views of health similarly suggest ways in which the local environment can be conceptualized as crucial for studying population health, since it is here that people's interactions with the local context build the social networks so vital to health outcomes (Cummins, Curtis, Diez-Roux, & Macintyre, 2007). For women's organizations the implications are that bringing women together to talk and work is a dialogical source of synergy for change.

The provisioning of a social space for women was an accomplishment in and of itself for all study sites. Nevertheless, it is the quality of the social space and its transformational capacity in the face of threats to its very existence that we are examining. Under such an analytical lens, what may be an integral part of the everyday features of this space takes on renewed importance. These are the same types of spaces that Weis and Fine (2000) refer to as sites of 'recuperation, resistance and the makings of "home" . . . not rigidly bound by walls or fences . . . where community intrusion and state surveillance are not permitted' (p. 57). Polletta (2000) refers to the free spaces of churches and fraternal organizations as the source of claims-making within the civil rights movement, because they were 'removed from the direct surveillance of authorities where people were able to envision alternative futures and plot strategies for realizing them' (p. 392). In similar fashion, Herr (1999) refers to 'the power of unencumbered space' for authentic changes within the school system.

Conceptualization of women's organizational work as collective provisioning of a vital social space suggests a dynamic connection between material services and social citizenship. This fluid connection challenges the dichotomies of public and private, strategic and practical, advocacy and service provision. In citizenship terms, the community organization provides a collective space (a melding of the private and the public) in which the foundations for social citizenship can be enacted in three mutually reinforcing ways: building solidarity, fostering respect; and connecting to strategic goals. The following sections elaborate these foundations, showing how they are attached seamlessly to meeting everyday provisioning responsibilities of women but are also are under attack from the pressures of neoliberal changes to their organizations.

Building Solidarity

Behind those deliberative activities that develop a 'collective voice' within an organization is the use of the social space as a place where personal troubles are shared and commonalities can be seen. One of the strongest themes in the interviews that emerged across all organizations is the value given by women to meeting 'others in the same situation.' Women expressed their desire to interact with staff members who have 'lived on the other side of the fence.' In more general terms, women in various organizations identified the consequences of sharing one's situation: (1) to know you are not alone; (2) to have a place to talk about your struggles and to have those struggles understood and validated by others; (3) to feel supported in the journey; and (4) to find some emotional support and relief from stress. These feelings and understandings thrive in the substrata of the social space that women's organizations provide for dialogue and discussion of one's personal plight. The work to provide this quality of social space was theorized in chapter 4 as the category of providing supportive cultures.

It is within the collective space that working through such emotions takes place. Here women confront the implications of a neoliberal regime that treats them as individualized clients who do not – but should – provision for themselves. The effect of such treatment is that women are made to feel devalued as persons, despite the fact that the provisioning in which women are engaged is socially organized in ways that disadvantage certain groups (Power, 2004). In protest, women describe how reclaiming understanding, validation, and support led to empowerment and liberation: 'They got together; they started telling their life stories . . . and that was the first time she realized that there were other older women who had the same kinds of experiences. And this was a totally liberating experience.'

Such story-telling can be seen as a kind of collective engagement in constructing and reconstructing the social meanings of experience that form kernels of resistance to daily injustices (Ewick & Silbey, 2003). It is through offering a collective venue to reflect on the conditions of their lives that women can begin to see that their problems are not rooted in individual shortcomings but in structural forces (Erbaugh, 2002; Finn, 2002; Lind, 1997; Reid, Allison, & Frisby, 2006; Susser, 1988).

Individualized citizenship is also behind the neoliberal discourse of 'active' citizenship; here volunteering is defined as the moral equivalent of employment (Fuller, Kershaw, & Pulkingham, 2008). The lone mothers interviewed by Fuller, Kershaw, and Pulkingham found that fulfilling the new forms of 'active' citizenship was seen as a means to escape from social stigma and reclaim a sense of social worth. Accordingly, one of our interviewees captured the sense of moral obligation underpinning the discourse of the active citizen: 'I would feel guilty . . . not doing hours or anything like that for the food.' Another woman mentioned she volunteered 'because I feel like a burden. I can't work, so I want to feel like I contribute.' Such bases for volunteering contrast with motivations that emphasize solidarity.

Across all six groups studied, more collectivist-oriented views of volunteering appeared to form a sense of solidarity. Shared experience was seen as critical for developing knowledge about one another, and it was anchored in a sense of responsibility to community. This approach to solidarity is based on a notion of volunteering as a shared struggle: you help others because you have been helped, and you care about others who share the same plight. In one woman's voice, her desire to volunteer came from knowing the situation of needing help: 'Because I've benefited from their programmes . . . I want to give back to them, because when I'm stepping out, there's four people coming in who are in my position.'

The commonality of experience is both the impetus to volunteer and the source of shared knowledge that is so valuable to women. It is a bargain struck among those in similar situations rather than enforced by government regulations that turn it into a 'compulsory altruism' that is required to obtain material benefits (Land & Rose, 1985).

Volunteering on the basis of solidarity corresponds to a social citizenship discourse rooted in a sense of responsibility to make a contribution to the community. Solidarity is realized through being part of something larger than oneself, and improving the community. 'I was brought up that you give 20 per cent back of every week to the community . . . In this regard the stewardship of the community helps me also, because I am part of that community and quality of life.'

This motivation goes beyond the quid-pro-quo framework of the social exchange approach or charity. Rather, it is seen as a form of 'paying forward,' a line of assistance that extends from one person to another and another.

Fostering Respect

Developing this kind of solidarity entails not just finding social support or a supportive network. It also involves using the social space to restore citizenship because a woman is not deemed unworthy by virtue of being in need or belonging to a marginalized group. Finding others in the same situation and having that situation validated carries with it the important message that 'there's nothing wrong with being in this situation.' Social support is inextricably tied to finding a place of self-worth. Even friendship is described in this way by one participant: 'What does it mean to have friends? . . . The world isn't so scary. Not everybody is out to hurt me.'

One aspect of a woman's capacity to engage in deliberative dialogue (Freeman, 2006) is her trust that others will not judge her harshly. Two quotes illustrate the kind of unconditional acceptance and respect that women receive in one organization: 'It's not "Well, let me see your bank account, let me see this, let me see that. Let me see this" . . . If a family's in need, then a family's in need. It takes a lot in order to ask.' 'That is the key – they treat us like we are capable and there's no judgment. Everybody works toward a common goal. It's not I am better than you or you are lower down here, or anything like that. There is no hierarchy here.'

Collective provisioning of a social space, based on non-hierarchical values and respect for women and their provisioning responsibilities, is central to supporting women's ability to make claims for service. The first step of learning to make better claims is being listened to and having one's situation understood and validated, with an effect that one study participant summed up well: 'You don't have to feel like a low-down person that you haven't been able to take care of your children. I am not made to feel any less of a mother. And that means quite a bit.'

Developing a sense of dignity protects women from conferring on themselves the neoliberal stereotype of an irresponsible citizen.

Although the main purpose of the social space is to validate and value women in their own right, their sense of shared situation and growth of dignity and self-worth lead to women feeling, as one woman expressed it, that they don't have to 'fight the system all by yourself.' Even if the main focus of the space is not on strategizing how to do so, women grow in their ability to develop a more critical world view (Stall & Stoecker, 1998).

Connecting to Strategic Goals

In an environment in which most advocacy projects have lost their funding and/or been overrun by increasing service demands and fewer resources, women's groups lose a whole gamut of advocacy opportunities for changing the political agenda. Yet we see evidence in our data that the social space within women's organizations nourishes the seeds of advocacy among women in small ways that provide a life-support system for social citizenship. Collective strategies for helping individual women to make better claims on the state resources to which they are entitled go against the tide of neoliberal strategies to discourage pursuit of entitlements. Marginalized women often came into the organizations in our study intimidated by bureaucratic institutions and fearful that even asking questions about eligibility rules or additional services would bring closer scrutiny of their individual case and endanger the assistance they were already receiving. Women shared their stories of resistance, of challenging arbitrary rules, by advising each other on how to negotiate with institutions and by sharing knowledge with the community about services that were not well known, as shown in the preceding chapters. They found allies, people with weight who would ask with them and go to bat for them.

Women's ways of working in these organizations contrast sharply with the more narrow service orientation of the neoliberal agenda that would cast women's organizations in the role of offering the 'quick fix' for the kinds of problems women face. Instead, within these organizations, women are given the courage to fight back against the threat of disentitlement. Townsend, Zapata, Rowlands, Alberti, and Mercado (1999) describe this as the power from within, which comes from 'a recognition that one is not helpless, not the source of all one's own problems, that one is restricted in part by structures outside oneself' (p. 30).

Participants' refusal to be discouraged and turned away from services for which they are eligible is not necessarily something we think of as citizenship activity. It does not, at first glance, appear to be strategic. It is, however, a means of fighting back against the marketization of citizenship and its connection with victim-blaming. Collective provisioning resists the fragmentation and individualization of neoliberal changes that reduce members to the status of individualized clients who do not and cannot provision for themselves or others. If women's organizations keep alive women's dignity and sense of solidarity, citizenship activity that starts here can lead to challenging dominant institutions and to becoming part of group advocacy.

For the women in our study, the connection to advocacy had a number of steps, beginning with participation in a collective space that challenged an individualized explanation for their situation and recast the notion of social citizenship to include not only the individual but the community and society as well. The next step in moving toward the ability to participate beyond their personal concerns was to connect private troubles to public issues. As participants in collective provisioning, women were aware of the connection between the immediate needs of those for whom they were responsible and the availability of services to meet those needs. They encountered an unresponsive bureaucracy (for example, the local social housing authority), and they gained confidence in their ability to engage with political authorities by starting with their awareness that they have to fight to be heard: 'The people, the problem of the people, we make . . . to go to . . . to talk with them [the member of Parliament] . . . We like to say to them, "This glass is broken." And they are not coming soon . . . Months, it takes them. Like, the shower is not properly working . . . they just write it down and they're gone.'

With this recognition, women can begin to construct new collective identities from which to challenge dominant institutions. Participants' primary institutional critiques were directed at the institutions immediately involved in their lives, such as social assistance, child benefits, and subsidized housing. The institution most criticized was the social assistance regime for its discriminatory treatment of people, unfair rules, bureaucracy, and withholding of information. However, within collective spaces, this critical focus can be extended to the effects of the broader welfare state, as well as labour market issues. As Erbaugh (2002) suggests, women's ways of organizing aim to transform their relationship to dominant institutions.

One woman's journey illustrates the ways in which collective provisioning – by opening an inviting, friendly, social space providing direct service – supported her in the first steps in an activist career that took her all the way to formal political activity. We introduced the story in chapter 4 when describing the collective provisioning work of resisting injustices. At that point we also argued that the story demonstrated the holistic, integrated nature of more and less visible collective provisioning dimensions. In this telling we show the pathways that began with the vital social space.

The trajectory followed by this woman through the political channels began with the help she received from the co-op in both material and strategic ways. A staff person there advocated for her when the social assistance office threatened to cut her off because she wasn't taking the typing and office skills courses they wanted her to take as part of her work requirement. Because of this support, she was able to remain in school and subsequently was inspired by a teacher to take action on the things about which she was passionate. One of these concerns was safety for her young son in a rough neighbourhood and was taken up with the police force that targeted drug dealers and prostitutes. After the provincial public housing bureaucracy had denied her application for subsidized housing on the basis of living in an unsafe neighbour-hood, she overtly challenged them. In the process, this woman met a provincial politician who was reviewing the social assistance system. Later this politician sponsored her to attend a social justice retreat.

What we have discovered is that women are challenging societal dis-courses on the worthy citizen as operationalized in how services are provided. We posit that there are links between the power to make a better claim and feeling a sense of solidarity with the community that contribute to the power to resist current definitions of the worthy citi-zen. Refusing to be denied services is a form of resisting a social con-struction of the non-worthy citizen (Ewick & Silbey, 2003; Neysmith & Reitsma-Street, 2005). By participating in organizations such as those in our study, members may be motivated by the interests of the house-hold, market, or state, but with the help of collectivities they can go beyond the concerns of these spheres that are too often divided into the false binaries of public and private. As Walby (2001) has pointed out, the 'politics of recognition' are lodged in struggles for equality that bring people together in complex interrelationships.

Women's collective provisioning leads to asking questions about the structures and practices of power and oppression that contribute to ex-ploitation and inequality. This suggests that a designation of service provision as reinforcing the status quo, and advocacy as challenging the status quo, may mask important advocacy that is happening in the way in which services are provided. In fact, receiving direct services that help women see that power imbalances can be managed empowers women to continue to fight for their rights. Women's organizations can be seen to provide a 'micro-mobilisation context' (Prokhovnik, 1998) that heightens women's consciousness of their common plight vis-à-vis the political and economic systems as they engage in their everyday activities. This should be seen as an effort to rejoin social citizenship and social rights.

Conclusion

We conclude that organizations, in provisioning for the full set of needs that women have, provide a public space that allows women to grow in critical understanding of their situation so that they can bring back into the public arena an articulation of their needs that have been privatized in the neoliberal era (Bashevkin, 2002; Schmidt, Bar, & Nirel, 2008). Community work takes place in a neoliberal environment that demands lowered expectations for service delivery and an individualizing approach to defining women's needs. To provide for greater solidarity and women's self-respect as building blocks for citizenship, women's groups are fighting for space to help women survive and at the same time challenge the conditions that make survival so difficult.

Collectively providing in the present may be both practical and strategic, especially in the ways women define provisioning and learn collectively to make better claims as citizens. In so doing, the women in our study are using their collective vital spaces to resist individualizing their concerns. For them, the collective space is an end in itself. It takes hard work and dedication to provision for the complex needs of women in ways that do not further isolate and alienate them. In bringing quality-of-life concerns into a public arena and making them visible (Finn, 2002; Susser, 1988), women are insisting to governments, and employers, that these material needs are a collective public responsibility. It is a space to fight back against an individualized regime and to find support in the fight.

We have argued that, in an environment in which citizenship has been disconnected from social rights, the work of helping women lobby for their own services and demand their rights is a way to connect their provisioning activity directly to their citizenship. The social spaces provided by women's organizations allow for dialogue that helps women define themselves as worthy citizens ready to challenge the notion of the autonomous individual citizen, as articulated in the way eligibility for services is determined. In an individualized citizenship regime, collective spaces are expected to take on a utilitarian function. They are spaces where individual citizens are shaped to become responsible employees and consumers in the marketplace, so that the group is a means to an end. Our findings show that women learn from one another in the vital social space that serves as an 'authentic public space' defined by Hummel (2002), as one in which citizenship can grow. The danger is that those vital social spaces that we have identified in our research will continue to shrink, weakening the catalytic collective provisioning that is so critical for binding practical and transformative strategies.

10 Sharing Life's Glories

In chapter 2 we used excerpts from 'Bread and Roses' to signal themes that we considered central to the dilemmas that women face as they strive to provision for those with whom they have relationships of responsibility. The fact that these well-known words are meaningful today signals the troubling persistence of the shape of work in women's lives. Bread is needed, and thus so are the means for acquiring it; the procurement of resources through precarious employment, demeaning social assistance requirements, and the informal labour market of many participants meant 'sweating from birth until life closes' just to make ends meet. However, participants also talked about the work they did that was associated with other dimensions of the provisioning responsibilities that they carried: the hours spent doing caring labour, volunteer work, maintaining health, ensuring safety, and making claims for themselves and others. These are documented, often in graphic detail, in the preceding chapters. This work, and the social significance of it, is far more than is usually captured under the apparently polar opposite terms of *breadwinner* and *caring*. As the data reveal, the former is but a small part of the work women do. Incorporating caregiving into the picture contributes to an important conceptual expansion. Nevertheless, much of the range and complexity of women's work remained below the surface, unnamed and undocumented. The research that informs this book set out to map this territory in some detail.

To pry open the concept of work, its meaning and worth, from the confines of the market, we began with the concept of *provisioning*, a term retrieved from an earlier approach to economics that focused on how humans materially provided for themselves. This wider approach to economics contrasts with its current definition as the allocation of scarce resources to satisfy wants within a market economy. Feminist economists such as Nelson (1993) and Power (2004) have revitalized the term to expose all the work that women do that is uncounted in the market economy. An important assumption in these writings is that such work is central, not peripheral, to economic life in the older sense of the word (Figart, 2007). Caring labour, household labour, and volunteer work are arenas of activity that have so far received the most documentation. To go beyond these established arenas into more unexplored areas, we followed pathways of responsibilities associated with relationship trails as we recorded individual and collective provisioning work that was connected to family, friends, neighbours, and community organizations.

After a careful assessment of this provisioning terrain, the question remains: so where are the roses? What was envisioned by the marchers as they talked of 'life's glories'? How can they be realized? Today such ideas might be captured by phrases such as *well-being* or *quality of life*. Admittedly, they are contestable conceptual tools, but they do have the virtue of encompassing more than merely income as measures of desirable outcomes in life. Glimmers of some of the invisible work done by individuals and collectivities of women seen when women's relationships are used as the compass, show the myriad ways in which women contribute to social reproduction, adding value to the lives of those for whom they have taken responsibility. Our point is that these are not sideshows around the central characters of the labour market. If the drama is about quality of life, the storyline consists of activities that are attached to relationships of responsibility, and paid work is one segment of it. Nevertheless, it cannot be ignored that in a market economy paid work is reified and many essentials of life are commodified. The resulting injustice is that having money would have allowed our participants to circumvent a lot of the relentless work they had to do that was not recognized or valued.

The plot thickens as we turn our attention to the script of neoliberal social policies that write off the provisioning of women as a free good, without considering its true costs and benefits. Feminist political economy has issued the proviso that without women's contribution to the economy, the burdens of social reproduction fall disproportionately on marginalized populations, and because the capitalist class benefits from this oppression, the state needs to intervene and support the essential work of women. Our study furthers arguments that the terms of citizenship need to be widened (Howell, 2007; Isin & Nielson, 2008;

Plummer, 2004; Stasiulis & Bakan, 2003) in ways that recognize the contributions and agency of women individually and collectively, in private as well as public spaces. Currently, social policies reward the full rights of citizenship to those who are fortunate enough to land the market-player parts – although it could be argued that some of these characters should be cast as villains in the citizenship drama.

The data from the research sites presented in the previous chapters suggest a number of important theoretical ideas that are discussed in this chapter. These we see as ingredients, the nutrients needed if the rose of citizenship is to be realized for women such as the participants in this study. We also indicate in this chapter methodological points that we think were conducive to revealing the many dimensions of provisioning. The chapter concludes by rejecting ideas of citizenship that are limited to market notions of rights and responsibilities and/or that recognize only engagement in formal voluntary organizations as participation in civil society. It presents a model of social provisioning in which the state is positioned as a key player with institutional, economic, and ideological power to shape the lives of its citizens.

Dimensions of Women's Working Lives

In chapter 2 we referred to the *range* of provisioning responsibilities that women carried. This general term was specified in chapters 3 and 4. In the former we articulated two major domains (activities and strategies), each encompassing six different types of work done by the individuals we interviewed. In chapter 4 the work required to keep community groups going was revealed and organized into three domains. As the quotes highlighted, women's work does not fall into silos, although to facilitate the mapping of this work we classified the data into categories and organized them along dimensions labelled individual and collective provisioning. This approach highlighted the complexity, as well as the amount, of work done, and made visible the fact that, despite neoliberal discourse denying its existence, women carry provisioning responsibilities in collective as well as individual spaces, in public and private spheres. Consider these categories as bookmarks in a provisioning story that needs to be written more fully as the language to describe these domains becomes more accessible to women. As language and concepts are clarified and developed into models, we anticipate that the borders of provisioning domains will be permeable, in several aspects.

In each chapter we underlined how the data make visible the existence of *pathways*, based on relationships of responsibility, between domains of work. This allowed us to track relationships without being stopped at the borders of family and/or paid work. Transgressing these borders revealed a range of relationships that could not be classified validly in one of the traditionally defined family, work, or volunteer spheres rather than another. It was not the sphere that determined the meaning of the relationship but rather the relationship that determined what responsibilities were assumed, how and why provisioning was done. As several of the quotes under transformative strategies suggest, participants speak of the desires and difficulties they face in negotiating their provisioning responsibilities, including those associated with commitment to the goals of the organization. They fulfil the responsibilities that these commitments entail through personal and organizational relationships. These trans-domain pathways follow relationships, and thus costs and benefits travel along with persons on these pathways (Emirbayer, 1997). These connections must be built into theory and policy models if they are to support women.

Another key finding is a clearer understanding of how current *boundaries* associated with ideas of public and private spheres are powerful shapers of women's lives. Fortunately, there is now a rich theoretical literature on boundaries (see Howell & Mulligan, 2005; Lamont & Molnar, 2002, for a review; Yuval-Davis & Stoetzler, 2002) that helped in exploring participants' responses. Our point is that women's provisioning requires that women attempt to cross these barriers. As does Dorothy Smith (1990), we argue that these borders and boundaries have presence and power when they are operationalized into policies and programmes and their effects are documented. The analyses in the preceding chapters show how boundaries operate in ways that result in women having to negotiate them – yet another work demand. This work is not a direct provisioning activity but is a necessary strategy to further both individual and collective provisioning. In a neoliberal society the market, state, family, and civil society spheres are real in the sense that there are powerful social structures defining them. The boundaries can be as solid as concrete, requiring determined hammering to get through them (recall in chapter 3 a participant's list of the work she did in response to the questioning of a social assistance official). The boundaries can be spongy, seemingly penetrable, but are impermeable when pushed – as when the grandmother is chastised by her son for taking a mental/physical health break in the form of a walk rather than staying in the house to care for the grandfather. Others can best be compared to fencing where there are openings, but what is on the other side is difficult to discern – one might squeeze through and land on safe ground, or fall into an abyss of the unknown. For example, job training seems to promise a way out of poverty, but our data and that of others suggest that it is more often a pathway to dead-end jobs with minimal pay. The work of figuring out the structure of boundaries and strategizing how to cross them is seldom recognized, or it gets named as something else when it is. For instance, finding out what is allowed, or not, under social assistance regulations is dubbed as 'exploiting the system'; setting limits on the demands of family for caring labour is called 'shirking family responsibilities.'

When well-being is equated with the market, employment, and individual consumption choices – and value is measured in dollars, *collective spaces* as arenas for support and action tend to fade from view. Ways of talking about these spaces – theories that capture their shape and activities – seem unnecessary when the dominant discourse is about markets, choice, and individual responsibility. In chapter 2 we noted how collective spaces where women could come together were disappearing. Funds to support them have diminished in the last decade, and those that remain are tightly hooked to delivering services, with accompanying accountability criteria. All chapters show that services are an important component of the resources that women access to meet their provisioning responsibilities.

Our concern was that the raison d'être of these organizations was being narrowed to that of a service agency – carrying on functions performed traditionally by the state or voluntary sector. Community capacity-building in any form was being squeezed out as funding criteria favoured short-term service programmes. We have purposefully documented the work that occurs in these spaces, to provide empirical evidence that there is much work in keeping groups going that is not counted in the costs of providing services. However, our concern goes beyond a call to recognize undocumented work, as important as that is. Viewing these events through a critical feminist lens suggests that these collective spaces are being shut down because they counter a market ethos and thus are seen to hinder the efficient operation of a market economy. In fact, it is in these collective spaces that women's provisioning is supported in order to keep individuals from placing even greater demands on the state and the economy.

Using a *methodology* that can document complexity is a critical ingredient in research that is aimed at building theory. While analysing data from multiple sites, one is constantly reminded of its complexity, how different types of provisioning work are related, and how classification schemes will change over time as new data are entered. We agree with McCall (2005) that categories are methodologically useful for documenting complexity – as long as they are recognized as place holders that reflect theoretical assumptions. In chapter 3 we noted how the final categories of provisioning activities and strategies used by participants were the result of coding that started separately within a few sites, followed by the development of cross-site draft categories to be used to code new data in these and the other sites. After all data were collected, two people very familiar with the sites examined codes and content, suggesting final naming for the categories of individual work. The naming of organizational work was also finally determined only after all the data had been collected and community advisory groups had debated the findings. Research team members then agreed upon the naming of the categories. Assuming the position that categories are best regarded as provisional, useful for a period of time, but needing to be modified as phenomena are better understood, the types of provisioning, and their names, done by women as individuals and as members of collectivities will change, we expect, as their breadth and depth become better understood. Furthermore, our understanding of how relationships shape the provisioning responsibilities carried by women is in its infancy. Hopefully the categories – the descriptors we are using, will soon be outgrown as research and theory about women's provisioning grow and mature.

Our choice of sites and approach to analysis were influenced by considerations of important structural inequalities and the effects of 'spheres' and their boundaries on the complexity of the work that women do and the relationships they maintain. Participants were purposefully sampled across six sites to reflect differences in geography, age, income, and organizational type. The women who participated in this research came from very different *social locations*. They brought to their provisioning responsibilities different priorities, experiences, and identities. The realities they faced differed. A woman of eighty-five with several chronic health conditions had struggles that were different from those of the refugee mother trying to raise a pre-schooler in a high-crime area. Thus, the specifics of their provisioning activities and the strategies they used to provide differed; the collective spaces that they found useful and to which they contributed also differed.

In recent years, the concept of intersectionality has been used to capture how this diversity affects people's lives and actions (see McCall, 2005; Simien, 2007). However, the concept can seem ambiguous, because it has been used in different ways. It is frequently employed to emphasize the fact that individuals have multiple dimensions to their identities, although many are rooted in social structures. For instance, an individual participant in our research might be young and poor, have one child, and be a second-generation immigrant from Jamaica. The attributes used to describe the participant in the previous sentence reflect both the diversity of individuals and the structural dimensions that define privilege and marginalization in Canadian society. However, an individual embodies only some aspects of each. Depending on what these are and how they come together, their relative importance/ influence will differ in people's lives. These intersections affect work and relationships and how they vary across social locations. It is important to articulate in theory and policy which dimensions of privilege and oppression are relevant, and why, and determine their relative importance vis-à-vis each other in affecting the quality of life of different groups of citizens.

Challenging Citizenship Claims

Discussions of citizenship reappeared in the eighties as global movements of goods and peoples brought into question the meaning of national borders and the entitlements of those who resided within them. Although this discussion originated in concerns about the meaning and power of nation states when flows of capital no longer recognize national borders, the debate has widened to include what constitutes the basis of citizenship claims and who can claim them. The 'what' is defined in terms of rights and responsibilities, while the 'who' can be found in policies on immigration and refugees (Dobrowolsky, 2008; Yuval-Davis, Anthias, & Kofman, 2005), transient workers (Sharma, 2006), and international caring labour chains (Browne & Braun 2008; Hochschild, 2000b). As the data from Jane's Place (chapter 6) revealed, responsibilities and accompanying funds flow regularly through relationships to kin in other countries. However, since most of the participants in our study were Canadian residents, in the following paragraphs we limit our focus to explicating how their rights and

responsibilities were filtered through gendered ideas of what constitutes citizen-like activities.

Marshall's classic post–Second World War articulation of the social
rights of citizenship within a welfare state underwent a sea change
during the eighties. Marshall's welfare state citizen enjoyed certain
entitlements based on the fact that 'he' lived within certain national
borders, that 'he' belonged to a nation state. However, Marshall's idea
of civil, political, and social rights, despite their social policy strengths,
were tied to notions of paid work (Marshall, 1950; Marshall & Bottomore, 1992). State benefits frequently stemmed from this connection.
Women's work, particularly unpaid caring labour, is excluded in debates and policies rooted in such a framework (Cohen & Pulkingham,
2009; Lister, 2003).

During the retrenchment of the 1980s, the importance of this exclusion of women's work became pronounced as neoliberal ideology took
hold and the idea of an active state, along with funding, retreated. The
entitlement-bearing citizen was transformed into a more active citizen,
and responsibilities were given more emphasis than rights (see, for
example, Etzioni, 1995). The consequences fell disproportionately on
women, whether as sole support mothers or as members and staff of
different types of publicly funded organizations (Dobrowolsky, 2008;
Dobrowolsky & Jenson, 2004; Jenson & Phillips, 2001). The decimation
of these organizations resulting from the rise of neoliberalism silenced
their critique of its effects on women. Canadian women have won some
visibility of their rights over the years – perhaps highlighted by the
insertion of equality clauses into the Charter of Rights and Freedoms
in 1982. However, even here, rights and claims focus on the individual.
Disappearing in such debates is the responsibility of the state to meet
the needs of its citizens. So dominant is the discourse of individual responsibility that it is difficult to see what/who fades from view in such
discussions. As chapters 4 and 9 show, collectivities offer critical spaces
for women to understand the actions of the state.

The new active citizen is expected to shoulder responsibilities by participating in paid work and in civil society. The effects of this expectation
on the well-being of women on social assistance is well documented
(Gazso, 2009; Little & Morrison, 1999). In a contorted twist of logic, for
those on social assistance who could not find employment, volunteer
activity was defined as a substitute arena for participation. However,
much formal volunteering privileges a culture characteristic of afflu-
ence rather than the informal volunteering that is more characteristic

of people with low incomes (Williams, 2003, as cited in Orton, 2006, p. 255). Most of the arenas in which our participants were involved as members and volunteers were viable options for them, because these organizations also provided material resources. In a nutshell, we are arguing that it is only the privileged who can afford to join organizations that do not help citizens meet their practical needs as well as addressing their strategic interests. If participation in civil society is limited to NGOs that separate the two, then the voluntary sector is yet another sphere with concrete borders that shut out women, such as those in this study, and thereby disconnect women from exercising their strategic interests. This is what social exclusion looks like locally.

Democracy allows for different ideals of civic life and many forms of engagement in different spaces for different people. Participation in meaningful groups exercising some form of democracy can take place in more arenas than party politics or formal voluntary organizations. A variety of groups that can be missed in such narrow definitions may include self-help groups such as NIMBY (not-in-my-back-yard) local interests (Schudson, 2006). Regardless of whether or not one agrees with the goals of such groups, they can be places in which to practise democracy and learn the skills of communication and working together. A variety of spaces are needed to facilitate learning that builds on the diverse capacities of individuals and communities. Even some seemingly therapy-focused groups, such as self-help networks, might lead to turning private troubles into public issues, although we lack empirical evidence showing how and when such private–public connections are made.

As previous chapters (particularly chapters 4 and 9) concluded, the collectivities we studied can foster the potential for making connections between individual problems and larger social forces. The family networks in which women with low incomes play key supportive roles are not likely to have the kinds of resources that can sustain them, and the people who rely on them and may drain their resources. The work of Dominguez and Watkins (2003) shows that ties with professionals in agencies were able to offer both instrumental and emotional support and that the latter proved to be unexpectedly robust. Our research also looks at how women from low-income neighbourhoods build relationships with people in community agencies (Fuller et al., 2008). Even when women were participating in the formal social service sector, their motivations for participation meshed material interests with a host of other strategic interests that can be interpreted as showing agency (Fuller, Kershaw, & Pulkingham, 2008) or the balancing of social support and social leveraging (Dominquez & Watson, 2003), even in relatively hostile environments for doing so.

Our data on women's work in collectivities allowed us to see that the provisioning of the social space was the catalytic source for women's ability to realize some of 'life's glories.' The organizations we studied made special efforts to involve participants in organizational processes and decision making, and thus to minimize the extent of differences among members. As a result, we could see that it was the interchanges among these women that had a catalytic effect on their growth. Change cannot happen if individuals are isolated by poverty or other types of social exclusion. Others are needed to imagine and discuss alternatives. In such arenas, 1 + 1 + 1 does not equal 3; interaction effects among participants result in conversations that are exponential – accompanied by the potential that different possibilities will emerge as a result.

Unfortunately, as we argued in chapter 9, current policy in Canada is following a model that equates not-for-profits with for-profit firms, that expects voluntary organizations to become more business-like so that they can take on the responsibilities being off-loaded onto them from government (Stivers, 2002, as cited in Campbell, 2005, p. 702). Closing down collective spaces means cutting off these relationship pathways and the associated linkages that make transformation possible. We argue that what is needed is an examination of the capacity of groups such as those in the six research sites to bolster participation and engage in a critical analysis of what is happening to poor women.

Re-Enter the State to Assume Responsibility for Social Provisioning

The lens of provisioning used in the previous chapters showed that rights and responsibilities came together in the lives of women; the division between the two in theory and policy debates did not hold in lived experience, although the tension did. The provisioning responsibilities of women were shown to be extensive and often costly to their own welfare. Women talked poignantly, and with distress, about the shrinking of these spaces in which they could debate and practise negotiations of rights and responsibilities and examine how these affect their lives – and those for whom they carry provisioning responsibilities.

Because we collected data at both the individual and collective levels, we were able to trace the importance of the collectivities for women's well-being. When we discuss the term *social provisioning*, we do not use it to refer to the individual level, as Marilyn Power (2004) did in her discussion of the networks in which women provision. We endorse her premise that, in order to understand women's work, one needs to look at caring and unpaid labour as fundamental to economic activity; use well-being as a measure of economic success; analyse economic, political, and social processes and power relations; include ethical goals and values as an intrinsic part of the analysis; and interrogate differences by class, race/ethnicity, and other dimensions of inequality (Power, 2004). We hope that this was visible in the methodology and analyses throughout the book. Our rationale for keeping the term *provisioning* as central to our study reflects a policy focus in which the concept of *social provisions* is used to describe some of the responsibilities carried by an active state so that not everything is left to the so-called active citizen. An active state is essential if future cohorts of women are not to continue marching for bread and roses.

Of particular concern is the retreat of the state, as evidenced by the withdrawal of social provisions since the 1980s. At the same time that a North American and European discourse was taking hold about the development of civil society as a cornerstone for democracy, the power of nation states was being transformed by a globalized economy. During this time, the state increasingly abdicated responsibility for social provisioning on the one hand, while on the other, the particular types of actions that defined the active citizen, and the spaces within which participation was recognized, shrank. Those spaces in which women were participating and meeting their provisioning responsibilities were not seen as 'real' centres of civil society participation. Thus women were not seen as responsible active citizens. Their organizations were shut down, while the state withdrew supports, and voluntary agencies were turned into service providers. Such are the dynamics of oppression in that they undermine women as active citizens.

In order to enhance the well-being of citizens such as the women who participated in this study, the starting place is to recognize that low-income women carry many provisioning responsibilities. They are not scrambling to offload them. Many, but not all, are assumed willingly because they are tied to meaningful relationships. What is sought is recognition that these commitments, and the associated work, do exist with consequences for the women doing the provisioning! Defining non-employed people as dependents excludes them from entitlements that accompany those seen as contributing members of society – those who are employed. Likewise, thinking in terms of what types of provisioning women do does not position individuals as simply givers or receivers of care. The concept is more concerned with highlighting how responsibilities flow along pathways of relationships.

Where women's rights are based on policies focused on getting women into low-paying jobs, women with provisioning relationships are just further burdened. It is the labour market that is the problem, not the women. Part of the answer is to establish policies that recognize that citizens live multi-dimensional lives. Paid work is privileged in a market economy because it is the arena for earning money – an activity that is valued and brings prestige. All other types of work are devalued. Thus employment policies are needed that modify the effects of this privilege. Currently, the contradictions between competing sets of demands can be avoided only by those women who have resources to buy some assistance with their unpaid work. The resulting inequities actually exacerbate the situation of poor women.

Gender-based incentives to promote equity have utilized Nancy Fraser's idea of the universal caregiver. This approach engages men in performing their fair share of caregiving if women are to succeed in the 'fight for bread.' However, as Olson (2003) cogently argues, even if a universal caregiver approach informs an active state policy approach, operationalizing such a model in a market economy where democracy is usually equated with an individual's right to exercise choice does not easily happen, even when active labour legislation encourages it. For example, until the mid-nineties Sweden's parental leave policy had salary replacement rates of up to 94 per cent. Despite such a strong incentive, examination of the Swedish experience revealed that income-replacement policies were not sufficient to attract men in the same numbers as women to take care leaves. Labour market priorities seemed to dominate individual and household decision-making. In this case, it revealed the dynamic that individuals incur costs beyond lost wages when they interrupt their labour force careers and, by contrast, shows the plight of poor women whose 'careers' begin with the testing grounds of women's collective efforts.

Paid work will continue to be privileged as the most valued approach to acquiring the needed resources for living. This will not disappear in a market economy, but a provisioning state can provide key resources that are now available only to households with higher incomes. The areas of child and elder care come readily to mind. Numerous studies document the need and the models used within and across countries. In Canada, women's groups have repeatedly argued that a viable national childcare policy is essential to women's autonomy. Yet multiple campaigns to institute one have met with stiff resistance over the years. Instead, a patchwork of tax benefits and subsidies keeps reappearing under different names. A parallel scenario is repeatedly enacted around calls for a national home- and community-care policy for elderly persons. These policy examples illustrate how class privilege interlocks with gender, race, class, and age to oppress particular groups of Canadians. The holistic concept of provisioning suggests that future research, and policies based on it, follow women's relationship pathways as trails to understanding citizens' need for both 'bread and roses.' Policies that position people as citizens who carry a range of individual and collective provisioning responsibilities would increase the capacity of women to choose to engage in various forms of participation, including politics. From such spaces, other possibilities can develop.

Conclusion

This book has focused on the provisioning work that women do. We have argued that this work is done as individuals and as members of collectivities. This work is tied to the responsibilities that women carry. No matter what the work is, or whether it is engaged in by choice or coercion, relationships are central. The sites in which the data were collected allowed us to explicate the amount and complexity of this provisioning work. Along with these empirical data from participants, each chapter interrogated the socio-political context within which individual and group-based provisioning was occurring. What becomes clear from a trans-site perspective is that the state continues to have a powerful presence in the lives of women like the participants in this study – and in the collectivities of which they were members. Funding policies hooked to narrow definitions of service programmes, and social assistance payments based on women positioned as part of a labour market pool, are technologies of ruling that regulate behaviour and suppress resistance.

In 2012, many of the premises of Marshall's welfare state, along with its gendered assumptions, no longer hold. What we support is the spirit, the commitment to collective well-being, that gave rise to it. Our concern about the current civil society / active citizen discourse is that it excludes segments of the population and loads responsibility onto individuals like our participants while letting the state elude its responsibility to do social provisioning. One should expect to look to the state for social provisions that enable, support, and in some cases relieve the provisioning work carried by citizens. The state has the power to intervene in all spheres, but in the current neoliberal regime support is limited to the market sector. Any illusions that the state has shrivelled in a market economy should have been wiped away after seeing state responses to the recession of 2008–9 when market forces seemed to be jeopardizing the welfare of several nation states. As noted in chapter 1, central governments were called on to infuse millions into financial and industrial markets. As this chapter is being written, it seems that the intervention did stabilize these sectors of the society. It is unnerving to witness how the types of behaviour that led to the crisis are reappearing – quite literally it is business as usual; the excesses are criticized but accepted as the price to be paid if a market economy is to grow. This is the political economic context within which low-income women struggle to meet their provisioning responsibilities. The point to be taken is that the character of the non-interventionist state in the neoliberal drama is a myth – a guise assumed until powerful market players call upon it to exercise the tremendous powers at its disposal. Those same powers can be used to promote the quality of life of all citizens.

Appendix: Principles and Practices in the 'Women Provisioning in Community' Research Project

MARGE REITSMA-STREET

Introduction

Academic and community members in this project examined the dimensions and consequences of women's individual and collective provisioning responsibilities in communities marginalized by age, race, or income.[1] A particular challenge in multi-site research is to create collective spaces in which members of research teams can effectively work together on common cross-site research matters while respecting community sensibilities and the learning obligations of students.

The principal investigator drafted the following document named 'Ways of Working' after discussion with researchers and students from four Canadian universities and site consultations with six community advisory groups. The memorandum of understanding was initially approved in December 2004, and revised in July 2006, after the issue of authoring articles was reviewed. In a subsequent amendment, the four academic co-investigators and authors of this book agreed to safeguard until 2011 the data from interviews with 100 women, and 138 key informants who participated in nineteen focus groups and/or interviews.

Preamble to 'Ways of Working'

There are exhilarating possibilities and challenging constraints that will significantly affect the quality of the research and working relationships within and across sites. The project is potentially complex, with dual obligations: to both conceptual and useful ideas; to both individual site teams and the cross-site team; and to both community and academic realities. There are significant differences in the capacities, financial resources, and privileges among project participants. We strive to nourish equality and trust while appreciating they cannot be assumed or taken for granted. Stereotypes, distrust, and envy may affect research relationships between those who live in or close to impoverished, economically insecure situations, and those who do not. Nor is it assumed that the reciprocity of benefits is equal. In particular, the focus of the project on theorizing the longer-term changes may not provide timely benefit for current community members. The project researchers hope that the good intent of curious persons who are committed to join with others for a substantial period of time on common purposes, questions, and principles will produce positive energy and learning, some benefits to community sites, and useful ideas that travel beyond the sites.

Principles

1. To develop conceptual and useful ideas about provisioning, women, and community.
2. To respect collective obligations and resources of the cross-site research project and those distinct to each site.
3. To communicate research findings in a timely manner to diverse audiences.
4. To promote training and mentoring opportunities for students to engage in community-based research.
5. To practise healthy ways of provisioning among ourselves and in the sites.

Processes

Cross-Site Team Relationships and Communication

A key factor in the facilitation of smooth and effective project operations with a cross-site team is adequate integration and communication throughout the project. We use team meetings, open communication channels, and cross-fertilization of specific studies to ensure that communication flows and strong relationships are facilitated. Meetings will occur annually with a focus on pulling all participants together to share experiences, data, and completed work, and to further facilitate the building of partnerships.

Several communications channels facilitate the flow of information throughout the project, including regular email, conversations, and meetings. A web board has been created, which is password protected. It can be accessed by all academic researchers attached to the project. The web board will serve as a hub for sharing data, posting papers for review, promoting project events and activities, and announcements. The structure and setup of the project are such that although each project is housed in one particular site, much of the research content is relevant to all sites.

Researcher Responsibilities

Each researcher takes the lead in a site to develop relationships, conduct research activities, work with students, assistants, and community members, and manage resources. Site teams will have more community members than researchers, to ensure there is adequate opportunity for discussion and negotiation of research activities relevant to a site.

Each researcher also gives direction and completes work for specific cross-site research and administrative tasks, including preparing academic publications and summaries for the popular press.

The principal investigator is responsible for managing the web board, for cross-site financial accounting, and for final accountability reports to the national Social Sciences and Humanities Research Council (SSHRC). The three co-investigators provide financial and other documents to the principal investigator on their site and university responsibilities.

Student Training and Employment

An important aim of the project is to train students and provide learning experiences for them to become better equipped for future research and community involvement. Over half the budget is devoted to student assistants. Student training and guidance is facilitated through site investigators, who involve their student research assistants in as many project activities as possible. Thus students have a research mentor who is a senior researcher with extensive experience in the training of students. Students are to have opportunities to experience research in the setting of the community partner, thereby expanding the traditional student research experience and building relationships for future research and participatory endeavours. The intent is to provide

opportunities to learn about models for community academic collaboration and participatory action research, as well as the nature of research careers in academic, community, and public sectors.

There are several doctoral students associated with the project who,
under the supervision of a project researcher, may create a site, with
attendant responsibilities and benefits including contributions to and
access to selected cross-site data.

Ethics

Each researcher negotiates with the respective site teams how to conduct research activities ethically in their community, and to submit appropriate applications to the respective university.

Every ethics application must include the names of the four academic
investigators, the granting agency, grant number, the project name, and
students' names where relevant.

Presentations and Publications for 2004–2008

1. Researchers, including students, and sites teams must include the
   'Women Provisioning in Community' Project name in all presentations and publications and acknowledge the funding of SSHRC
   Grant 410–2004–0233. It is expected that appreciation is expressed to
   those who make conceptual and practical contributions to a work.
2. Site summaries or short documents of findings written in accessible
   language are prepared and distributed in a timely manner. Annually there is one cross-site summary document approved by the
   cross-site team.
3. Papers using data from a site that are authored by a project researcher, including students, are to be circulated so the relevant site
   team has adequate opportunity for input, correction, and comment.
   Site teams or organizational boards, however, are not required nor
   expected to approve papers authored by researchers on a site. Authorship, errors, and omissions remain with university researchers.
   These academic authored papers must not identify sites.
4. Sites may write their own summaries and use project data on the
   organization with individual identification removed. These site-
   authored presentations and papers are to be approved by the site
   research teams and/or boards and may identify the site by name.
   Also, each site determines what opportunities are required for

those who contributed to the research to know about the findings and to be informed that their experiences and ideas are 'going somewhere.'

5. For each cross-site academic publication and presentation that uses data from more than one site, one (or two) researchers become the lead author(s). There are to be adequate opportunities for project investigators to give input into academic conference papers or publications based on cross-site data and conceptual work. The lead author will use input to make revisions. Other contributors will be named as authors, in order of the level of contribution or in alphabetical order if contributions are equivalent. 'Contribution' includes writing sections of a paper or substantial involvement in preparation of data and analysis. All authors or investigators, however, do not have to sign off on the final paper. Whenever possible, author order and contributions to a project will be decided in advance of the work being done before the first draft. Authorship is explicitly discussed again before a paper submitted for publication.

6. Student papers using data from their site for course work and thesis are authored solely by the student. One of their committee members or faculty supervisor will be a project co-investigator. Student submissions for academic publication using data from their site may be co-authored, and must be reviewed, but not necessarily approved, by a project co-investigator.

7. Researchers may be the sole author of papers based on their own site, inviting others to participate as they wish, giving authorship or acknowledgments where appropriate.

8. Site researchers, including students, are to provide copies of papers and publications to their site and the cross-site team regularly, until 2010, and to inform the principal investigator or designate they have done so. A full list of papers, presentations, and seminars to *all* audiences will be submitted by the principal investigator to the funding agency in March 2008 (or March 2009, if an extension is required).

9. [Approved 3 August 2006] We will have a discussion early on in the writing of papers for refereed academic journals and conference papers about who the authors are of a particular paper, and possible acknowledgments. Just before submission for publication, there will be a second opportunity for discussion of authorship, with a decision made by at least two people – the lead author and one other author – about who the authors are and the order of the names.

10. [Approved 3 August 2006] Our guiding principle is to remain generous (i.e., including as many authors and acknowledgments as possible) in as many ways as possible in the production of academic and popular work. In the early drafts of all written papers, and in flyers, brochures, and any written material, we will include a listing of authorship and acknowledgments, and acknowledge granting agency support.

Ownership, Storage, and Access to Research Data

1. Project researchers are responsible to 'clean' their site data before sharing data and uploading them to the electronic web board. Clean data removes identifying information on individuals, organizations, and cities. Any lists linking pseudonyms or codes with names are to be kept separate from consent forms and the data.
2. Cleaned site data on the provisioning of women and organizations collected by project researchers through interviews, discussions, focus groups, field notes, and analytical memos are to be shared among the investigators for cross-site analysis. Researchers are not expected to share tapes and personal research journals.
3. The principal investigator is manager of the web board hosted by the University of Victoria. The project has web board space approved to 1 January 2008. Extension is negotiable. The four investigators must decide by consensus who will have password access to the data stored on the web board.
4. Researchers, including students, will erase tapes of interviews, focus groups, and discussions no later than March 2007, or earlier if there are concerns about maintaining a respondent's confidentiality or safety. Researchers, again including students, are responsible to inform the principal investigator and a member of their site team they have done so.
5. Site researchers are responsible to destroy their electronic and paper copies of site data, along with consent forms no later than 2010 [amended 4 August 2010 to 2011] and to inform the principal investigator and a member of their site team they have done so. The principal investigator is responsible to destroy data on the web board by that year, and is to inform the investigators she has done so.

6. A copy of cleaned data on the community and site organization
   from focus groups, field notes, and interviews with key informants
   may be given to the site team for its use. Absolutely no data on
   individual women will be given to a site team.

Review and Endings

This document and our experience of working together will be reviewed early in 2006.

It is expected that dilemmas, surprises, and conflicts may arise in
the site and cross-site teams, such as tension between the benefits of
conceptual investigations and those immediately helpful to a site. It is
hoped that prompt discussion and consultation using the intent of the
project research principles and proposal will encourage a compromise.

Data analysis and preparation of materials at the site level will end by
March 2007 – unless monies other than those from the original granting
agency are used, or the granting agency provides an extension. Each
site is responsible for evaluating, celebrating, and ending their project
activities.

The work of the final year of the grant is cross-site analysis and publication. By March 2008 all original money must be spent, and the principal investigator submits a report. The cross-site team decides how it
wishes to end the project. There is also to be discussion and decisions
about future collaboration on publications and use of the research data
after 2008.

Notes

1. Introduction: Conceptualizing the Work of Women in the Twenty-First Century

1 The sites were also selected for feasibility and mutual interest. There were six researchers, each responsible for a site situated geographically, histori- cally, and culturally close to them. The researchers already had established relationships with the sites, and, with the help of community advisory pan- els, approached the members and decision-makers to invite their participa- tion in the study. The selection of participants and the details of the research data procedures varied by group, depending on the advice of the commu- nity advisory groups who had agreed to work alongside the researchers for the duration of the study.

2 Transcriptions, with confidential information removed, were uploaded to a password-protected web board, facilitating cross-site analysis of a large qualitative database over time by researchers and assistants living in dif- ferent cities. The qualitative software program N*Vivo was used to help manage the data and to ensure consistent analysis across the six sites. Within each site and across sites, the co-authors engaged in iterative analy- sis to code specific categories of responsibilities, to examine themes, and to explore interpretations. There were several rounds of analysis to ensure saturation of categories and validity of themes for each of the subsequent chapters (Boeije, 2002; Glaser & Strauss, 1967). The analyses relevant to a chapter are presented therein. In brief, interview and focus-group tran- scripts from the three sites discussed in chapter 8 (Cascade, Hands-On, and Pont Place) were subjected to bottom-up open coding to generate concepts. These guided the coding done in the other three sites: Gen-Y (chapter 5), Jane's Place (chapter 6), and Heracane (chapter 7). After all data

were collected and coded, a top-down thematic coding across all sites was undertaken by one researcher for the individual provisioning schema presented in chapter 3. A similar process occurred for finalizing the categories on collective provisioning presented in chapter 4.

2. Securing the Future by Positioning the Past in the Present

1 The following sections draw heavily on an article by two of the authors: Neysmith & Reitsma-Street (2005).
2 *Workfare* is a term used widely to define welfare-to-work programmes throughout Canada and the United States. If a person on social assistance is considered 'employable,' then the person is required to look for work, participate in programmes such as employment support and employment placement, *and/or* do community service. These schemes have been widely critiqued on the basis that the jobs are low paid / short term, and dead end; the community service aspect is coercive and divisive. See, for example, Quaid (2002).

3. Provisioning Responsibilities of Women: Relationships Shape the Work

1 The text that follows was originally published in Neysmith, Reitsma-Street, Baker Collins, Porter, & Tam (2010).

4. Collective Provisioning: Naming the Work of Vital Spaces

1 In the first round of analysis, the principal investigator and one associate completed an intensive open coding of the responsibilities and activities emerging from several focus groups collected in the pilot site for the project. Names and descriptions of collective provisioning categories were drafted and debated in the site and across the sites. In the second round, open coding was conducted in four sites on women's perspectives of the work of organizations, using N*Vivo qualitative software on individual interviews. Researchers in each site generated additional categories to the point of saturation, providing names, descriptions, and examples for debate in cross-site meetings, and subsequent electronic discussions (Bringer, Johnston, & Brackenridge, 2004). Next, one researcher took the description of categories generated from the four sites and completed a top-down closed coding of all the focus groups and key informant interviews transcripts in those sites. The purpose of this step was to confirm, revise, and

explicate the categories thus far. In the final round of analysis, evidence that disconfirmed or revised the categories of collective provisioning was explored in data from women interviewees and organizational informants in the fifth and sixth sites – as these included significant racial diversity in membership, while differing significantly in governance, size, and purpose.

5. Producing Racial Knowledge in Community Programmes for 'At Risk' Young Women

1 This term is used to recognize that racial categories are constructed as a result of dynamic social and historical processes.

6. Provisioning for Children in a Low-Income Community

1 The interviews with the Riverview women were part of a study that examined how Canadian child-care policy assists and constrains low-income women's strategies of provisioning for their children (Cerny, 2009). The interviews at both sites were conducted between 2005 and 2007. The names of women used throughout this chapter are pseudonyms.

7. Revealing Older Women's Provisioning Responsibilities

1 An earlier version of this chapter was published in Neysmith & Reitsma-Street (2009).
2 There may be an opportunity emerging to expose some of the responsibilities borne by older women globally as the grandmothers of South Africa become internationally recognized for their role in raising young children whose parent's generation has been decimated by HIV/AIDS.
3 As in the other sites, before starting the interview an information and consent form was signed by all participants. This process included a verbal and written explanation of the concept of *provisioning*, as well as why we were using it rather than *work* or *care* in the interview. Participants were given a sheet of Bristol board and coloured markers and encouraged to draw diagrams of people and provisioning relationships. This allowed participants to determine where to start mapping their provisioning responsibilities, while it served as a visual stimulus for the interviewer to probe the associations among specific persons, relationships, and changing responsibilities over time.
4 It is worth noting that in this interview the interviewer was white and the focus was on age and gender, not race discrimination. As DeVault (1995)

has shown in her own research, race may shape the content and organization of a conversation but remain invisible in the data and analysis if it is not part of the framework. Such a dynamic seems to be operating in this case example.

8. Counting the Costs of Provisioning for Women Living on Low Incomes

1 An earlier version of this chapter was published in Baker Collins, Neysmith, Porter, & Reitsma-Street (2009), which can be found at http://www.tandfonline.com.
2 As explained in chapters 3 and 4, the categories emerging from these three sites were used to do initial coding of data for the rest of the sites. The categories presented in tables 3.1, 3.2, and 4.1 reflect final coding decisions. In the following sections we have left much of the original organization of the data because it reflects what emerged strongly among these low-income groups of women. The reader will see common threads in the types of provisioning work done, even though the final wording of categories is somewhat different and the relative importance of some types of provisioning (some categories) might be less present in these three sites than in others.

9. Collective Spaces as Incubators of Citizenship

1 This chapter draws on arguments that appeared in Baker Collins, Reitsma-Street, Porter, & Neysmith (2011), which can be found at http://www.tandfonline.com.
2 The systemic underfunding of the non-profit community sector (Eakin, 2004) has been compounded by a shift from funding the general mission of organizations to funding specific, short-term projects, resulting in much more staff time spent in writing project proposals and in demonstrating effective, efficient outcomes (Arai & Reid, 2003; Ilcan & Basok, 2004; Richmond & Shields, 2005). The consequences of this shift are instability, volatile funding, and huge swings in revenue (Scott, 2003).
3 This goal has recently been quietly added back to the Status of Women Canada's mandate, and the description now includes 'work to advance equality for women.'
4 Molyneux (1998), whose distinction between practical and strategic interests has been used extensively (see Moser, 1991), takes up the ways in which this distinction has been used in response to critiques of it. Molyneux affirms that strategic interests are defined as those 'involving claims to transform social relations in order to enhance women's position and to secure a more

lasting re-positioning of women within the gender order and society,' and practical interests are defined as those based on the 'satisfaction of needs arising from women's placement within the sexual division of labour' (p. 232). Molyneux asserts that in some cases these distinctions have been applied in a way that assumes a too rigid and hierarchical character, with practical interests set against strategic. This application does not leave room for exploring the links between practical and strategic interests.

Appendix: Principles and Practices in the 'Women Provisioning in Community' Research Project

1 See, for example, Neysmith, Reitsma-Street, Baker Collins, & Tam (2010).

References

Acklesberg, M.A. (1988). Communities, resistance, and women's activism: Some implications for a democratic policy. In A. Bookman & S. Morgen (Eds.), *Women and the politics of empowerment* (pp. 297–313). Philadelphia: Temple University Press.

Adam, B. (2002). The gendered time politics of globalization: Of shadowlands and elusive justice. *Feminist Review, 70*(1), 3–9.

Adams, J., & Padamsee, T. (2001). Signs and regimes: Rereading feminist work on welfare regimes. *Social Politics: International Studies in Gender, State & Society, 8*(1), 1–23.

Adams, R. (2003). *Social work and empowerment* (3rd ed.). New York: Palgrave Macmillan.

Adkins, L. (2005). Social capital: The anatomy of a troubled concept. *Feminist Theory, 6*(2), 195–211.

Aptheker, B. (1989). *Tapestries of life: Women's work, women's consciousness and the meaning of daily experience.* Amherst, MA: University of Massachusetts Press.

Arai, S.M., & Reid, D.G. (2003). Impacts of a neo-liberal policy shift on citizenship and the voluntary sector: A policy delphi with social planning organizations. *Canadian Review of Social Policy, 52,* 67–92.

Armstrong, P., & Armstrong, H. (2003). *Wasting away: The undermining of Canadian health care* (2nd ed.). Toronto: Oxford University Press.

Aronson, J., & Neysmith, S. (2006). Obscuring the costs of home care: Restructuring at work. *Work, Employment & Society, 20*(1), 27–45.

Baker Collins, S. (2004). Welfare and well-being: The treatment of social relationships in the administration of income assistance in Ontario. *Critical Social Work, 5*(1).

Baker Collins, S., Neysmith, S., Porter, E., & Reitsma-Street, M. (2009). Women's provisioning work: Counting the cost for women living on low income. *Community, Work & Family, 12*(1), 21–37.

Baker Collins, S., Reitsma-Street, M., Porter, E., & Neysmith, S. (2011). Women's community work challenges market citizenship. *Community Development, 42*(3), 297–313.

Bakker, I. (Ed.). (1996). *Rethinking restructuring: Gender and change in Canada.* Toronto: University of Toronto Press.

Bakker, I. (2003). Neo-liberal governance and the reprivatization of social reproduction: Social provisioning and shifting gender orders. In I. Bakker & S. Gill (Eds.), *Power, production and social reproduction* (pp. 66–82). London: Palgrave Macmillan.

Bakker, I. (2007). Social reproduction and the constitution of a gendered political economy. *New Political Economy, 12*(4), 541–56.

Bannerji, H. (2000). *The dark side of the nation: Essays on multiculturalism, nationalism and gender.* Toronto: Canadian Scholars' Press.

Barker, D.K. (2005, Summer). Beyond women and economics: Rereading 'women's work.' *Signs: Journal of Women in Culture and Society, 30*(4), 2189–209.

Barrig, M. (1994). The difficult equilibrium between bread and roses: Women's organizations and democracy in Peru. In J.S. Jaquette (Ed.), *The women's movement in Latin America: Participation and democracy* (2nd ed.) (pp. 151–75). Boulder, CO: Westview.

Bashevkin, S.B. (2002). *Welfare hot buttons: Women, work and social policy reform.* Toronto: University of Toronto Press.

Beck, U. (1992). *Risk society: Towards a new modernity.* London: Sage.

Beck, U. (2000). Risk society revisited: Theory, politics, and research programmes. In B. Adam, U. Beck, & J. Van Loon (Eds.), *The risk society and beyond: Critical issues for social theory* (pp. 211–29). London: Sage.

Beneria, L. (1995). Toward a greater integration of gender in economics. *World Development, 23*(11), 1839–50.

Beneria, L., Floro, M., Grown, C., & MacDonald, M. (2000). Introduction to globalization and gender. *Feminist Economics, 6*(3), vii–xviii.

Bettie, J. (2003). *Women without class: Girls, race and identity.* Berkeley, CA: University of California Press.

Bezanson, K., & Luxton, M. (Eds.). (2006). *Social reproduction: Feminist political economy challenges neo-liberalism.* Montreal & Kingston: McGill-Queen's University Press.

Biggs, S. (2004). Age, gender, narratives, and masquerades. *Journal of Aging Studies, 18*(1), 41–58.

Blackstone, A. (2004). 'It's just about being fair': Activism and the politics of volunteering in the breast cancer movement. *Gender & Society, 18*(3), 350–68.

Boeije, H. (2002). A purposeful approach to the constant comparative method in the analysis of qualitative interviews. *Quality & Quantity, 36*(4), 391–409.

Bolton, S.C. (2000). 'Emotion here, emotion there, emotional organizations everywhere.' *Critical Perspectives on Accounting, 11*(2), 155–71.

Brah, A. (2002). Global mobilities, local predicaments: Globalization and the critical imagination. *Feminist Review, 70*(1), 30–45.

Brannen, J. (2005). Time and the negotiation of work–family boundaries: Autonomy or illusion? *Time & Society, 14*(1), 113–31.

Breitkreuz, R.S. (2005). Engendering citizenship? A critical feminist analysis of Canadian welfare-to-work policies and the employment experiences of lone mothers. *Journal of Sociology & Social Welfare, 32*(2), 147–65.

Bringer, J.D., Johnston, L.H., & Brackenridge, C.H. (2004). Maximizing transparency in a doctoral thesis: The complexities of writing about the use of QSR*NVIVO within a grounded theory study. *Qualitative Research, 4*(2), 247–65.

Brodie, J. (2002). Citizenship and solidarity: Reflections on the Canadian way. *Citizenship Studies, 6*(4), 377–94.

Brodie, J. (2008). We are all equal now: Contemporary gender politics in Canada. *Feminist Theory, 9*(2), 145–64.

Brown, L.M. (2003). *Girlfighting: Betrayal and rejection among girls.* New York: New York University Press.

Browne, C.V., & Braun, K.L. (2008). Globalization, women's migration and the long-term-care workforce. *Gerontologist, 48*(1), 16–24.

Brush, L.D. (2002). Changing the subject: Gender and welfare regime studies. *Social Politics: International Studies in Gender, State & Society, 9*(2), 161–86.

Byrne, D.S. (1999). *Social exclusion.* Milton Keynes, UK: Open University Press.

Callahan, M., Brown, L., MacKenzie, P., & Whittington, B. (2004, Fall/Winter). Catch as catch can: Grandmothers raising grandchildren and kinship care policies. *Canadian Review of Social Policy, 54*, 58–78.

Callero, P.L. (2003). The sociology of the self. *Annual Review of Sociology, 29*, 115–33.

Calliste, A. (2000). Resisting professional exclusion and marginality in nursing: Women of colour in Ontario. In M.A. Kalbach & W.E. Kalbach (Eds.), *Perspectives on ethnicity in Canada: A reader* (pp. 303–28). Toronto: Harcourt Canada.

Campbell, A. (2006). Proceeding with care: Lessons to be learned from the Canadian parental leave and Québec daycare initiatives in developing a national childcare policy. *Canadian Journal of Family Law, 22*, 171–222.

Campbell, K.B. (2005). Theorizing the authentic: Identity, engagement and public space. *Administration & Society, 36*(6), 688–705.

Campbell, M., & Gregor, F. (2002). *Mapping social relations: A primer in doing institutional ethnography*. Walnut Creek, CA: AltaMira.

Caragata, L. (2009). Lone mothers: Policy responses to build social inclusion. In M.G. Cohen & J. Pulkingham (Eds.), *Public policy for women: The state, income security, and labour market issues* (pp. 161–83). Toronto: University of Toronto Press.

Carroll, W.K., & Ratner, R.S. (1996). Master frames and counter-hegemony: Political sensibilities in contemporary social movements. *Canadian Review of Sociology, 33*(4), 407–35.

Carroll, W.K., & Ratner, R.S. (2001). Sustaining oppositional cultures in 'post-socialist' times: A comparative study of three social movement organizations. *Sociology, 35*(3), 605–29.

Castells, Manuel (1996). *The rise of the network society* (Vol. 1). Oxford: Blackwell.

Cerny, J. (2009). *Low income mothers, provisioning and childcare policy: A vision of shared caring*. Unpublished doctoral dissertation, University of Toronto, ON.

Chesney-Lind, M., & Irwin, K. (2008). *Beyond bad girls: Gender, violence and hype*. New York: Routledge.

Chunn, D., & Gavigan, S. (2004). Welfare law, welfare fraud, and the moral regulation of the 'never deserving poor.' *Social & Legal Studies, 13*(2), 219–43.

Cities Centre. (2008). *Statistics Canada census data 1971 to 2006*. Unpublished manuscript, Cities Centre, University of Toronto, ON.

City of Toronto. (2005a). *Child care service plan 2005–2009*. Toronto Children's Services. Retrieved from City of Toronto website: http://www.toronto.ca/children/report/ccsplan/ccsplan_05.htm.

City of Toronto. (2005b). *Strong neighbourhoods task force recommendations*. Toronto Staff Report to the Policy and Finance Committee, October 2005.

City of Toronto, United Way of Greater Toronto and Social Planning Council of Metropolitan Toronto. (1997). *Profile of a changing world: The 1996 community agency survey*. Toronto: United Way.

Clement, G. (1996). *Care, autonomy and justice: Feminism and the ethic of care*. Boulder, CO: Westview.

Cohen, M.G., & Brodie, J. (Eds.). (2007). *Remapping gender in the new global order*. London: Routledge.

Cohen, M.G., & Pulkingham, J. (Eds.). (2009). *Public policy for women: The state, income security, and labour market issues*. Toronto: University of Toronto Press.

Cohen, R. (2000). Mom is a stranger: The negative impact of immigration politics on the family life of Filipina domestic workers. *Canadian Ethnic Studies, 32*(3), 76–88.

Collins, P.H. (2000). *Black feminist thought: Knowledge, consciousness, and the politics of empowerment* (2nd ed.). New York: Routledge.

Cornwall, A., & Gaventa, J. (2001). *From users and choosers to makers and shapers: Repositioning participation in social policy.* IDS Working Paper 127. Brighton, UK: Institute of Development Studies, University of Sussex.

Craig, L. (2007). Is there really a second shift, and if so, who does it? A time-diary investigation. *Feminist Review, 86*(1), 149–70.

Creese, G., & Strong-Boag, V. (2005, March 5). *Losing ground: The effects of government cutbacks on women in British Columbia, 2001–2005.* Retrieved 9 November 2006: http://www3.telus.net/bcwomen/archives/losingground.

Crouch, C., Eder, K., & Tambini, D. (2001). Introduction: Dilemmas of citizenship. In C. Crouch, K. Eder & D. Tambini (Eds.), *Citizenship, markets, and the state* (pp. 1–20). Oxford: Oxford University Press.

Cumming, S.J., & Cooke, M. (2009). 'I work hard for no money': The work demands of single mothers managing multiple state-provided benefits. *Canadian Review of Social Policy, 60/61,* 75–90.

Cummins, S., Curtis, S., Diez-Roux, A.V., & Macintyre, S. (2007). Understanding and representing 'place' in health research: A relational approach. *Social Science & Medicine, 65*(9), 1825–38.

Daly, M. (2002). Care as a good for social policy. *Journal of Social Policy, 31*(2), 251–70.

Day, T. (1995). Symposium on feminist economics: Introduction. *Canadian Journal of Economics, 28*(1), 139–42.

Deere, C.D., Safa, H., & Antrobus, P. (1997). Impact of the economic crisis on poor women and their households. In N. Visvanathan, L. Duggan, L. Nisonoff, & N. Wiegersma (Eds.), *The women, gender and development reader* (pp. 267–77). Halifax, NS: Fernwood Publishing.

Delgado, R., & Stefancic J. (2001). *Critical race theory: An introduction.* New York: New York University Press.

Desforges, L., Jones, R., & Woods, M. (2005). New geographies of citizenship. *Citizenship Studies, 9*(5), 439–51.

DeVault, M.L. (1991). *Feeding the family: The social organization of caring as gendered work.* Chicago: University of Chicago Press.

DeVault, M.L. (1995). Ethnicity and expertise: Racial-ethnic knowledge in sociological research. *Gender & Society, 9*(5), 612–31.

Dobrowolsky, A. (2008). Interrogating 'invisibilization' and 'instrumentalization': Women and current citizenship trends in Canada. *Citizenship Studies, 12*(5), 465–79.

Dobrowolsky, A., & Jenson, J. (2004). Shifting representations of citizenship: Canadian politics of 'women' and 'children' *Social Politics: International Studies in Gender, State & Society, 11*(2), 154–80.

Dolbin-MacNab, M.L. (2006). Just like raising your own? Grandmothers' perceptions of parenting a second time around. *Family Relations, 55*(5), 564–75.

Dominelli, L. (2006). Racialised identities: New challenges for social work education. In K. Lyons & S. Lawrence (Eds.), *Social work in Europe: Educating for change.* Birmingham, UK: Venture.

Dominguez, S., & Watkins, C. (2003). Creating networks for survival and mobility: Social capital among African-American and Latin-American low-income mothers. *Social Problems, 50*(1), 111–35.

Donath, S. (2000). The other economy: A suggestion for a distinctively feminist economics. *Feminist Economics, 6*(1), 115–23.

Douglas, M. (1992). *Risk and blame: Essays in cultural theory.* London: Routledge.

Drevland, R. (2007). Women's activism and the marketing of the nonprofit community. In M.G. Cohen & J. Brodie (Eds.), *Remapping gender in the new global order* (pp. 151–65). London: Routledge.

Dua, E., Razack, N., & Warner, J.N. (2005). Race, racism, and empire: Reflections on Canada. *Social Justice, 32*(4), 1–10.

Dua, E., & Robertson, A. (Eds.) (1999). *Scratching the surface: Canadian anti-racism feminist thought.* Toronto: Women's Press.

Dyck, I., Kontos, P., Angus, J., & McKeever, P. (2005). The home as a site for long-term care: Meanings and management of bodies and spaces. *Health & Place, 11*(2), 173–85.

Eakin, L. (2004). *Community capacity draining: The impact of current funding practices on non-profit community organizations.* Toronto: Community Social Planning Council of Toronto.

Edin, K., & Lein, L. (1996). Work, welfare and single mothers' economic survival strategies. *American Sociological Review, 62*(2), 253–66.

Edin, K., & Lein, L. (1998). The private safety net: The role of charitable organizations in the lives of the poor. *Housing Policy Debate, 9*(3), 541–73.

Ehrenreich, B., and Hochschild, A.R. (Eds.). 2003. *Global woman: Nannies, maids, and sex workers in the new economy.* New York: Metropolitan Books.

Elliott, A. (2002). Beck's sociology of risk: A critical assessment. *Sociology, 36*(2), 293–315.

Ellis, K. (2004). Dependency, justice and the ethic of care. In H. Dean (Ed.), *The ethics of welfare: Human rights, dependency and responsibility* (pp. 29–48). Bristol, UK: Policy.

Elson, D. (1992). From survival strategies to transformation strategies: Women's needs and structural adjustment. In L. Beneria & S. Feldman (Eds.), *Unequal burden: Economic crises, persistent poverty and women's work* (pp. 26–48). Boulder, CO: Westview.

Elson, D. (2000). Gender at the macroeconomic level. In J. Cook, J. Roberts, & G. Waylen (Eds.), *Towards a gendered political economy* (pp. 77–97). New York: St Martin's.

Emirbayer, M. (1997). Manifesto for a relational sociology. *American Journal of Sociology, 103*(2), 281–317.

England, P., & Folbre, N. (2003). Contracting for care. In M.A. Ferber & J.A. Nelson (Eds.), *Feminist economics today: Beyond economic man* (pp. 61–80). Chicago: University of Chicago Press.

Erbaugh, E.B. (2002). Women's community organizing and identity transformation. *Race, Gender & Class, 9*(1), 8–32.

Esping-Andersen, G. (1999). *Social foundations of postindustrial economies.* New York: Oxford University Press.

Essed, P., & Goldberg, D.T. (Eds.). (2002). *Race critical theories: Text and context.* Malden, MA: Blackwell Publishers.

Etzioni, A. (Ed.). (1995). *New communitarian thinking: Persons, virtues, institutions and communities.* Charlottesville: University of Virginia Press.

Evans, P.M. (2007). (Not)Taking account of precarious employment: Workfare policies and lone mothers in Ontario and the UK. *Social Policy & Administration, 41*(1), 29–49.

Everingham, C. (2002). Engendering time: Gender equity and discourses of workplace flexibility. *Time & Society, 11*(2–3), 335–51.

Ewick, P., & Silbey, S. (2003). Narrating social structure: Stories of resistance to legal authority. *American Journal of Sociology, 108*(6), 1328–372.

Feldman, S. (1992). Crises, poverty, and gender inequality: Current themes and issues. In L. Beneria & S. Feldman (Eds.), *Unequal burden: Economic crises, persistent poverty and women's work* (pp. 1–25). Boulder, CO: Westview.

Ferber, M.A., & Nelson, J.A. (Eds.). (2003). *Feminist economics today: Beyond economic man.* Chicago: University of Chicago Press.

Figart, D.M. (2007). Social responsibility for living standards: Presidential address, Association for Social Economics, 2007. *Review of Social Economy, 65*(4), 391–405.

Finn, J.L. (2002). Raíces: Gender-consciousness community building in Santiago, Chile. *Affilia, 17*(4), 448–70.

Fitzpatrick, T. (2004). Social policy and time. *Time & Society, 13*(2–3), 197–219.

Franzway, S. (2001). *Sexual politics and greedy institutions.* Annandale, NSW: Pluto Press Australia.

Frazer, H. (2005). Setting the scene Europe-wide: The challenge of poverty and social exclusion. *Community Development Journal, 40*(4), 371–83.

Fraser, N. (1997). *Justice interruptus: Critical reflections on the 'postsocialist' condition.* New York: Routledge.

Freeman, C. (2000). *High tech and high heels in the global economy: Women, work, and pink-collar identities in the Caribbean.* Durham, NC: Duke University Press.

Freeman, M. (2006). Nurturing dialogic hermeneutics and the deliberative capacities of communities in focus groups. *Qualitative Inquiry, 12*(1), 81–95.

Frost, L. (2001). *Young women and the body: A feminist sociology.* New York: Palgrave.

Fuller, S., Kershaw, P., & Pulkingham, J. (2008). Constructing 'active citizenship': Single mothers, welfare, and the logics of voluntarism. *Citizenship Studies, 12*(2), 157–76.

Gardiner, J. (1997). *Gender, care and economics.* Basingstoke, Hampshire, UK: Macmillan.

Gazso, A. (2009). Gendering the 'responsible risk taker': Citizenship relationships with gender-neutral social assistance policy. *Citizenship Studies, 13*(1), 45–63.

George, U. (1998). Caring and women of colour: Living in the intersection of race, class and gender. In S. Neysmith (Ed.), *Women's caring: Feminist perspectives on social welfare* (pp. 3–22). Toronto: Oxford University Press.

Gibson, P.A. (1999). African American grandmothers: New mothers again. *Affilia, 14*(3), 329–43.

Giddens, A. (1994). *Beyond left and right: The future of radical politics.* Cambridge: Polity.

Giddens, A. (1998). *The third way: The renewal of social democracy.* Cambridge: Polity.

Giddens, A. (Ed.). (2001). *The global third way debate.* Cambridge: Polity.

Gilligan, C. (1982). *In a different voice: Psychological theory and women's development.* Cambridge, MA: Harvard University Press.

Giri, A.K. (1995). The dialectic between globalization and localization: Economic restructuring, women and strategies of cultural reproduction. *Dialectical Anthropology 20*(2), 193–216.

Gittell, M., Ortega-Bustamante, I., & Steffy, T. (2000). Social capital and social change: Women's community activism. *Urban Affairs Review, 36*(2), 123–47.

Glaser, B.G., & Strauss, A.L. (Eds.). (1967). *The discovery of grounded theory: Strategies for qualitative research.* New York: Aldine de Gruyter.

Glendinning, C., & Means, R. (2004). Rearranging the deckchairs on the Titanic of long-term care: Is organizational integration the answer? *Critical Social Policy, 24*(4), 435–57.

Glenn, E.N. (2002). *Unequal freedom: How race and gender shaped American citizenship and labor.* Cambridge, MA: Harvard University Press.

Gonick, M. (2003). *Between femininities: Ambivalence, identity, and the education of girls.* Albany, NY: State University of New York Press.

Goodman, C.C., & Silverstein, M. (2006). Grandmothers raising grandchildren: Ethnic and racial differences in well-being among custodial and co-parenting families. *Journal of Family Issues, 27*(11), 1605–26.

Grahame, K.M. (2003). 'For the family': Asian immigrant women's triple day. *Journal of Sociology & Social Welfare, 30*(1), 66–90.

Gunn, S. (2006). From hegemony to governmentality: Changing conceptions of power in social history. *Journal of Social History, 39*(3), 705–20.

Gurstein, P., & Vilches, S. (2009). Revisioning the environment of support for lone mothers in extreme poverty. In M.G. Cohen & J. Pulkingham (Eds.), *Public policy for women: The state, income security, and labour market issues* (pp. 226–47). Toronto: University of Toronto Press.

Hankivsky, O. (2004). *Social policy and the ethic of care.* Vancouver: UBC Press.

Hanlon, N., Rosenberg, M., & Clasby, R. (2007). Offloading social care responsibilities: Recent experiences of local voluntary organizations in a remote urban centre in British Columbia, Canada. *Health & Social Care in the Community, 15*(4), 343–51.

Hannah-Moffat, K. (2002). *Governing through need.* Paper presented at the British Society of Criminology Conference, University of Keele, Keele, Staffordshire, UK.

Harvey, D. (2007). *A brief history of neoliberalism.* Oxford: Oxford University Press.

Haylett, C. (2003). Class, care and welfare reform: Reading meanings, talking feelings. *Environment and Planning, 35*, 799–814.

Hennessy, J. (2009). Choosing work and family: Poor and low-income mothers' work – family commitments. *Journal of Poverty, 13*(2), 152–72.

Herd, P., & Harrington Meyer, M. (2002). Care work: Invisible civic engagement. *Gender & Society, 16*(5), 665–88.

Hermer, J. & Mosher, J. (2002). *Disorderly people: Law and the politics of exclusion.* Halifax: Fernwood.

Herr, K. (1999). The symbolic uses of participation: Co-opting change. *Theory into Practice, 38*(4), 235–40.

Himmelweit, S. (2002). Making visible the hidden economy: The case for gender-impact analysis of economic policy. *Feminist Economics, 8*(1), 49–70.

Hochschild, A.R. (2000a). Global care chains and emotional surplus value. In W. Hutton & A. Giddens (Eds.), *On the edge: Living with global capitalism* (pp. 130–46). London: Jonathan Cape.

Hochschild, A.R. (2000b). The nanny chain. *American Prospect, 11*(4), 32–6.

Hoskyns, C., & Rai, S.M. (2007). Recasting the global political economy: Counting women's unpaid work. *New Political Economy, 12*(3), 297–317.

Howell, J. (2005). Introduction. In J. Howell & D. Mulligan (Eds.), *Gender and civil society: Transcending boundaries* (pp. 1–22). New York: Routledge.

Howell, J. (2007). Gender and civil society: Time for cross-border dialogue. *Social Politics: International Studies in Gender, State & Society, 14*(4), 415–36.

Howel, J., & Mulligan, D. (Eds.). (2005). *Gender and civil society: Transcending boundaries*. New York: Routledge.

Hummel, R. (2002). Critique of 'public space.' *Administration & Society, 34*(1), 102–7.

Hyatt, S.B. (2001). From citizen to volunteer: Neoliberal governance and the erasure of poverty. In J. Goode & J. Maskovsky (Eds.), *The new poverty studies: The ethnography of power, politics, and impoverished people in the United States* (pp. 201–35). New York: New York University Press.

Ilcan, S., & Basok, T. (2004). Community government: Voluntary agencies, social justice, and the responsibilization of citizens. *Citizenship Studies, 8*(2), 129–44.

Isin, E., & Nielsen, G. (Eds.). (2008). *Acts of citizenship.* Toronto: University of Toronto Press.

Jaggar, A.M. (1998). Globalizing feminist ethics. *Hypatia, 13*(2), 7–31.

Jaggar, A.M. (2005). Arenas of citizenship: Civil society, state and the global order. *International Feminist Journal of Politics, 7*(1), 3–25.

Japel, C., Tremblay, R., & Côté, S. (2005). Quality counts! Assessing the quality of daycare services based on the Quebec Longitudinal Study of Child Development. *Choices, 11*(5), 1–44.

Jenson, J., & Phillips, S.D. (2001). Redesigning the Canadian citizenship regime: Remaking the institutions of representation. In C. Crouch, K. Eder, & D. Tambini (Eds.), *Citizenship, markets and the state* (pp. 69–89). Oxford: Oxford University Press.

Jensen, L., Cornwell, G.T., & Findeis, J. (1995). Informal work in non-metropolitan Pennsylvania. *Rural Sociology, 60*(1), 91–107.

Jones, M., Graham, J., & Shier, M. (2008). Linking transportation inadequacies to negative employment outcomes. *Canadian Review of Social Policy, 60/61*, 91–108.

Kaplan, E.B. (1997). *Not our kind of girl: Unraveling the myths of black teenage motherhood.* Berkeley, CA: University of California Press.

Kershaw, P. (2006). *Carefair: Rethinking the responsibilities and rights of citizenship.* Vancouver: UBC Press.

Kershaw, P. (2010). Caregiving for identity is political: Implications for citizenship theory. *Citizenship Studies, 14*(4), 395–410.

Klein, S., & Long, A. (2003). *A bad time to be poor: An analysis of British Columbia's new welfare policies*. Vancouver: Canadian Centre for Policy Alternatives BC Office.

Koehn, D. (1998). *Rethinking feminist ethics: Care, trust and empathy*. New York: Routledge.

Kreigher, S. (1999). Feminist lessons from the grey market in personal care for the elderly. In S. Neysmith (Ed.), *Critical issues for future social work practice with aging persons* (pp. 155–86). New York: Columbia University Press.

Lamont, M., & Molnar, V. (2002). The study of boundaries in the social sciences. *Annual Review of Sociology, 28*, 167–95.

Land, H., & Rose, H. (1985). Compulsory altruism for some or an altruistic society for all? In P. Bean, J. Ferris, & D. Whynes (Eds.), *In defense of welfare*. London: Tavistock.

Langley, P., & Mellor, M. (2002). 'Economy,' sustainability and sites of transformative space. *New Political Economy, 7*(1), 49–65.

Larner, W. (2000). Neo-liberalism: Policy, ideology, governmentality. *Studies in Political Economy, 63*, 5–26.

Lather, P. (1993). Fertile obsession: Validity after postmodernism. *Sociological Quarterly, 34*(4), 673–93.

Lee, M., & Ivanova, I. (2009). BC Budget 2009. September Update BC Commentary No. 12(3). BC Office: Canadian Centre for Policy Alternatives.

Levitas, R.A. (1996). The concept of social exclusion and the new Durkheimian hegemony. *Critical Social Policy, 16*(46), 5–20.

Lewis, J. (2001). Decline of the male breadwinner model: Implications for work and care. *Social Politics: International Studies in Gender, State & Society, 8*(2), 152–69.

Light, D.W. (2001). Managed competition, governmentality and institutional response in the United Kingdom. *Social Science & Medicine, 52*(8), 1167–81.

Lind, A. (1997). Gender, development and the urban social change: Women's community action in global cities. *World Development, 25*(8), 1205–23.

Lind, A. (2005). *Gendered paradoxes: Women's movements, state restructuring, and global development in Ecuador*. University Park, PA: Pennsylvania State University Press.

Lister, R. (2001). Towards a citizens' welfare state: The 3 + 2 'R's of welfare reform. *Theory, Culture & Society, 18*(2–3), 91–111.

Lister, R. (2003). Investing in the citizen-workers of the future: Transformations in citizenship and the state under New Labour. *Social Policy & Administration, 37*(5), 427–43.

Lister, R. (2007). Inclusive citizenship: Realizing the potential. *Citizenship Studies, 11*(1), 49–61.

Little, M.J.H. (1998). *No car, no radio, no liquor permit: The moral regulation of single mothers in Ontario, 1920–1997.* Toronto: Oxford University Press.

Little, M.J.H., & Morrison, I. (1999). The pecker detectors are back. *Journal of Canadian Studies 34*(2), 110–36.

Littlewood, P., & Herkommer, S. (1999). Identifying social exclusion: Some problems of meaning. In Paul Littlewood (Ed.), *Social exclusion in Europe: Problems and paradigms* (pp. 1–21). Aldershot, UK: Ashgate.

Lorde, A. (1984). The master's tools will never dismantle the master's house. In A. Lorde (Ed.), *Sister outsider: Essays and speeches* (pp. 110–13). Santa Cruz, CA: Crossing.

Lowen, C., & Reitsma-Street, M. (2006). *Impact of performance-based funding on provisioning an employability program for women who experienced abuse.* Presentation at the Canadian Association of Schools of Social Work Conference, York University, Toronto, ON.

Lowndes, V. (2000). Women and social capital: A comment on Hall's social capital in Britain. *British Journal of Political Science, 30*, 533–7.

Luxton, M., & Corman, J. (2001). *Getting by in hard times: Gendered labour at home and on the job.* Toronto: University of Toronto Press.

MacDonald, M. (1995). Feminist economics: From theory to research. *Canadian Journal of Economics, 28*(1), 159–76.

Mahon, R. (2002). Child care: Toward what kind of 'Social Europe'? *Social Politics: International Studies in Gender, State & Society, 9*(3), 343–79.

Marshall, T.H. (1950). *Citizenship and social class and other essays.* Cambridge: Cambridge University Press.

Marshall, T.H., & Bottomore, T.B. (1992). *Citizenship and social class.* London: Pluto.

Martin, P.Y. (1990). Rethinking feminist organizations. *Gender & Society, 4*(2), 182–206.

Mason, R. (2007). Building women's social citizenship: A five-point framework to conceptualise the work of women-specific services in rural Australia. *Women's Studies International Forum, 30*(4), 299–312.

Masson, D. (2000). Constituting 'post-welfare state' welfare arrangements: The role of women's movement service groups in Quebec. *Resources for Feminist Research, 27*(3/4), 49–69.

McBride, K.D. (2005). *Collective dreams: Political imagination and community.* University Park, PA: Pennsylvania State University Press.

McCall, L. (2005). The complexity of intersectionality. *Signs: Journal of Women and Society, 30*(3), 1771–800.

McCormack, K. (2004). Resisting the welfare mother: The power of welfare discourse and tactics of resistance. *Critical Sociology, 30*(2), 355–83.

McDowell, L. (2002). Transitions to work: Masculine identities, youth inequality and labour market change. *Gender, Place and Culture, 9*(1), 39–59.

McIntyre, L., Glanville, N.T., Raine, K.D., Dayle, J.B., Anderson, B., & Battaglia, N. (2003). Do low-income lone mothers compromise their nutrition to feed their children? *Canadian Medical Association Journal, 168*(6), 686–91.

Meier, P., & Lombardo, E. (2008). Concepts of citizenship underlying EU gender equality policies. *Citizenship Studies, 12*(5), 481–93.

Meinhard, A.G., & Foster, M.K. (1997). *Competition or collaboration: Preliminary results of a survey of women's voluntary organizations.* Toronto: Centre for Voluntary Sector Studies, Ryerson University Faculty of Business.

Meinhard, A.G., & Foster, M.K. (2003). Differences in the response of women's voluntary organizations to shifts in Canadian public policy. *Nonprofit and Voluntary Sector Quarterly, 32*(3), 366–96.

Miles, D. (2004–5). Feminist activism in northern territory women's services. *Women against Violence: An Australian Feminist Journal, 17*, 33–40.

Mills, A.J. (1998). Organization, gender and culture. *Organization Studies, 9*(3), 351–69.

Mink, G. (1998). Feminists, welfare reform, and welfare justice. *Social Justice, 25*, 147–57.

Minkler, M. (1999). Intergenerational households headed by grandparents: Contexts, realities, and implications for policy. *Journal of Aging Studies, 13*(2), 199–218.

Mirchandani, K. (2006). Gender eclipsed? Racial hierarchies in transnational call centres. *Social Justice, 32*(4), 105–19.

Mirza, H.S. (1992). *Young, female and black.* London: Routledge.

Misztal, B.A. (2005). The new importance of the relationship between formality and informality. *Feminist Theory, 6*(2), 173–94.

Mohanty, C.T. (2003). 'Under Western eyes' revisited: Feminist solidarity through anti-capitalist struggles. *Signs: Journal of Women in Culture and Society, 28*(2), 499–535.

Molyneux, M. (1998). Analysing women's movements. In C. Jackson & R. Pearson (Eds.), *Feminist visions of development: Gender analysis and policy* (pp. 65–88). New York: Routledge.

Molyneux, M. (2002). Gender and the silences of social capital: Lessons from Latin America. *Development & Change, 33*(2), 167–88.

Morgen, S., & Maskovsky, J. (2003). The anthropology of welfare 'reform': New perspectives on U.S. urban poverty in the post-welfare era. *Annual Review of Anthropology, 32*, 315–38.

Moser, C.O.N. (1989). Gender planning in the Third World: Meeting practical and strategic gender needs. *World Development, 17*(11), 1799–825.

Moser, C.O.N. (Ed.). (1991). *Gender planning in the Third World: Meeting practical and strategic gender needs*. Bloomington, IN: Indiana University Press.

Moser, C.O.N., & Holland, J. (1997). *Household responses to poverty and vulnerability: Vol. 4. Confronting crisis in Chawama, Lusaka, Zambia*. Washington, DC: World Bank for the Urban Management Program.

Mosher, J., Evans, P., & Little, M. (2004). *Walking on eggshells: Abused women's experiences of Ontario's welfare system*. Toronto: Ontario Association of Interval and Transition Houses.

Murray, K.B., Low, J., & Waite, A. (2006). The voluntary sector and the realignment of government: A street-level study. *Canadian Public Administration, 49*(3), 375–92.

Naples, N.A. (1992). Activist mothering: Cross-generational continuity in the community work of women from low-income urban neighborhoods. *Gender & Society 6*(3), 441–63.

Naples, N.A. (Ed.). (1998). *Community activism and feminist politics*. New York: Routledge.

National Council of Welfare. (2010). Welfare incomes 2008. National Council of Welfare. http://www.ncw.gc.ca/l.3bd.2t.1ils@-eng.jsp?lid=91.

Nelson, J.A. (1993). The study of choice or the study of provisioning? Gender and the definition of economics. In M.A. Ferber & J.A. Nelson (Eds.), *Beyond economic man: Feminist theory and economics* (pp. 23–36). Chicago: University of Chicago Press.

Nelson, J.A. (1996). *Feminism, objectivity and economics*. London: Routledge.

Nelson, J.A. (1998). Labour, gender and the economic/social divide. *International Labour Review, 137*(1), 33–46.

Nelson, J.A. (1999). Of markets and martyrs: Is it OK to pay well for care? *Feminist Economics, 5*(3), 43–59.

Nelson, J.A. (2006). Can we talk? Feminist economics in dialogue with theorists. *Signs: Journal of Women in Culture and Society, 31*(4), 1051–74.

Nelson, J.A., & England, P. (2002). Feminist philosophies of love and work. *Hypatia, 17*(2), 1–18.

Nelson, M.K. (1999). Between paid and unpaid work: Gender patterns in supplemental economic activities among white, rural families. *Gender & Society, 13*(4), 518–39.

Neysmith, S. (Ed.) (2000). *Restructuring caring labour: Discourse, state practice and everyday life*. Toronto: Oxford University Press.

Neysmith, S., Bezanson, K., & O'Connell, A. (2005). The myth of community, family and friends. In S. Neysmith, K. Bezanson, & A. O'Connell (Eds.), *Telling tales: Living the effects of social policy in Ontario* (pp. 144–69). Halifax, NS: Fernwood.

Neysmith, S., & Reitsma-Street, M. (2000). Valuing unpaid labour in the third sector: The case of community resource centres. *Canadian Public Policy, 26*(3), 331–46.

Neysmith, S., & Reitsma-Street, M. (2005). Provisioning: Conceptualizing the work of women for 21st century social policy. *Women's Studies International Forum, 28*(5), 381–91.

Neysmith, S., & Reitsma-Street, M. (2009). The provisioning responsibilities of older women. *Journal of Aging Studies, 23*(4), 236–44.

Neysmith, S., Reitsma-Street, M., Baker Collins, S., Porter, E., & Tam, S. (2010). Provisioning responsibilities: Connecting work to relationships. *Canadian Review of Sociology, 47*(2), 149–70.

Ng, R. (1981). Constituting ethnic phenomenon: An account from the perspective of immigrant women. *Canadian Ethnic Studies, 13*(1), 97–108.

Ng, R. (1996). *The politics of community services: Immigrant women, class and state.* 2nd ed. Toronto: Fernwood.

Ng, R. (2002). Freedom from whom? Globalization and trade from the standpoint of garment workers. *Canadian Woman Studies, 21/22*(4 & 1), 74–81.

O'Connor, J.S., Orloff, A.S., & Shaver, S. (1999). *States, markets, families: Gender, liberalism and social policy in Australia, Canada, Great Britain and the United States.* Cambridge: Cambridge University Press.

Odih, P. (2003). Gender, work and organization in the time/space economy of just-in-time labour. *Time & Society, 12*(2/3), 293–314.

Oliker, S.J. (1995). The proximate contexts of workfare and work: A Framework for understanding poor women's economic choices. *Sociological Quarterly 36*(2), 251–72.

Olson, K. (2002). Recognizing gender, redistributing labour. *Social Politics: International Studies in Gender, State & Society, 9*(3), 380–410.

Orpana, H.M., Lemyre, L., & Gravel, R. (2009). *Income and psychological distress: The role of the social environment.* Catalogue no. 82003XPE, 20(1). Ottawa: Health Reports, Statistics Canada.

Orton, M. (2006). Wealth, citizenship and responsibility: The views of 'better off' citizens in the UK. *Citizenship Studies, 10*(2), 251–65.

Osborne, K., Baum, F., & Ziersch, A. (2009). Negative consequences of community group participation for women's mental health and well-being: Implications for gender aware social capital building. *Journal of Community & Applied Social Psychology, 19*(3), 212–24.

Pahl, R.E., & Wallace, C. (1985). Household work strategies in economic recession. In N. Redclift & E. Mingione (Eds.), *Beyond employment: Household, gender and subsistence* (pp. 189–227). Oxford: Blackwell.

Parada, H. (2004). Social work practices within the restructured child welfare system in Ontario. *Canadian Social Work Review, 21*(1), 67–76.

Perrons, D. (2000). Care, paid work, and leisure: Rounding the triangle. *Feminist Economics, 6*(1), 105–14.

Peters, H., & Kwong-Leung, T. (2004). B.C. women standing up against neoliberal encroachment: The use of international advocacy. *Canadian Review of Social Policy, 54*, 122–7.

Peterson, V.S. (2002). Rewriting (global) political economy as reproductive, productive and virtual (Foucauldian) economies. *International Feminist Journal of Politics, 4*(1), 1–30.

Petrzelka, P., & Mannon, S.E. (2006). Keeping this little town going: Gender and volunteerism in rural America. *Gender & Society, 20*(2), 236–58.

Pettman, J.J. (1996). *Worlding women: A feminist international politics.* New York: Routledge.

Phipps, S.A., & Burton, P.S. (1995). Sharing within families: Implications for the measurement of poverty among individuals in Canada. *Canadian Journal of Economics, 28*(1), 177–204.

Piven, F.F., Acker, J., Hallock, M., & Morgen, S. (2002). *Work, welfare and politics: Confronting poverty in the wake of welfare reform.* Eugene, OR: University of Oregon Press.

Plaza, D. (2000). Transnational grannies: The changing family responsibilities of elderly African Caribbean-born women resident in Britain. *Social Indicators Research, 51*(1), 75–105.

Plummer, K.. 2004. *Intimate citizenship: Private decisions and public dialogues.* Montreal and Kingston: McGill-Queen's University Press.

Polletta, F. (2000). The structural context of novel rights claims: Southern civil rights organizing, 1961–1966. *Law & Society Review, 34*(2), 367–406.

Porter, E., Neysmith, S.M., Reitsma-Street, M., & Baker Collins, S. (2009). Reciprocal peer interviewing. *International Review of Qualitative Research, 2*(2), 291–312.

Power, M. (2004). Social provisioning as a starting point for feminist economics. *Feminist Economics, 10*(3), 3–19.

Prentice, S. (2007). Less access, worse quality. *Journal of Children and Poverty, 13*(1), 57–73.

Prokhovnik, R. (1998). Public and private citizenship: From gender invisibility to feminist inclusiveness. *Feminist Review, 60*, 84–104.

Putnam, R.D. (2000). *Bowling alone: The collapse and revival of American community.* New York: Simon & Schuster.

Quaid, M. (2002). *Workfare: Why good social policy ideas go bad.* Toronto: University of Toronto Press.

Rankin, K.N. (2002). Social capital, microfinance, and the politics of development. *Feminist Economics, 8*(1), 1–24.

Ray, R.E., & Chandler, S. (2001–2). Narrative approach to anti-aging. *Generations, 25*(4), 44–8.

Rebick, J. (2005). *Ten thousand roses: The making of a feminist revolution.* Toronto: Penguin.

Reid, C., Allison, T., & Frisby, W. (2006). Finding the 'action' in feminist participatory action research. *Action Research, 4*(3), 315–32.

Ricciutelli, L., Miles, A.R., & McFadden, M.H. (Eds.). (2004). *Feminist politics activism and vision: Local and global challenges.* Toronto: Inanna.

Richmond, T., & Shields, J. (2005). NGO–government relations and immigrant services: Contradictions and challenges. *Journal of International Migration and Integration, 6*(3–4), 513–26.

Room, G.J. (1999). Social exclusion, solidarity and the challenge of globalization. *International Journal of Social Welfare, 8,* 166–74.

Rudiman, D.L. (2006). Shaping the active, autonomous and responsible modern retiree: An analysis of discursive technologies and their links with neoliberal political rationality. *Ageing & Society, 26,* 9–35.

Rummery, K. (2009). A comparative discussion of the gendered implications of cash-for-care schemes: Markets, independence and social citizenship in crisis? *Social Policy & Administration, 43*(6), 634–48.

San Martin, R.M., & Barnoff, L. (2004). Let them howl: The operation of imperial subjectivity and the politics of race in one feminist organization. *Atlantis: A Women's Studies Journal, 29*(1), 77–84.

Schild, V. (2000). Neo-liberalism's new gendered market citizens: The 'civilizing' dimension of social programs in Chile. *Citizenship Studies, 4*(3), 275–305.

Schmid, H., Bar, M., & Nirel, R. (2008). Advocacy activities in nonprofit human service organizations. *Nonprofit & Voluntary Sector Quarterly, 37*(4), 581–602.

Schudson, M. (2006). The varieties of civic experience. *Citizenship Studies, 10*(5), 591–606.

Scott, K. (2003). *Funding matters: The impact of Canada's new funding regime on nonprofit and voluntary organizations.* Ottawa: Canadian Council on Social Development.

Scourfield, P. (2006). 'What matters is what works'? How discourses of modernization have both silenced and limited debate on domiciliary care for older people. *Critical Social Policy, 26*(1), 5–30.

Sevenhuijsen, S. (2004). Trace: A method for normative policy analysis from the ethic of care. In S. Sevenhuijsen & A. Švab (Eds.), *The heart of the matter* (pp. 13–46). Metelkova: Institute for Contemporary Social and Political

Studies, Liubliana. http://www2.arnes.si/~ljmiri1s/eng_html/publications/pdf/MI_politike_symposion_the_heart.pdf.

Sharma, N.R. (2006). *Home economics: Nationalism and the making of 'migrant workers' in Canada*. Toronto: University of Toronto Press.

Silliman, J. (1999). Expanding civil society, shrinking political spaces: The case of women's nongovernmental organizations. In J. Silliman & Y. King (Eds.), *Dangerous intersections: Feminist perspectives on population, environment and development* (pp. 133–62). Cambridge, MA: South End.

Simien, E. (2007). Doing intersectionality research: From conceptual issues to practical examples. *Politics and Gender, 3*(2), 264–71.

Smith, D.E. (1987). *The everyday world as problematic: A feminist sociology*. Boston, MA: Northeastern University Press.

Smith, D.E. (1990). *The conceptual practices of power: A feminist sociology of knowledge*. Toronto: University of Toronto Press.

Solomon, B. (2003). A 'know it all' with a 'pet peeve' meets 'underdogs' who 'let her have it': Producing low-waged women workers in a welfare-to-work training program. *Journal of Contemporary Ethnography, 32*(6), 693–727.

Staeheli, L.A. (2004). Mobilizing women, mobilizing gender: Is it mobilizing difference? *Gender, Place & Culture, 11*(3), 347–72.

Staeheli, L.A., & Clarke, S.E. (2003). The new politics of citizenship: Structuring participation by household, work, and identity. *Urban Geography, 24*(2), 103–26.

Stall, S., & Stoecker, R. (1998). Community organizing or organizing community? Gender and the crafts of empowerment. *Gender & Society, 12*(6), 729–56.

Standing, G. (1999). Global feminization through flexible labor. *World Development, 27*(3), 583–602.

Stasiulis, D., & Bakan, A. (2003). *Negotiating citizenship*. New York: Palgrave Macmillan.

Statistics Canada. (2005a). *Cornerstones of community: Highlights of the National Survey of Nonprofits and Voluntary Organizations*. Catalogue no. 61–533-XIE. Ottawa: Statistics Canada.

Statistics Canada. (2005b). *General Social Survey: Cycle 19 (Time Use)*. Catalogue no. #12M0019XCB. Ottawa: Statistics Canada.

Statistics Canada. (2005c). *Women in Canada: A gender-based statistical report*. Catalogue no. 89–503. Ottawa: Statistics Canada.

Statistics Canada. (2008a). *Canada's ethnocultural mosaic, 2006 Census*. Catalogue no. 97–562-X. Ottawa: Statistics Canada.

Statistics Canada. (2008b). *The Canadian labour market at a glance*. Catalogue no. 71–222-X. Ottawa: Labour Statistics Division, Statistics Canada.

Statistics Canada. (2009a). *Caring Canadians, involved Canadians: Highlights from the 2007 Canada Survey of Giving, Volunteering and Participating.* Catalogue no. 71–542-XPE. Ottawa: Statistics Canada.

Statistics Canada. (2009b). *Census tract (CT) profiles, 2006 Census.* Catalogue no. 92–597-XWE. Retrieved Statistics Canada website: http://www12.statcan. ca/census-recensement/2006/dp-pd/prof/9^#^=^#91/index.cfm?Lang=E.

Statistics Canada. (2009c). *Income and psychological distress: The role of the social environment.* Catalogue no. 82–003.XPE. Ottawa: Statistics Canada.

Statistics Canada. (2009d). *Low income cut-offs for 2008 and low income measures for 2007.* Minister of Industry. Income Statistics Division, Income Research Paper Series. Retrieved from Statistics Canada website: http://www. statcan.gc.ca/pub/75f0002m/75f0002m2009002-eng.pdf.

Stolle, D., & Lewis, J. (2002). Social capital: An emerging concept. In B. Hobson, J. Lewis, & B. Siims (Eds.), *Contested concepts in gender and social politics* (pp. 195–229). Cheltenham, UK: Edward Elgar.

Stratigaki, M. (2004). The co-optation of gender concepts in EU policies: The case of 'reconciliation of work and family.' *Social Politics: International Studies in Gender, State & Society, 11*(1), 30–56.

Susser, I. (1988). Working class women, social protest and changing ideologies. In A. Bookman & S. Morgen, *Women and the politics of empowerment* (pp. 257–71). Philadelphia, PA: Temple University Press.

Swift, K.J. (1995). *Manufacturing bad mothers: A critical perspective on child neglect.* Toronto: University of Toronto Press.

Swift, K.J., & Callahan, M. (2009). *At risk: Social justice in child welfare and other human services.* Toronto: University of Toronto Press.

Tam, S. (2007). *Young women's provisioning: A study of the social organization of youth employment.* Unpublished doctoral dissertation, University of Toronto, ON.

Tang, K., & Peters, H. (2006). Internationalizing the struggle against neoliberal social policy: The Canadian experience. *International Social Work, 49*(5), 571–82.

Taylor, R.F. (2004). Extending conceptual boundaries: Work, voluntary work and employment. *Work, Employment & Society, 18*(1), 29–49.

Taylor, V. (1999). Gender and social movements: Gender processes in women's self-help movements. *Gender & Society, 13*(1), 8–33.

Teghtsoonian, K. (2003). W(h)ither women's equality? Neoliberalism, institutional change and public policy in British Columbia. *Policy, Organisation & Society, 22*(1), 26–47.

Thomas, J. (1996). *Time, culture, and identity: An interpretative archaeology.* London: Routledge.

Thompson, J.A., & Bunderson, J.S. (2001). Work-nonwork conflict and the phenomenology of time: Beyond the balance metaphor. *Work and Occupations, 28*(1), 17–39.

Timonen, V., Convery, J., & Cahill, S. (2006). Care revolutions in the making? A comparison of cash-for-care programmes in four European countries. *Ageing & Society, 26*(3), 455–74.

Toronto Police Service. (2007). *Annual statistical report*. Retrieved from Toronto Police Service website: http://www.torontopolice.on.ca/publications/files/reports/2007statsreport.pdf.

Townsend, J.G., Zapata, E., Rowlands, J., Alberti, P., & Mercado, M. (Eds.). (1999). *Women and power: Fighting patriarchies and poverty*. London: Zed Books.

Tronto, J.C. (1993). *Moral boundaries: A political argument for an ethic of care*. New York: Routledge.

Twigg, J. (2004). The body, gender and age: Feminist insights in social gerontology. *Journal of Aging Studies, 18*, 59–73.

Ungerson, C. (2004). Whose empowerment and independence? A cross-national perspective on 'cash for care' schemes. *Ageing & Society, 24*(2), 189–212.

Ungerson, C., & Yeandle, S. (Eds.). (2007). *Cash for care in developed welfare states*. Houndmills, UK: Palgrave Macmillan.

UNICEF. (2008). *The child care transition: Innocenti report card 8*. http://www.unicef.ca/portal/SmartDefault.aspx?at=2250.

United Way Toronto. (2007). *2007 Annual report to the community*. http://unitedwaytoronto.com/downloads/aboutUs/AR2007/2007_UWT-AnnualReport.PDF.

Vobruba, G. (2000). Actors in processes of inclusion and exclusion: Toward a dynamic approach. *Social Policy and Administration, 34*(5), 601–13.

Vosko, L.F. (Ed.). (2006). *Precarious employment: Understanding labour market insecurity in Canada*. Montreal & Kingston: McGill-Queen's University Press.

Vosko, L.F. (2009). Precarious employment and the challenges for employment policy. In M.G. Cohen & J. Pulkingham (Eds.), *Public policy for women: The state, income security, and labour market issues* (pp. 374–95). Toronto: University of Toronto Press.

Walby, S. (2001). From community to coalition: The politics of recognition as the handmaiden of the politics of equality in an era of globalization. *Theory, Culture & Society, 18*(2/3), 113–35.

Waring, M. (1988). *Counting for nothing: What men value and what women are worth*. Wellington, NZ: Bridget Williams Books.

Weeks, W., in collaboration with Women's Services. (1994). *Women working together: Lessons from feminist women's services*. Melbourne: Longman Cheshire.

Weigt, J. (2006). Compromises to carework: The social organization of mothers' experiences in the low-wage labor market after welfare reform. *Social Problems, 53*(3), 332–51.

Weis, L., & Fine, M. (2000). *Speed bumps: A student-friendly guide to qualitative research*. New York: Teachers College Press.

Weldon, S.L. (2005). The dimensions and policy impact of feminist civil society: Democratic policy-making on violence against women in the fifty U.S. states. In J. Howell & D. Mulligan (Eds.), *Gender and civil society: Transcending boundaries* (pp. 196–221). London: Routledge.

White, E. (2002). *Fast girls: Teenage tribes and the myth of the slut*. New York: Scribner.

Williams, C.C. (2008). Developing a culture of volunteering: Beyond the third sector approach. *Journal of Voluntary Sector Research, 1*(1), 25–43.

Williams, C.C., & Windebank, J. (2003). Reconceptualizing women's paid informal work: Some lessons from lower-income urban neighbourhoods. *Gender, Work & Organization, 10*(3), 281–300.

Williams, F. (2001). In and beyond new labour: Towards a new political ethics of care. *Critical Social Policy, 21*(4), 467–93.

Wray, S. (2003). Women growing older: Agency, ethnicity and culture. *Sociology, 37*(3), 511–27.

Yuval-Davis, N. (1999). The 'multi-layered citizen': Citizenship in the age of 'globalization.' *International Feminist Journal of Politics, 1*(1), 119–36.

Yuval-Davis, N., Anthias, F., & Kofman, E. (2005). Secure borders and safe haven and the gendered politics of belonging: Beyond social cohesion. *Ethnic & Racial Studies, 28*(3), 513–35.

Yuval-Davis, N., & Stoetzler, M. (2002). Imagined boundaries and borders: A gendered gaze. *European Journal of Women's Studies, 9*(3), 329–44.

Index

Cornwell, Gretchen T., 124
covering (head scarves), 78–9
culture: cultural traits, 67–8; role of
grandmothers, 109–10; as support,
73
Cumming, Sara J., 96

Desforges, Luke, 141
DeVault, Marjorie, 67, 173–4n4
dignity, 145
disabled, 103
discrimination. *See* racism
domestic sector: and citizenship,
140–1; domestic labour, 18–19; as
safety net, 126
Dominguez, Silvia, 157
Donath, Susan, 126

economics and economic activity:
earlier conceptions of economics,
149–50; effects of global trends
on individuals, 67; government
support of elite, 26, 45–6; market
citizenship, 134–5; market theory,
14–15, 25, 41, 150; purpose of, 4–5;
shift to informal economy, 126,
128–30. *See also* employment
Edin, Kathyrn, 124
education: on anti-discrimination,
77–8; children's education, 89;
choices in, 77–8; debt and, 71;
desire for, 89; foreign credentials,
91; of low-income women, 91;
required volunteer work, 31;
youth employment programme,
80–1
elderly: caring labour for, 102;
economic relationship with, 124.
See also aging; older women
Elson, Diane, 126

employment: citizenship as right
to, 136; collective provisioning
sites, 48; domestic labour, 18–19;
employability programme, 50–1,
58–9, 138; female breadwinner
model, 17–20; female dominated
professions, 67; of Gen-Y interviewees, 69–71, 81–2; informal
work, 124, 129; job training, 153;
link to citizenship, 156; market
theory, 15; moral superiority
of paid work, 100, 159–60;
multiple jobs, 90; racism and,
65–6, 78–9; racism in, 67; self-
employment, 73; service sector
employment, 18–19; small-scale
entrepreneurial activity, 118–19;
volunteering as moral equivalent
to, 142–3; workfare, 172n2. *See also*
economics and economic activity;
market citizenship
empowerment, 5
Erbaugh, Elizabeth, 146
Esping-Anderson, Gosta, 17–18
extended present, 114

fathers, 113
female breadwinner model, 17–20
female dominated professions, 67
financial stress, 125
Findeis, Jill L., 124
Fine, Michelle, 141
fitness, 106–7
food cooperatives: benefits of
involvement, 33; effect of
government regulations, 139;
need for, 124–5, 125–6. *See also*
collective provisioning
foreign credentials, 91
Fraser, Nancy, 160